Computer Literacy for School Administrators and Supervisors

Stephen Radin
New York City Public
   School System
Harold M. Greenberg
South Shore High School,
   New York City

LexingtonBooks
D.C. Heath and Company
Lexington, Massachusetts
Toronto

Library of Congress Cataloging in Publication Data

Radin, Stephen.
    Computer literacy for school administrators and supervisors.

    Includes index.
    1. Education—Data processing—Handbooks, manuals, etc. 2. School
management and organization—Data processing—Handbooks, manuals, etc.
3. Computer-assisted instruction—Handbooks, manuals, etc.
I. Greenberg, Harold M. II. Title.
LB1028.43.R33   1983   370'.28'5   82-48597
ISBN 0-669-06330-4

Published simultaneously in Canada

Printed in the United States of America

International Standard Book Number: 0-669-06330-4

Library of Congress Catalog Card Number: 82-48597

This book is dedicated to our wives,
Helen Radin and Adeline Greenberg.
Their constant support as editors and critics
and their unlimited patience
made this book possible.

Contents

Contents

Contents

Figures

Figures

Introduction

The worldwide community recognizes and accepts the mushrooming computer revolution. Once identified primarily with engineering staffs and the multimillion-dollar corporate world of big business, computers have become part of our everyday existence. Telephone bills and operator voice messages advising of the misdialing of telephone numbers are accepted computer functions. For example, the voice message, "the number you have dialed, 2-5-3-1-2-6-5, has been changed to 2-5-1-4-3-4-7," often is delivered by a computer. Utility bills enter our homes on computerized statements without fanfare. Computer-printed college transcripts are now accepted as normal fare without even a thought to the process that generates them. Service-station-inspection printouts on the condition of automobiles are already gaining similar acceptance by the public. Computer monitoring of cardiac patients no longer creates any surprise. Small-business owners and individuals in the privacy of their homes utilize small, personal computers for a variety of tasks and as the means for accessing needed information. Our language has already begun to accommodate terminology normally associated with computers. It is no longer uncommon to hear such words as *data, input, output, program, parameter, printout, generate,* and *interface.*

Computer games now rival television viewing of national sporting events. Pac-Man "widows and widowers" now sympathize with their Sunday-football counterparts. Airlines utilize computers to provide passengers with information about arrivals and departures and their presence is considered to be as normal as takeoffs and landings. Many of the nation's cross-country trains are now run by computer. Many accountants now utilize computers for providing a variety of data rather than rely solely on the more primitive calculators for arriving at important conclusions.

The computer has also continued to have an impact on the lifestyles of human beings. Buddhist priests can now meditate by computer and rabbis can consult ancient *responsas* (religious decisions), to gain insight into the thinking of sages on perplexing problems, by pressing a key on a computer terminal. Attorneys may ask computers to provide information about the liberal or conservative bent of prospective jurors. A physician can input a description of symptoms exhibited by a patient and instantaneously receive a printout that provides not only one or more possible diagnoses but also the most up-to-date treatments used successfully by other physicians with patients having the same symptoms and similar body structures. Office managers may work from their homes and communicate with office staffs located miles away, as a result of convenient telephone connections with centralized computer facilities. Parents are sending their children to summer camps that feature computer education. Teenagers have made fortunes designing computer games and toys. Operas are being composed with the assistance of computers.

Civilized communities recognize that computers mean change. They also recognize that computers mean problems. Furthermore, they realize that computers have shortcomings, which if not harnessed and controlled may affect adversely some of the values and behavior patterns civilization cherishes. Attempts to stand up to the waves and resist their inevitability, their power, and their flow is to invite disaster. Flexibility, intelligent caution, and considered decision making are needed.

It is only natural that our schools, reflecting the best and worst of our many community lifestyles, have to face the dilemma of either rejecting computers or accepting their potential for improving our quality of life.

To assist those in positions of educational leadership to cope effectively with the challenges of the computer revolution, we will offer practical approaches for resolving many difficult questions. Among these are: How can schools utilize computers to assist in performing labor-saving chores? How can computers assist in providing varieties of instantaneous, up-to-date information? How can computers be used to assist in upgrading productivity? How can schools meet the expectations and demands of students, parents, and other members of the community that approaches to education keep pace with those technological changes that have become a normal, familiar part of their daily lives?

This book strives to provide insights and some practical approaches to these and other relevant questions. Concerned school administrators and supervisors now have available to them a meaningful, realistic guide for the harnessing of computers for coping effectively with the many difficult problems encountered in educating our nation's youth.

Acknowledgments

We wish to acknowledge the enthusiastic support of Ralph T. Brande, Community Superintendent of District 22, Brooklyn, New York; the assistance of Fred Zahn, Allen Argoff, Bernard A. Walker, Peter Ferrara, Michael Gluck, Sidney Greenberg, and Dr. Alan Greenberg; and the influence of C. Edwin Linville, former principal of Taft High School, Bronx, New York.

**Computer
Literacy
for School
Administrators
and Supervisors**

1

An Overview of Computer Utilization in Our Schools

The Birth of a Powerful Tool

Computers have captured the imagination of the people of the United States. As inevitably as rock yielding to the elements, technologically oriented societies have yielded to the promise that computers could be harnessed to serve humanity beneficially. As one outgrowth of the many technological changes that assaulted human imagination during the Second World War, individual creativity pursued the idea that electrical impulses could be channeled constructively to the performance of a variety of tasks denied the limitations of human endurance, intellect, and capability. As the process continued to evolve, the increasing sophistication of such tasks became related to human need, perseverence, and imagination.

Initially the province of engineers who were able to think in terms of high-level mathematics and unfathomable symbols, computers were associated with intangible giant corporations such as the International Business Machines Corporation (IBM) and The Rand Corporation. The uses to which such organizations put computers were hardly part of the ken of most of society. There was talk, there were rumors, and there were occasional reports by the media of unusual advances in technology, but most people had neither the time nor the inclination to think that one day computers serving the needs of high-level industry would or could become a commonplace part of the day-to-day lifestyle of our world.

Computers were thought of as massive pieces of equipment—secretly stored and maintained by high-priced technicians in sterile laboratories, handled by an elite group, and understood by even fewer intellects in the genius category. These conceptions may have been correct. At the outset, the reception accorded by the public to the idea of computers was that of a wait-and-see posture tempered with an element of trepidation.

As with most new phenomena, a significant segment of society approached computers with mistrust. Many initially feared that computers might replace people in jobs and that, eventually, computers would come to control human beings. Regarding these fears, the reality is that computers were not designed to replace people. Rather, one of the principal objectives in the development of computers was to permit the liberation of human beings from frustration, from the degrading burden of thankless repetition, and from dehumanization. Harnessed, computers would permit some restoration of the dignity of human labor.

In the Charlie Chaplin film classic, *Modern Times*, the protagonist spends each waking day working unthinkingly on an assembly line, turning the same wrench in the same direction, a never-ending process.

By the end of the work shift, his hand involuntarily continues to move, mechanically, in the same direction to which it had become accustomed. Essentially this human being has been turned into a machine. Such films had their impact. Some individuals became determined to alleviate the plight of such human misery and began the search for labor-saving devices. Among the labor-saving devices that were developed are computers. Their proper utilization would permit human beings to devote creative energies toward more productive achievements. Society willed it and technology delivered.

Can Computers Control Us?

A major fear—that computers will one day come to control society—is understandable but untenable. Computers—made of inanimate materials, having no brain with which to think, and possessing no Achilles' heel, the gamut of human emotions—can only be the servant of human beings not their master. The computer can only perform those tasks that have been assigned to it by people. Therefore, only man can control himself and those things he creates. Computers cannot control human beings; they can, however, become the focus of man's greed and refusal to control the values and behavior of the social community in which he lives.

If, for example, computers have been equipped to provide moments of pleasure through a variety of technological games, and human beings refuse to monitor the amount of time they spend playing such games, thereby limiting exposure to other worthwhile endeavors, then, in this sense, computers will certainly appear as though they have come to control us. Making the computer the scapegoat, however, is unjustified.

As technology became oriented toward the consumer, what had been previously associated with unproven rumor and incomprehensible possibilities became more familiar to the public at large. That computers could be utilized to predict almost instantaneously the outcome of national elections staggered the imagination. In retrospect, perhaps it was the reality of Sputnik or the race to the moon—or perhaps it was the repetitious appearance on the television screen of the National Aeronautics and Space Agency's (NASA) sterile space-age headquarters with human beings monitoring sophisticated computer terminals in an endless series of countdowns—that finally broke down resistance and succeeded in moving the age of computers into our living rooms.

Simultaneously, perhaps it was the increasing popularity of science fiction, the supercharged atmosphere associated with James Bond and the ultramodern equipment he utilized in his exploits, and the popularity of such television series as "Star Trek" that promoted increasing public receptivity to the infinite possibilities offered by computers and eventually made their harnessing a reality. Soft-spoken, reasoned, intelligent individuals such as Walter Cronkite served to reassure the public about technological developments through consistent, creditable reporting. As a result, fears were allayed and—in what seemed to be an endless succession of revelations—transistor radios, tape recorders, cassette players, computer punchcards, and digital clocks became a familiar part of our daily lifestyle.

It was only a question of time before the human mind would conceive of and find a way to create microscopic tools that in turn would create new, more sophisticated microscopic tools. Robots, once conjured up in the incredible world of science fiction, are now a reality whose time has come. In quickening progressions, youth responded to such stimulation and each succeeding generation became more comfortable with and increasingly enticed by the challenges posed by the incomprehensible.

Computer Potential

Computers undertake those mechanical tasks that in the past often spelled agony for human beings. They have the capability of offering a huge memory bank with capacity for permanent storage of information on either magnetically coated plastic disks or tapes. They permit either the modification or retrieval of stored information. The computer permits the searching through of stored information to pinpoint and find specific blocks of information with particular characteristics. For other laborious tasks, the computer accomplishes with ease the sorting of information.

Computers in the Schools

Two examples will suffice to illustrate the computer's potential in an educational environment. At the beginning of each semester, in most of our schools, a secretary is assigned the task of preparing lists of teachers assigned to particular homeroom classes. Within the space of just a few days, the data may change several times. To effect the numerous corrections properly, the secretary must presently retype the entire listing. The utilization of a computer eliminates the tedious repetition inherent in such chores with a minimum of human effort and frees the secretary for more productive assignments.

A supervisor may wish to create a listing of students by reading level to facilitate class organization. The process involved in the preparation of such a listing is time consuming and tedious. The utilization of a computer permits a quick, painless completion of such a task and once again frees the individual to whom it has been assigned for more satisfying, productive work assignments.

It is evident that computers and the ideas with which they have become associated are now accepted and commonplace. In reality, in those fields in which computers have been accepted, there are often increased opportunities for the employment of human beings in new, upgraded capacities. Viable statistical studies attest to the fact that in those companies and organizations that have utilized the services of computers, there has been considerable growth in both corporate and employee income as well as in levels of employment. Rather than replacing people, the adoption of computers seems to be creating a need for additional employees, although in changed roles and assignments.

On the heels of the successful harnessing of computers by private industry and government agencies, a significant number of school districts throughout the nation have begun the process of bringing computers into their schools. Within the next few years, it is expected that in significantly increasing numbers, local school boards will be seeking insight into ways in which to utilize advantageously the blessings wrought by this computer-dominated technological revolution. As indicated, a variety of chores needed by school organizations are mechanical in nature and are thus ideally suited to the talents of the computer.

There are other tasks that are performed more efficiently by people. It is for administrators and supervisors to assess the needs of the schools under their jurisdiction and to determine those projects to be assigned to computers. Computers that have been utilized effectively in schools essentially fall into two categories. One group is referred to as *dedicated computers*. Such machines are capable of performing only one specific assigned task. The second group is identified as *programmable computers*. Such machines are those that can be programmed or instructed to perform a variety of multidimensional assignments. It is the latter group, the multifaceted, programmable computer that offers school administrators and supervisors the widest possible range of alternatives and is the powerful tool needed for upgrading productivity.

Becoming Outdated

Because improvements in computer technology seem to be a constant, the question of becoming *outdated* even before personnel have become proficient in using expensive equipment already purchased continues to plague those who are charged with the responsibility for making the investment of dollars for such equipment. There can never be a so-called safe time for investment that rules out the possibility of equipment becoming technologically outdated. Seemingly, the plausible approach is to assess the current technological scene, to make necessary decisions for the securing of the most appropriate equipment, to attend to the proper training of personnel, and then to monitor changes in available equipment with a view to upgrading when times become economically feasible. If goals can be identified clearly at the outset, then the administration can select equipment that best meets the specific needs of the school. As long as those needs do not change significantly, such equipment cannot become outdated. As new problems arise, adjustments may have to be made with supplementary equipment. Because the original equipment will always be capable of solving the problems for which it was initially purchased, fears of obsolescence are unfounded.

One of the possibilities for school utilization of the multifunctional or programmable computer is that it can be supplied with a commercially available program that converts the machine into a *word processor*. Word processors permit typing on a familiar, standardized typing keyboard as well as the modification, storage, and printing of written documents. Used in this capacity, the multifaceted computer becomes temporarily a dedicated computer. While controlled by a word-processing program it can perform only those tasks for which it was designed. It cannot be utilized, for example, to assist teachers in providing drill-and-practice exercises for students at the same time that it is being used to process words. It cannot be used to develop lists of student names and addresses while it is functioning in this mode. This topic is covered in greater depth in chapters 2 and 7.

A well-chosen, table-model programmable computer not only can serve as a word processor as efficiently as commercially available dedicated machines but is also capable at other times of performing a seemingly infinite variety of burdensome tasks within a school.

Community and Other Pressures to Develop
Computer-Based Programs

Not a day seems to pass without the appearance in a major periodical—or the mention on a radio broadcast or on a major television newscast—of developments related to computers. Students at all levels of education are hardly immune to such news items. Each day, supervisors and administrators throughout the nation face the reality that many youngsters are willing to devote countless hours to play such Atari Corporation computer games as Pac-Man and Space Invaders, which they learn to play so proficiently.

Why a series of electrical impulses disguised as colorful, animated cartoon characters succeeds in capturing the imagination, energy, time, attention, and perserverence of such a large segment of our youth continues to confound, frustrate, and elude us. Why these same youngsters who develop such proficiency with computer games face difficulties in reading, math, and the conjugation of verbs in foreign language also continues to perplex educators nationally.

Perhaps it would be advantageous to come to terms with the times and with the reality of the computer's appeal to youth and its ability to help solve problems. Rather than resist what has become increasingly apparent, administrators and supervisors might well consider the merits of utilizing the possibilities of the computer revolution to improve communication with students, to motivate them, and to upgrade the quality and variety of approaches to instruction. Students, their parents, and the community at large have come to expect that schools will continue to reflect the times as they are, the changing values, and the behavior patterns of those whose education they are charged with overseeing. Schools have never and ought never to be isolated from trends and developments in society. The utilization of computers is expected. It is essential, however, that responsible officials be aware of both the positive and negative impact that exposure to computers in education can have on students, staff, and the community. Such awareness can significantly influence the ways in which the solving of problems is approached.

Computer Literacy

To make educationally sound decisions regarding the acquisition and utilization of computers, it is essential that school administrators and supervisors develop some degree of proficiency in *computer literacy*. Although there are several interpretations as to what constitutes computer literacy, the most widely accepted definition encompasses four principal components: (1) defining the term *computer*, its basic parts, their interrelationship, and the means by which computers communicate with human beings; (2) the history of the computer with an understanding of those pressures that motivated its evolution and multidimensional applications for resolving continually developing technological problems; (3) cognizance of the positive and negative impact of computers on society; and (4) controlling the computer with quality programming that achieves a desired objective proficiently and accurately.

Without such knowledge, school administrators and supervisors are at a tremendous disadvantage when dealing with the wide range of educational problems before them. To develop viable, proficient project utilization for computers in administration, supervision, and instruction, computer literacy is essential. Chapter 11 is devoted entirely to computer-literacy education.

Definition of Terms

At this point it is advantageous to define a number of terms used frequently in the computer industry that we will be using throughout the book.

1. *BASIC* refers to one of the more popular languages that are used to communicate with some computers (*B*eginners *A*ll *P*urpose *S*ymbolic *I*nstruction *C*ode).
2. A *calculator* is a piece of equipment that can only perform numerical calculations.
3. *Hardware* refers to physical pieces of equipment such as computers, printers, disk drives, cathode-ray-tube (CRT) screens, cassette recorders, and such.
4. A *program* is a collection of instructions to be performed by the computer.
5. A *programmer* is an individual who creates a set of instructions that causes the computer to perform either a specific function or a collection of functions.
6. A *commercial program* is a program designed to cause a computer to accomplish specific tasks. It may be purchased from organizations outside the school.
7. An *in-house-program* is one that is written by an individual within an organization.
8. *Software* is a term that describes a set of instructions that direct a computer to perform a specific task or collection of tasks.
9. *Supplies* are expendable materials such as paper, labels, unused diskettes, and so forth.
10. A *user* is an individual who knows how to operate a computer that has been preprogrammed and who does not necessarily have to comprehend how a computer functions or how a program is designed.

The Parts of a Computer

What is a computer? A computer is a plastic, silicon, and metal device, which contains within it a variety of interrelated parts connected by wires that serve to receive, transmit, and store messages and information via electrical impulses. Those computers that have been most widely accepted for use in schools contain four principal parts: (1) the central processing unit (CPU), (2) input devices, (3) output devices, and (4) storage devices. We will be using an anthropomorphic analogy to illustrate the interrelation of the various parts of a computer.

C.P.U.

The central processing unit constitutes the so-called brains of the machine. It is responsible for receiving information, manipulating that data, attending to the achievement of specific assigned tasks, and transmitting the resulting information to the computer user. The CPU performs some functions analogous to those of the traffic police officer or the transit switchperson. It must monitor the activity of all of the computer's components and coordinate them so that the entire system functions as an integrated unit.

CPUs come in three sizes and are known as microprocessors, mini processors, and main-frame processors. They each are designed to accommodate different-sized computers. The three types of computers are known as main-frame computers (the largest computers, serving the needs of major corporations and the information-processing needs of government), minicomputers (desk-size computers—the basic school computer of the 1970s), and microcomputers (table-model computers about the size of electric typewriters). It is the latter (the microcomputer) that seems best suited to the needs of most schools today.

At the heart of the microcomputer is a single integrated-circuit chip, one of many mounted on a board within the plastic housing unit. Chips range in size from approximately one inch to three inches in length and from one-fourth of an inch to one inch wide. The larger computers that are designed to perform more extensive, complicated functions are composed of a series of many such boards. Each manufacturer uses a different model integrated-circuit-chip processor, each with its own unique advantages and disadvantages but essentially performing the same function. The construction of such chips is of no importance to those charged with the decision as to which computer to purchase. It is, however, important to become aware of the most popular available brands of microcomputers, namely TRS8O, Apple, Pet, Atari, Commodore, Digital Equipment, and the IBM. Each offers a variety of advantages and disadvantages.

Input Devices

The microprocessor at the core of each computer must be able to receive and transmit information if it is to interact with the computer user. To *speak with* or communicate with a computer, a user has to be able to send electronic messages to the computer via one of several languages that the computer has been programmed to *understand*. Among the more common languages are BASIC, FORTRAN, COBOL, PL/1, Pascal, LOGO, and PILOT, to name just a few. Input devices are used by the processor to obtain information from a computer user. The most familiar forms of input device are typewriter keyboards and computer-card readers.

Generally microcomputers use keyboards as input devices as contrasted with the larger main-frame machines, which usually use both keyboards and card readers. Therefore, input devices are utilized by computer users and programmers to transmit information to the computer. The typewriter keyboard is the mechanism used to speak directly to the CPU by typing instructions, which are translated into specific electrical impulses that the computer has been programmed to understand. A keypunch machine is used to prepare punched cards containing many holes seemingly placed in haphazard arrangements. Such cards are familiar because they are similar to the telephone and utility bills that arrive in the mail at many of our homes and offices. The holes on the card are read electronically by an electro-

Source: Courtesy of Commodore Business Machines, Inc.

Figure 1-1. Input Device, Commodore VIC 20

Figure 1-2. Input Device: Joystick

mechanical light-sensing device known as a *card reader* and the information is then transmitted to the CPU. There are other input devices, but they are used far less often in schools.

Output Devices

Output devices are machines that are attached to the central processing unit and that the processor uses to transmit information to the computer programmer or user. The most common forms of output devices are cathode-ray-tube screens (the familiar television screen and known by computer experts as CRTs) and printers (machines that translate the computer's electrical impulses into the English alphabet and then proceed to print that information on paper for the computer user to see and use). With such devices, a processor can either supply information or inform the user of problems or specific needs in the system in a clear visual format.

Storage Devices

Storage devices are of basically two varieties known generally as *temporary storage devices* and *permanent storage devices*. Temporary storage devices retain computer information only as long as the power is left on. When the

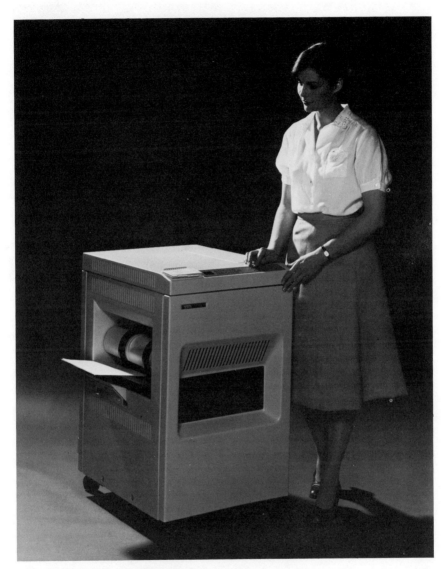

Source: Courtesy of Digital Equipment Corporation.
Figure 1-3. Laser Page Printer

computer system's power is turned off, temporary storage devices immediately lose the ability to retain the information that had been stored. Integrated-circuit chips are generally utilized for temporary storage of information. Each chip is currently technologically able to store in excess

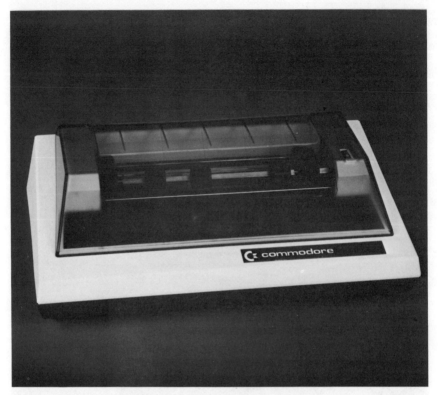

Source: Courtesy of Commodore Business Machines, Inc.
Figure 1-4. Microcomputer Printer

of one-million pieces of information and storage capacity is doubling approximately every three years.

In most computers currently in use, the less-advanced 16,000-fact storage chip is common. Although these chips are powerful tools, they are also volatile. For that reason there are more permanent forms of storage available. The standard unit of storage is called the *byte*. One byte represents the amount of memory that can retain a single character of information (for example, one letter of the alphabet or a keyboard symbol). One *kilobyte* is equal to 1,024 storage units. Thus a 48K microcomputer is capable of retaining in excess of 49,000 characters in its temporary memory at any one time (that is, $48 \times 1,024 = 49,152$).

Whereas microcomputers smaller in capacity than 48K can serve well for the resolution of many school tasks, the 48K capability ensures potential performance of even the most complex computer operations required by most schools. It is advisable to resist the urge to purchase more machine than is actually needed.

Permanent storage generally is accomplished on magnetic media, most commonly in the form of tape or disk. A variety of tapes in different sizes is employed. Most familiar is the smaller standard-size cassette, the length of which is measured in time (for example, 30 minutes; 60 minutes; 90 minutes; 120 minutes). Large-reel tape, referred to as *mag tape*, is the other familiar form of permanent storage on tape. The second mode of permanent storage is *disk*, a soft, flat, round, magnetically coated, plastic sheet housed permanently within a flat, square, plastic protective jacket. Such disks are either five-and-one-quarter-inch square, resembling the familiar 45-rpm phonograph record or are eight-inch square. These mini diskettes, generally referred to as *floppy diskettes* differ in their storage capacities. Hard-sectored disks are physically larger and have a significantly greater

Source: Courtesy of Zilog Corporation.

Figure 1-5. Z80 Microprocessor Chip in Its Protective Case

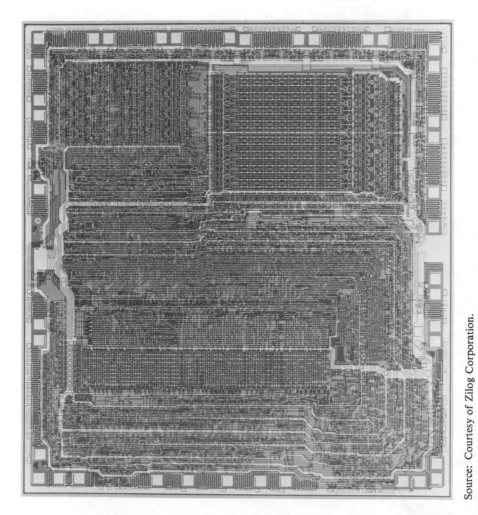

Figure 1-6. Z80 Microprocessor Chip out of Its Protective Case, with Internal Parts Visible

storage capacity. The type needed is dependent on the specific requirements of each particular microcomputer and the application for which it is intended. These permanent storage devices function much in the same way as does tape by allowing information or data to be stored magnetically. One major difference, however, is that disks permit the transfer of information more rapidly than tape. The input and output of data may be accomplished at a faster rate.

It is important, at this point, that administrators and supervisors become cognizant of other fundamental computer terms. Because there are a large variety of tasks that the computer may be asked to perform, it is essential that these broad categories be explored and understood. Familiarity with these concepts will ensure that sound educational decisions can be made. There are five principal categories for the assignment of tasks to be handled by the computer in most schools: (1) central administration, (2) supervision, (3) instruction: drill and practice (computer-assisted instruction), (4) instruction: tutorial programs, and (5) computer-literacy education.

1. *Central-administration* computing chores permit the computer user to perform a wide variety of clerical tasks and provide authorized personnel with rapid and easy access to desired information.
2. *Supervisory* computing chores permit the user to perform a variety of clerical chores related to the instruction process and provide personnel with rapid and easy access to desired information. The permanent-storage function of which computers are capable permit the saving of valuable file-cabinet storage space.
3. *Instruction: drill-and-practice* chores permit the computer user to obtain assistance with the instructional process. In this capacity, computers do not teach but, rather, assist the teacher. Computers are utilized to provide individualized drill and practice sessions for students of varying levels of ability and in all subject areas.
4. *Instruction: tutorial programs* permit the computer to actually teach content. In this capacity, computers may be utilized to introduce new material to students of varying ability levels with special identifiable problems. This mode is particularly useful in independent-study programs and for reteaching individually concepts not previously grasped by students.
5. *Computer-literacy education* permits the computer to be utilized in the instruction of students in the operation and control of computers, the history of computers, and the social blessings and problems brought to communities by virtue of computer utilization. Students are taught how to write programs, which may then be tested by actual experimentation. Among others, one major result of such involvement is to make students aware of possible future viable careers.

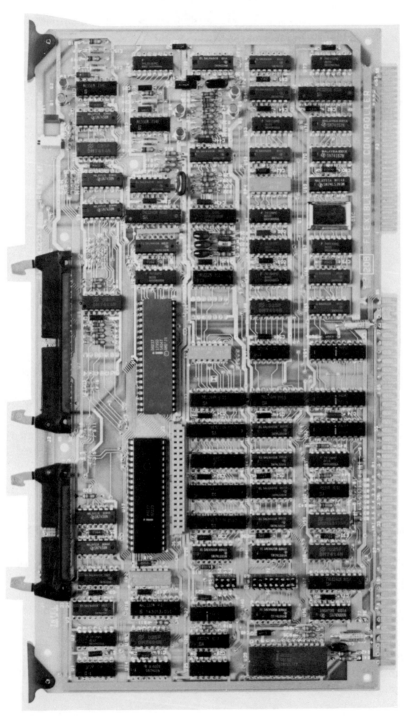

Figure 1-7. Multi-Chip Board

Source: Courtesy of Intel Corporation.

Source: Courtesy of Motorola, Inc.

Figure 1-8. Storage Device: RAM Chips

Source: Courtesy of Texas Instruments, Inc.
Figure 1-9. Storage Device: Cassette Recorder

Each of the above categories suggests the need for careful consideration by administrators and supervisors prior to planning the initiation of possible school computer facilities. It must be determined at the outset precisely which function or functions are most appropriate for a particular school environment.

Security

It is essential to explore the problem of security maintenance when planning a computer facility. Not only must hardware and supplies be made secure from vandalism and theft but also the data banks of information that the computer is able to provide must be made available only to those individuals who are delegated the authority to know. The integrity and the privacy of individuals are cardinal principles in a democratic society that must be safeguarded.

The unscrupulous must be prevented from accessing information to which they are not entitled and that they might sell or exchange for personal

Source: Courtesy of International Business Machines Corporation.
Key: A—Keyboard input device for IBM Personal Computer.
B—CRT output device for IBM Personal Computer.
C—Diskette drive permanent storage device for IBM Personal Computer.
D—CPU and memory chips (under the keys) for IBM Personal Computer.
E—Printer for IBM Personal Computer

Figure 1-10. Complete Administrative Computer System

gain. The tapes or disks that store what may be confidential information must be secured. A well-designed computer facility is one in which security is easily and effectively maintained.

Training

Another vital consideration that must be examined at the inception of planning a computer facility is the proper preparation, involvement, selection, training, and utilization of staff. It is advisable to discuss plans with faculty and staff at the outset so that avenues for their input may be provided. The structure and design of the computer facility only can benefit from such input, feelings of identification, and commitment by the staff. Only well-trained and properly motivated people can make a computer facility function effectively. It is essential to avoid alienation. Rumor, inuendo, and fear can only have an adverse effect on the success of the operation.

If the computer facility involves articulation with and assistance from outside agencies, it is important to determine at the outset the roles that each will be expected to play. We will discuss this in greater detail in the next chapter.

It is increasingly evident that U.S. society and other technologically oriented nations are becoming more and more involved with computers and with computer-related activities. Over the past two centuries, we have been transformed from a society that was more than 80-percent agrarian at its inception into one that is now more than 60-percent information oriented. A recent study suggests that 20 percent of the U.S. urban working force is engaged in night-time labor. A host of businesses now maintain twenty-four-hour facilities to service this segment of the labor force. Night-time labor is necessitated to keep expensive computers working twenty-four hours a day, seven days a week. As a society, we are adapting to the new economics that emanate from the computer presence. It is expected that significant social adjustments will become necessitated as well.

A recent issue of a major national magazine reported that within the very near future, human beings will have made available to them a new variety of computer-oriented products designed once again to elevate the quality of life and the standard of living. Video cameras can record images electronically on magnetic disks rather than on film, thereby permitting the consumer to view snapshots on a television screen rather than having to develop film. A major international corporation expects to market a microwave oven that recites recipes.

Current stereophonic systems may become obsolete with the expected introduction of a compact digital audio disc-and-player system utilizing lasers. Such promise seems to demand that administrators look and listen.

Schools can no longer afford to disregard the possibilties afforded by the utilization of computers. Society that fails to keep pace with the times falls behind. Those school systems that choose not to adjust to changing technology deny the computer the opportunity to assist in the reduction of a variety of burdensome tasks; they fall behind and fail their students, staff, and community.

2

The Gamut of Possibilities for Computer Utilization

Preparing to Receive the New Machines

Many schools throughout the nation are already involved with the utilization of computers for assisting with administrative and instructional chores. Because the decision to assign computers to an active role in schools is a phenomenon that reaches back only to the early 1970s, very few administrators are knowledgeable about the wide spectrum of possible applications available and therefore have not taken fullest advantage of the entire menu of choices. Even in those educational institutions now identified as computerized schools, administrators seem to have relegated computers to only a few limited functions. The machines do little but sit idle for much of the time and are highly underutilized. Though computers, even in this limited capacity, have handled assigned tasks to the satisfaction of administrators and seem in most cases to justify the initial investment, each school would do well to establish a kind of computer think-tank committee, composed of administrators, supervisors, teachers, secretaries, students, and parents. Such a group would be assigned the principal tasks of determining how most effectively to extend the talents of these tireless pieces of equipment, to evaluate periodically their performance, and to monitor changes in computer technology in order to continue to remain aware of possible new applications.

School computer utilization falls naturally into five major areas: (1) central administration, (2) supervision, (3) insruction: drill and practice, (4) instruction: tutorial programs, and (5) computer literacy. Each of these categories opens for consideration a wide range of possible applications.

Central Administration

The central administration in a school can secure computer assistance in two essential areas: (1) word processing and (2) data-file maintenance. Within each of these categories, there are a large variety of possible applications to choose from.

Word processing is an umbrella term for those activities usually associated with the professional clerical tasks normally handled by a school's secretarial staff. Using a computer in the capacity of word processor (alluded to previously in chapter 1), secretaries can type letters, lists, and other documents into a computer, modify them, and have them printed

23

automatically and instantaneously on paper for immediate use. A photocopy of such material may then be stored in traditional file cabinets or saved permanently on a five-and-one-quarter-inch magnetic diskette (approximately the size of 45-RPM record), on an eight-inch magnetic diskette (with a larger storage capacity), on hard disk (the granddaddy of storage devices), or on a tape. Each blank five-and-one-quarter-inch diskette has the capacity to save up to 180,000 characters (typewriter-key strokes), the approximate equivalent of five chapters in this book. One hard disk can store up to 80 million characters (a small library). One side of a thirty-minute cassette has the capacity to save up to approximately 135,000 characters. Each time any key on the computer keyboard is struck, an electronic impulse registers the equivalent of one character. It is advisable to set up an entry system—either a notebook log for identifying the specific document and its exact place of storage or a computer program that may be written to serve as an electronic index for data saved on permanent diskettes or cassettes. Should the document be needed for reference in the future, the easily accessible diskette or cassette will permit either its viewing on the computer screen or its reprinting on paper. In addition to its greater capacity for the saving of data, the diskette permits the subsequent accessing of that data at a significantly more rapid rate than does the cassette. The space saving in filing cabinets can be highly significant and the possibility of misplacing data is minimized.

Unlike the traditional procedure for preparing documents on a typewriter, modifications are accomplished instantaneously by a word processor. Individual characters, words, sentences, and paragraphs may be modified easily. The word processor then allows for the rearrangement of words, sentences, and paragraphs at the touch of a single key stroke. For example, the word processor permits deletion, insertion, overtyping, and block movement of words, phrases, sentences, and paragraphs to newly selected locations within the document, which may be examined on the screen and again edited and modified before being printed automatically on selected qualities of paper. As changes are made, the computer accommodates each such change by rearranging the balance of the document automatically. The time saved in endless corrections and retyping frees the secretary for other work.

Costly supplies (for example, correction tape and whiteout) become unnecessary. It has been estimated that word processing results in the saving of from 20 percent to 50 percent of the time usually required for the traditional electric-typewriter preparation and modification of school documents. This time-saving factor is cumulative because schools frequently reuse the same or similar letters, notices, and bulletins each year. Rather than retype the entire document, the secretary retrieves the document from the diskette or cassette and loads it into the computer by pressing a few keys in sequence, affects appropriate modifications, again saves the revised document on the diskette or cassette, makes notations in the log index, and then prints it on paper. The process of typing itself is significantly faster on a word processor than on a traditional typewriter. One specific example is in order to illustrate the process. Each year it is customary in most senior-high schools to issue a college-night bulletin. Rather than spend time searching through file-cabinet drawers for the previous year's bulletin from which to type the new document, the secretary can instead retrieve a copy of the previous bulletin from the computer in approximately ten seconds; immediately visualize it on the screen, change the date, the scheduled meeting time, and the names of the current college representatives in a few minutes; and then print out the newly revised bulletin in a few additional seconds. Afterthoughts and additional modifications by the supervisor should obviate resentments generally brought on by the tedious redoing of the same work.

Once finalized on the screen, the bulletin can then be directed by the word processor to be printed precisely according to instructions (for example, automatic centering; automatic single, double, or triple spacing; automatic correctly placed hyphenations; and the specific number of lines per page). The insertion of a diskette with a commercially available dictionary program permits the bulletin to be proofread electroncially so that any errors in spelling that may have been missed may be automatically corrected. The entire process is completed in a few minutes. Requirements that a document either be typed once or used as the prototype for subsequent versions to be generated suggest that word processing is the most sensible technique for increasing productivity. Its speed of operation permits the completion in seconds of those changes that improve the overall cosmetic appearance of the document. Eyesores like whiteout and uneven spacing are avoided. The excessive time needed for retyping with possible new mistakes, reproofing, and correcting often encourages administrators to accept less than perfect copy. They no longer need compromise or accept less. Word processing allows for continuing modification without retyping the entire document. In addition, because properly functioning computers generate very few errors, word-processed documents tend to be freer of errors than their unprocessed ancestors. The time for administrative word processing in schools is now.

Other school-administration documents—generally a variety of repetitive clerical chores that lend themselves to word processing—include letters, bulletins, notices, annual and weekly calendars, organization sheets, conference agendum and minutes, teacher and supervisor evaluation reports, faculty profiles, pupil-suspension reports, performance objectives, survey reports, and bibliographies. Word processors can also be utilized effectively for the creation of schedules that can be modified each year. For example, testing coordinators arrange schedules showing student names, room assignments, and proctors. Such annual schedule changes need only accommodate name changes rather than necessitating complete revision. Additionally, among the onerous tasks to which secretaries may be assigned is the typing of endless lists that seem to be forever in need of constant revision. Such lists encompass transportation address verification, lunchroom-program procedures, medical-office reports (student handicaps), scores on standardized examinations (mathematics and reading), student admissions and discharges, candidates for graduation, class-placement statistical reports (overall averages), and identification of students who failed to return textbooks. One example, perhaps will illustrate the point. The secretary assigned the task of preparing a listing showing official classes, official rooms, and assigned teachers, usually requiring a succession of changes, would welcome a word processor.

At each level, elementary, middle school or junior-high school, and senior-high school, the central administration is not only besieged by such clerical chores as those described above but also often requires current access to information—and often on a cumulative basis. It is advantageous to store such data electronically in computers in an ongoing process, thereby creating a series of data banks or data files. Whereas it would be extremely cumbersome if not impossible for human beings to maintain such data files because of the large mass and variety of information constantly being accumulated, a computer is ideally suited to performing this data-file maintenance. Its memory bank is extensive and as data is deposited or entered into the computer, it is not only stored in the machine's memory but is also saved on diskettes for subsequent instant retrieval at the touch of a key. Administrators, therefore, can design needed data collections and may manipulate them to achieve specific objectives. Several examples will serve to illustrate the advantages of using a computer for this task.

A treasury-file management program allows a school administrator to store and manage the school's treasury information. With the computer configured properly, the amounts on all checks written and on all bills incurred would be recorded in a computer data file and stored for subsequent retrieval. Periodically the administrator can ask the computer to list all transactions that were made by a particular individual or involved a particular vendor, and the machine would respond by printing out the requested information in date sequence. The computer can also generate its output list in accordance with specific amounts of money. This feature allows for a quick search of the data file for specific information and for a listing to be generated on paper.

Should a vendor maintain that a bill has not been paid, the administrator can easily determine which specific purchases were made from that vendor and the exact dates that the checks were drawn. On occasions when a school has been billed for a purchase not yet received, the computer can generate a list of all back-ordered items so that payment is made for only those items received. Therefore, greater efficiency results.

Another data file might include complete teacher profiles. This would allow the payroll secretary to print out a teacher seniority list according to date of employment and area of specialization. Such a data file could also be utilized to identify individuals who have served in a particular capacity to assist administrators in providing for an equitable rotation of assignments.

An inventory data file of supplies and hardware permits immediate identification of items and quantities distributed to individuals, items in short supply, and prices.

A school's college office can maintain a continuing college-profile data bank for use by students who intend to apply for admission. Such a file would include information about previous applicants: academic averages, Scholastic Aptitude Test (SAT) or Achievement College Test (ACT) scores (verbal and math), achievement-test scores, colleges to which applications were sent, and decisions by colleges (acceptances or rejections). A student wishing to assess the chance for admission to a particular college may ask the computer for a record of all students who previously applied to that school. The student may then compare his or her statistics with those of previous applicants to help determine chances for acceptance.

A student-profile data bank can be developed by storing information about each child admitted to a school. Once begun, the process of data-file maintenance is continuous. The computer can be asked to store in its memory the following categories of information: the student's full name, home address, home telephone number, parents' names, emergency telephone number, ethnic data, socioeconomic data (for example, welfare need, free-transportation need, free-lunch need, and so on), physical handicap, language difficulty, specific talents, standardized scores in reading and mathematics, textbook-return record, and dean's office record of infractions.

The administration, as needs arise, can then access a variety of data for completing required government ethnic-survey reports, for informing faculty as to student disabilities, and for the preparation of burdensome organization reports. Zip codes can serve as a source of information about the number of students residing in poverty areas, needing free-transportation passes, and free lunch. Such data can be useful in ascertaining if a school qualifies for special funding under a specific federal program. At the touch of a key, administrators can access information about a student's record of disciplinary infractions and can then determine whether parents should be notified, if suspense proceedings are in order, or if referral for counseling is indicated. The total number of students in each grade, monitored by additional admissions and discharges, is immediately and accurately available. Pupil-personnel services can determine at a glance those students in need of remedial assistance in reading and mathematics.

A program data file containing information about the kinds of classes on each subject area (for example, American history, Western civilization, electives, and such), the number of classes in each subject area, the numbers of students opting for those classes, teacher-subject assignments, and teacher noninstructional assignments, can yield invaluable information: (1) teaching coverage per teacher, (2) teaching coverage per department, (3) distribution of students by subject area, (4) distribution of students in regular, honors, and repeater classes, (5) average class size per subject area, (6) class size within subjects in each academic area, (7) daily program of average student, (8) curriculum index, and (9) the degree of efficiency by which an administration utilizes its budget capabilities.

Chapter 7 will provide several computer programs for setting up data files similar to those described in this chapter.

Supervision

Generally, junior- and senior-high schools are organized by departments, each supervised by either an assistant principal or a chairperson. In times of budgetary restriction, costly supplies such as paper, the lifeblood of many departments, are severely limited. Much time is also devoted to duplicating, collating, and stapling large varieties of teacher-made materials. Because much individual time and effort is expended in the preparation and typing of spirit-duplicator and mimeograph stencils, teachers are reluctant to reproduce the number of copies that are actually needed for students in their classes. Most teachers, anticipating students losing the material, often duplicate more than is actually needed for their classes and sometimes even duplicate sets of papers for use in future years. Though much is eventually thrown away, because the material either becomes obsolete, no longer seems useful, or loses the interest of the teacher, resulting in significant time and material waste, there is ongoing need for filing—cabinet storage space. In times of economic contraction, there is among teachers, cooperative planning, preparation of materials (for example, readings, documents, charts, graphs, outline maps, cartoons, and examinations), and the request for large printing runs. Such cooperation, admirable for its brainstorming advantages, also has by its very nature an adverse effect on individual creativity. The word processor provides opportunity for the return to such individual creativity because it offers the opportunity to eliminate the need for such extensive cooperation among teachers.

The computer, used as a word processor, once again offers to supervisors and administrators tremendous advantages. Documents such as performance objectives, generally required annually, may be prepared, printed and saved on diskette for future reference, evaluation, and revision. Multipage courses of study can be written, similarly saved on diskette, and retrieved, modified, and printed as needs arise, thus avoiding the waste of having multiple copies cumbersomely stored in already burgeoning file cabinets. Multipage calendars of lessons for each course of study, invaluable as teacher guides for implementing curricula, lend themselves to the word processor. Such documents are easily prepared, printed, and saved on diskette for reference, evaluation, and revision. As a word processor, the computer can be used to prepare, print, and save teacher-observation reports, again saving file-cabinet storage space and increasing efficiency. The supervisor of a department each term often must prepare lists of students in each grade needing assignment to rooms for uniform and standardized examinations. The word processor is an invaluable ally for such burdensome tasks, as is a computer preprogrammed to manage data files.

Supervisors of departments can also utilize a computer for data-file maintenance. Inventory data files can be developed to keep track of textbook titles, per-textbook cost, names of students to whom such textbooks were issued, names of subject class teachers, numbers of textbooks requested by teachers for each subject class, and the numbers of textbooks returned from each subject class at the end of each term or school year. The supervisor has available instantaneously information about numbers of textbooks either lost or not returned, teacher effectiveness in controlling textbook loss, information on which to base textbook-ordering estimates, and the names of students who may be required to pay penalties for such loss. The supervisors of such departments as business education, industrial arts, fine arts, music, and physical education are faced with the ongoing problem of maintaining extensive inventories of equipment and supplies. The computer is ideal for this use. The individual assigned to supervise or coordinate the activities of the school library or multimedia center is similarly faced with inventory problems related to equipment (for example, phonographs, film and filmstrip projectors, cassette players and recorders, overhead projectors, and opaque projectors), software (for example, films, filmstrips, filmloops, phonograph records, maps, and globes), and books. Again the computer is an ideal tool for inventory data-file maintenance.

Supervisors can develop computer files for lesson plans in each subject area that can be used for teacher-training programs and for per-diem or long-term substitute teachers. a resource data file can be prepared so that teacher-made materials can be instantaneously accessed for each subject taught. Teacher-prepared-examination data files can be developed for each subject area. Even more impressive is the possibility for developing a quality question data bank for each subject taught from which teachers may select specific questions for unit examinations. The supervisor can also prepare and maintain a teacher-profile data bank containing information relevant to college courses, specific areas of academic interest, courses taught each semester, years of teaching experience, student level preferred (for example, honors, regular, slow or repeater), and subject area preferred. Such a data file permits the supervisor to access relevant information for decision making in teacher program assignments, selection of individuals for cocurricular activities, and identification of individuals to spearhead the development of a viable elective or pull-out program. The computer's utilization for data-file maintenance is extremely helpful for upgrading the process of effective supervision. Specific data-file maintenance programs in chapter 8 will illustrate the advantages of such computer assistance in supervision.

Instruction: Drill and Practice

The computer's flexibility offers unique opportunities for assisting teachers with the instructional process. It provides the teacher with still another tool with which to reach students, one with which they are familiar, one that offers little threat to ego and social status, and one to which they respond positively. Computers do not replace teachers, textbooks, workbooks, spirit-duplicator stencils, or the chalkboard; they merely offer another mode for meeting the particular needs of certain youngsters. In situations where the pupil-to-teacher ratio is high, the computer can be a potent assistant for providing individualized instruction. Computer-aided instruction (CAI) has proved effective for reinforcement of skills and concepts already presented by the teacher. It permits remediation experiences for the reticent child who may feel more secure and less threatened when working alone with a machine that doesn't criticize. It offers the teacher the opportunity to help those alienated students who might respond favorably to a nontraditional approach. It is suited to students who learn at a slower rate and need additional help beyond the group situation as well as those who need a more advanced or enriched program than that available to their classmates.

When the teacher becomes aware that certain students have not mastered specific aspects of content and skills already presented (this is usually ascertained from examinations, from student writing samples, and from evaluation of student recitations), and there seems to be little time for reteaching if the course of study is to be completed by the majority of students in class, CAI provides individualized instructional assistance. It also reaches those children whose home academic environment is less than ideal and where parental assistance may be lacking. CAI has proved effective for children with dyslexia and other learning disabilities, with physical handicaps, and with other special-education limitations.

Computers have been placed in a centrally located classroom for sharing by teachers on a grade. In some schools, CAI activities are organized so that computers may be moved from room to room either on a schedule or on a need basis. More often, computers are located centrally in department offices, in libraries or multimedia centers, in reading laboratories, and in mathematics laboratories. Students may reserve time with a computer to reinforce learning through practice.

There are essentially two types of computer-aided instruction. One approach involves the use of the computer to generate a series of questions without the machine storing a record of the student's correct or incorrect answers. For example, one program instructs the student to type in the antonyms to a series of words. The student is afforded the opportunity to practice a skill that has been previously presented to the entire class. The computer, acting as a patient, noncritical coach, informs the student after each question whether the answer provided was correct or incorrect.

A second approach in computer-aided instruction involves drill and practice with a file-management feature (the so-called computer-managed-instruction mode). Student scores are maintained by the computer, permitting teachers to identify those children who showed weakness in a skill area that was practiced. The file-maintenance feature also allows the computer to create new assignments for students based on those questions incorrectly answered. Many schools throughout the nation have experienced considerable success with computer-aided instruction.

Computer-aided instruction programs can be developed in most curriculum areas. Opportunities for its use in reading include phonics (for example, blends, silent *e*, hard and soft *c*, and vowel sounds), comprehension skills (for example, main idea, inference, recall of facts, and sequencing), and vocabulary development (for example, synonyms, antonyms, homonyms, and dictionary skills). In the language-arts program, CAI may be used for correct usage, spelling, punctuation, parts of speech, sentence structure, paragraphing, and letter writing to mention just a few possible areas. Several examples of its use in mathematics are problem solving, shape recognition, arithmetic operations, percentage, ratio, metrics, basic number facts, and money concepts. In the social studies program, CAI is appropriate for interpreting maps, globes, and charts; use of reference books; use of index and table of contents; using library facilities; and reviewing units of work (for example, the Constitution, the Civil War, and so on). In science, CAI can be effective in reading thermometer scales, interpreting weather maps, and classification within the animal kingdom. CAI has also been utilized effectively in the fine arts, industrial arts, and business education. Several CAI programs will be discussed in chapter 9.

Instruction: Tutorial Programs

Computers can be used effectively in specific situations to introduce and teach new bodies of content. Students sit in front of a console and respond to programmed questions by typing responses on a standard computer keyboard. Unlike programs in drill and practice described above, in tutorial programs the computer is geared to analyze each student response and then to proceed depending on the nature of the response. For example, a student, Mary Smith, learning about the U.S. Constitition is asked by the computer, "Which article of the Constitution is concerned with the executive branch of government?" If the student responds, "Article II," the machine may proceed by displaying on its screen, "You are correct, Mary, try the next question." If, however, Mary did not know the correct answer and guessed by typing "Article III," the computer might print on its screen, "Mary, please open your textbook to page 435 and review each of the Articles of the Constitution." Another alternative is for the computer to reveal the correct answer and then present the question again at a later time.

Computers used in tutorial programs have been placed most effectively in centralized locations such as the library or multimedia center, department offices, and in reading and mathematics laboratories, or in one corner of a classroom. Procedures are established for students to reserve computer time. Tutorial programs are often extremely effective with students who have had a history of repeated failure in particular subject areas. A student may have failed a unit examination. The teacher, because of time pressures, may not reteach the unit to the unsuccessful students in the class. Availability of computer assistance would encourage the teacher to assign students to a computer session for such reteaching. On occasion a student has a prolonged absence from school for a variety of legitimate reasons (for example, illness, parent divorce, court appearances, special problems, and such), and needs to catch up on work missed. In addition to make-up assignments in the textbook, the computer can be utilized for such instruction. Often, students who have moved from other communities are admitted to class at various times during the term. Units of work vary from school to school and from teacher to teacher. The computer can assist such students in making the adjustment and in catching up with the rest of the class. Some students have become alienated after repeated failures and may respond positively to computer-oriented tutorial programs. The computer also is effective in assisting students with a review of units of work for uniform or standardized examinations. It is ideally suited for students engaged in either advanced work or in independent study programs. In reading and mathematics laboratories where the pupil-to-teacher ratio may be high, the computer may assist with individualized remedial reading and mathematics instruction. Several suggested computer tutorial programs will be discussed in chapter 10.

Computer Literacy

Computer literacy may be defined as a planned sequential approach to enlightening individuals about computers (previously discussed in chapter 1).

Attention needs to be given to students at each stage of their educational development about the term *computer* and its construction, the history of the computer, the positive and negative impact of the computer on society, and learning to program the computer proficiently and meaningfully. The narrower definition, often assigned by some, that suggests that computer literacy means "learning to communicate with and use a computer" is inadequate. It lacks the comprehensiveness of the first definition and thereby falls short. It is appropriate in an increasingly computer-oriented world society that students, faculty, and community become familiar with terminology associated with computers (for example, input and output devices, bytes, bits, magnetic diskettes, programs, and so on). It is important that the community become aware of the history of computers so that the uniqueness and ingenuity of the human being is better appreciated. It is essential, if we are to educate self-disciplined, self-sustaining, responsible, contributing, healthy individuals who are expected to take their place in society, to create an awareness of the potential positive and negative impact that computers may have. The impact on social relationships, standard of living, and self-fulfillment of each individual in a technologically oriented society must be explored. The setting of goals and limits has to be encouraged. Lastly, informed citizens must become cognizant of approaches for harnessing the computer to do the bidding of society for the accomplishment of good rather than evil. Because computers are continuing to affect lifestyles, the values to which we aspire, and the behavior of communities individually and collectively, it is essential that computer-literacy education becomes a fundamental part of the educational process.

The future promises continuing computer involvement in international communication, recreation, entertainment, medical treatment, law practice, transportation, and energy systems. On a personal, individual basis, computers are familiar adjuncts in the construction of wrist watches, clock radios, cameras, and stereo systems.

One case in point illustrates clearly the need for continuing computer-literacy education. A senior secretary in a New York City business office was offered a promotion after many years of service with the firm. The employer arranged for the introduction of a computer to assist with office functions. The secretary was provided with the machine and a manual of operations. After many frustrating hours spent in trying to learn the necessary material in the manual, the secretary sadly gave up the attempt. Initial exposure to the new machine instilled a sense of fear, foreboding, and expectation of failure. To cope with such fear and to provide for the needs of contributing citizens, computer literacy and exposure to new phenomena such as computers is vital.

A government bureau recently reported that the world of work has become more than 60 percent involved with information processing. With such changes continuing to affect the job market, intelligent, adequate education must be provided. Specific attention will be devoted to computer-literacy education in chapter 11.

3

Involving School Personnel and the Community: Developing Avenues of Communication

It is advisable to begin generating a climate of inquiry and receptivity at the earliest possible moment once the decision has been made to bring computers into the school. Fortunately, much of the groundwork has already been laid by the mass media. Familiarity of faculty and staff members with items of computer output encountered in day-to-day living (for example, utility bills and such) also assists the administration with establishing a positive, wholesome climate for generating appropriate discussion.

Developing Interest

Although most individuals in a school may be ignorant of the technical aspects of the computer revolution and may have genuine reservations about becoming involved personally with computers and their supportive equipment, there is usually present a natural curiosity about such phenomena. Special television-documentary programs, frequent stories on the news, and regular coverage of developments, often with color photos in weekly national magazines, whet the appetite and suggest an urgency to consider the appropriateness of adopting the latest technological equipment for daily utilization in schools. And yet there is the need to overcome understandable fears and resistance. Many individuals regard themselves as hopelessly inadequate when it comes to dealing with machines. There is an underlying concern that expensive equipment is fragile, sensitive, and subject to expensive, irreparable damage for which they may be held personally liable. There is reluctance, therefore, to touch and handle. Some people suffer from a fear of computers. As reported in the *New York Daily News* on 7 September 1982 this fear is known medically as *Cyberphobia*. It was further reported that this phobia may cause in those vulnerable either nausea, hysteria, stomachaches, or cold sweat. One recent study cited, which was conducted at Saint Joseph's University in Philadelphia, Pennsylvania, revealed that at least 30 percent of the nation's office workers suffer some distress when in the presence of computers. As a result, computer therapy classes are already being offered. There is a need for reassurance and for education to explode misconceptions and myths. A sensible plan of action seems to be in order.

35

It is important to make faculty and staff aware of the many possible applications for which computers may be utilized. It is particularly important to reach out to those individuals who indicate receptivity toward the adoption of computers. There is no more potent ally than positive attitudes expressed with conviction by peers. Prior to initiating the development of a computer facility, it is advisable to plan for a succession of presentations at faculty and small-group conferences (the latter for individuals who wish to attend voluntarily). Follow-up discussions and analyses may be engaged in at either departmental or grade-level conferences.

Speakers from within the school and community are useful for motivating discussion and inquiry and for generating a sense of challenge, excitement, and immediacy. Guest speakers from other schools, local colleges, and universities should be invited to make presentations to the faculty, to the student body at special large-group instructional sessions, and to the parents at evening conferences. It is helpful if these speakers are dynamic individuals who bring to the attention of the audience some of the experiences of personnel in other schools. These experts then become the sounding boards for expression of overt and latent fears. The ensuing discussions may reveal those individuals who are receptive to the introduction of computers and who may become supportive personnel.

Films and other audio-visual materials are readily available from computer manufacturers and from various hardware and software vendors. These firms either employ or hire educational consultants who have been trained to make effective presentations. Care must be taken, however, to ensure that these guest speakers adhere to prearranged guidelines to make their presentations educationally valuable rather than a platform for sales.

An alert administration will arrange for the videotaping of quality television shows about the revolution in technology (for example, the NBC special, "Japan versus U.S.A.—The Hi-Tech Shootout") and utilize such documentaries as the springboard for faculty conferences.

Other formats that may be useful are debates or panel discussions dealing with the possible impact of the computer revolution on society. Not only are significant issues raised but also the process of computer-literacy education (discussed in chapters 1 and 2) is begun. Such discussions invariably turn to a consideration of the wisdom of bringing computers into the school. Allowance for question-and-answer sessions by the staff permits the open exploration of the myriad of possibilities with computer utilization.

Such sessions encourage freedom in the expression of doubts and misgivings. The staff should be given every opportunity to vent feelings at the earliest possible moment. Such expression provides the opportunity in an open forum for administrators to clarify misconceptions, to abolish rumors, to allay fears, and to encourage the raising of relevant questions. Such discussions provide for the amplification and dissemination of relevant information. Such sessions are also valuable for stimulating thinking, revitalizing interest, welcoming involvement, and securing commitment. Most important, a cadre of staff will be identified eventually as the nucleus on which to build the school's computer facility.

The gamut of possibilities for utilizing computers to make the school an easier and more interesting place in which to function usually is considered at such meetings. The staff is led to accept the challenge of being able to do more for the student body as well as for themselves. An informed, committed faculty that has been made part of the process at the inception of the plan to computerize can be a formidable ally in swaying others in the community.

Many firms are willing to make multiple copies of computer-related literature available to schools. Many of these publications are well written, can serve to enlighten the faculty and staff and may be another approach for extending computer-literacy education. The field is changing so rapidly that unless the staff keeps up with new developments and the latest applications, their information is soon outdated. The school library can subscribe to a variety of quality computer magazines that are helpful in furthering the education of the staff. To help make the selection easier, appendix B provides an annotated listing of many of the most popular magazines.

The administration must eventually come to terms with the need to recognize those individuals who are to become the groundbreakers for the computer facility. Several generally held misconceptions need to be dispelled. Many believe, erroneously, that a background in mathematics is a prerequisite for learning to operate computers. Others still cling to the belief that computers can only handle problems in engineering, mathematics, and physics. Though both contain some element of truth, these widely held views are erroneous. No previous training is needed to prepare for successful involvement in the field of educational computing.

Who Should Be Involved?

Furthermore, computers today are much more than mere calculators. Their functions have been expanded significantly over the past few years. Not only can computers perform numerical calculations, but they are extremely adept in handling concepts and problems involving words. Computers are able to assist in analyzing sentence structure. They can be utilized to strengthen skills in reading comprehension. Some computers can actually talk and pronounce words in a modern language. Some computers are able to respond to the physical movements of handicapped persons who cannot type evenly. Computers are used by the blind to read by sound. Computers are being used for music composition. Companies are using computers to monitor the production of phonograph records to detect accurately the sources of technological defects so that an improved product may result.

People with the potential for learning about computers may be linguists, sound experts, artists, musicians, teachers of modern languages, or typists (some of the best computer students at the college level are English or modern-language majors). Any reasonably intelligent, interested individual can learn to operate computers. It would be a terrible error in judgment to consider only a particular segment of the professional staff for computer training.

Selection of Personnel

The problem of accurately identifying the best people for such initial involvement sometimes causes difficulty. A useful approach is to isolate first the projects or functions targeted for adaptation to computers. Once such designations have been ascertained, the specific areas for computer placement in the school become localized. It may be that the workload of the secretary to the administrative assistant has been causing bottlenecks. It may be that the supplies secretary has been experiencing difficulties with maintaining inventories. The school treasurer may have indicated that assistance is needed with the maintenance of accounts. The increase in guidance services expected by students and their parents may have focused in on the need for computer assistance. The individual in charge of the reading laboratory may require computer assistance. Once priorities have been established, the problem of where to place computers has been resolved.

Should the individuals in these agencies indicate either reluctance to the idea of using computers or resentment at having to learn the skills necessary to use them, then the decision of where to initiate projects or whom to train may have to be reconsidered. Should this not be the problem, and there are several candidates from which to choose, then it becomes a matter of identifying those people who would be the most likely to succeed. Consideration should be given to individuals who have either expressed or indicated interest in using computers. Personal conversations may identify more clearly those people who have the enthusiasm and the aptitude for harnessing the computer. The staff might be invited to complete a questionnaire designed to ascertain attitudes toward bringing computers into the school. Should choices become difficult, it is advisable to review each candidate's profile, receptivity to supervision, experience, and record of attendance and punctuality.

It is essential to select a back-up staff for training to allow for possible changes in school organization. Without such back-up, sudden illness or decision to leave results in the computer project coming to a halt until the training of other individuals may be effected. It is also essential at the outset that at least one or two supervisors be trained. Supervisors cannot effectively oversee a computer project if either they become too dependent on the individuals under their supervision or if those individuals truly know more about computer utilization than the supervisors under whom they work. In order that the administration retain its prerogatives and options, it is important that supervisors actively take an interest in and stay on top of developments. To lead effectively, the supervisor must know why and know how. To avoid becoming overdependent on any individual, back-up personnel are necessary.

Personnel Training

Arranging for the training of personnel that have been selected is the second problem that an administration must address. A well-regarded approach is the planning of a series of school or district-wide workshops. Such workshops are usually informal, led by an individual with computer experience and expertise, welcome staff input and constructive suggestions, and encourage the sharing of ideas. Some administrators arrange for experts teaching in colleges and universities to offer inservice courses in their schools. The onsite location of such courses, making travel elsewhere unnecessary, helps to attract staff. It is at such workshops and inservice courses that immersion in available current literature is wedded to theory and combined with practical applications. Some colleges and universities offer excellent computer-training courses and it is advisable to bring such information to the attention of the staff. Some manufacturers of computers, hardware, and software are willing to underwrite training programs. Often they are prepared to send expert consultants to individual schools or to offer training at central locations to accommodate the staffs of several schools. Sometimes, these firms make their own plant sites available for training courses.

In some schools, when budgetary allocation permit, teachers who are selected for involvement in computer-training programs, are relieved either from some of their classes or from nonteaching assignments. In some of the more affluent suburban school districts, staff members are offered financial remuneration for the time and energy they expend. It is incumbent on the administration to provide a climate that encourages growth.

Periodically, it is advantageous to provide opportunities for individuals undergoing computer training to act as resource personnel and to share their knowledge, skills, and insights. They should be encouraged to speak to colleagues at department and faculty conferences, to students at specially arranged assemblies (and eventually to students in computer-education courses), and to parents at evening conferences. They should be asked to speak at meetings of the various community organizations (for example, social, professional, and political groups, churches, and temples). Such personnel should be given the opportunity to write articles in school and community newspapers. After they have gained the necessary expertise, they should be afforded the opportunity to preside at newly developing workshops and to teach inservice courses. In such ways is the process of computer-literacy education advanced.

Outside Assistance

It is of the utmost importance for the school administration to be alert to opportunities for developing ongoing channels of communication with outside agencies and individuals. Such efforts may result in the recruitment of allies who may assist with computer project development and who may also wish to avail themselves of some of the newly acquired services that the school's computers and personnel can provide. In times of economic contraction, the administration cannot afford to ignore the possibilities for securing additional financial assistance and supplementary resources.

Many parent-teacher associations have been involved actively in the purchase of much-needed computing equipment. Individuals active in such organizations are often motivated to call on personal contacts to help the school secure necessary equipment. Many community business people have given time, energy, hardware, supplies, and funds to assist schools in initiating and in developing their computer-education facilities.

Businesses in the community have a vital interest in assisting schools to develop computer-education programs. Their contributions are recognized within the community. Often, they are singled out for recognition and the awarding of plaques at testimonial dinners or at PTA functions. Their business organizations are given wide publicity for their involvement in the school and in furthering the educational process for the community's youth. Often, free advertising is provided in school publications and by word of mouth. These business people are afforded the loyalty of parents and build the loyalties of young people who will one day become customers. Even more important, perhaps, better-educated students possessing the skills demanded by industry provide a better-prepared work force from which to choose. Business leaders often donate to schools some of their firm's equipment that may have become obsolete but may be perfectly suitable for educating students. Often, community business people offer the schools computer paper, which although used (usually only on one side), may be ideally suited to the practicing needs of students. Often, business leaders offer schools the assistance of highly trained personnel who can be utilized in the ongoing process of staff training. Community businesses often make their plants available for training visits by staff members and for student experiential excursions.

Colleges and universities are engaged actively in ongoing teacher-training programs on the undergraduate and graduate levels. It is the conviction of most of such higher-education institutions that the training process of future teachers should include computer education because the individuals who will be entering the profession will have to be computer literate in order for them to function effectively. It is futile to contest the power of the tide. It is in the interest of the colleges and universities to assist community elementary and secondary schools in developing meaningful, quality computer-education programs. As with businesses, many colleges and universities have substantial amounts of equipment that, as a result of continuing developments in computer technology, have become obsolete. Such equipment is still highly usable for computer-education programs in community schools. The colleges and universities are afforded the benefits of tax writeoffs once such donations of equipment have been accepted. Such obsolete computer equipment has permitted many schools to begin computer-education programs that they otherwise might not have been able to afford. Large national firms such as telephone companies and utilities have also provided necessary groundbreaking computer equipment for many school districts.

Utilizing Internal Strengths

As computer-literacy-education programs in the schools take hold, students will learn how to write computer programs. As the programs they write become more sophisticated, not only will they become more meaningful and useful but they also will provide concrete evidence of student growth. To give young adults in senior-high school status and responsibility, they can be asked to assist junior-high school students in the community with the writing of a variety of drill-and-practice programs. Similarly the youngsters in junior-high school can be encouraged to assist elementary-school students in the community with writing less sophisticated but viable drill-and-practice programs. Many elementary-school administrators encourage their more able computer-literacy students to write drill-and-practice programs for their schoolmates who are in need of remediation. Such involvement benefits older children who are encouraged to create such computer programs and also benefits the children who are to make use of the programs generated within their own school.

Many schools also arrange for young programmers to visit those classes, or even other schools, in which their computer programs are actually in use. Not only does it afford these youngsters much needed recognition and status but it also provides them with the opportunity to identify first hand any weaknesses they may discern in the programs they have written, to make necessary amendments, and to develop skills for developing better-quality computer programs. Such visits certainly promote the most meaningful kind of articulation between schools.

Many youngsters bring to school a surprisingly sophisticated awareness of computers. They are actively involved with a large variety of commercially available computer games. They seem much less afraid of a computer-oriented environment than many adults. In addition, they seem to welcome opportunities to demonstrate to the establishment the expertise they have attained. They often seem to delight in knowing more than the adults who are their teachers. If, therefore, sensitive administrators were to take advantage of this mind set, the interests, abilities, needs, and energies of many of our students could be channeled toward desirable ends. For example, a variety of extracurricular activities could be developed to accommodate such objectives.

By mobilizing the leadership of more able students, a dynamic faculty advisor could motivate large numbers of interested youngsters to develop original computer games and to then arrange competitions (with prizes) at no significant financial cost to their parents. Interschool competitions would follow naturally. Other groups of students who might be theory-oriented could be encouraged to write sophisticated programs needed by agencies within the school. Such youngsters could be encouraged to enter a variety of local, state, and national program-writing contests. The development of such natural interests might instill in our nation's youth an awareness of potential marketable skills for future occupational decision making. Students also should be encouraged to participate in local computer clubs, to attend community conferences sponsored by private firms and colleges, to attend lectures, to participate in ongoing programs involving computers, and to attend local computer shows.

There are possibilities for the school administration to extend to parents and other adult members of the community opportunities for learning about computers and for creating an awareness of specific applications for personal problem solving with which computers can assist. Adult-education courses are ideal for bringing the community into the school and for extending computer-literacy education.

Efforts to involve school personnel and the community in the development of a viable computer-education program are the outgrowth of carefully considered planning. It is advisable that school administrators and supervisors secure as much information as possible before attempting to set meaningful short-range and long-range goals. Colleges, universities, corporations, local and state departments of education, community libraries, and federal agencies are ideal sources of current information. Such data is necessary for identifying those school problems that computer utilization can help to resolve. Only then can administrators and supervisors determine the possible nature of a pilot project and undertake the setting of goals.

Establishing Priorities

Priorities have to be established. Decisions have to be made as to whether the school will begin with the word-processing advantages offered by the computer, whether the school simultaneously will undertake projects in CAI, or whether a more ambitious program in computer-literacy education is to be initiated. A determination will have to be made assigning the computer either to central-administration problems or to the needs for tutorial instruction. Such decisions, by their very nature, involve the setting of priorities within the school. Local community school boards at the district level may insist on having some meaningful input into the decision-making process.

Specific situations have to be evaluated. The feelings of personnel cannot be neglected. Choices will have to be made. For example, if there are teachers who have expressed interest in utilizing the computer in the remedial-reading laboratory and a secretary is not yet prepared to accept computer assistance, then the likely decision is that the computer will be assigned to the reading laboratory for at least part of the time. With equipment comes the inevitable cost. As we will suggest in later chapters, sharing helps a great deal.

The process of cost assessment will be given comprehensive attention in chapters 4 and 5. At this point in the early planning stages, it is enough to know that in reality, a school often needs considerably less equipment than is generally advised by sales personnel. It will also stand the administration in good stead to remember that because computer technology is changing rapidly, it is advisable to proceed slowly. A computer that is manufactured by one company may be best for a particular school. The most appropriate supplementary printer or disk drive, however, may be manufactured by another company. Through experience it was learned in the 1960s that electronic components can be mixed and matched, as are the more familiar stereo components, often resulting in better quality for much less money than had the equipment been purchased from the same manufacturer. This principle holds true for computer equipment as well. We will help you in later chapters to make some of these critical decisions.

Caveat emptor still prevails. One U.S. company that is known for an excellent computer at a reasonable price sells its printers at much more than the usual market price (when compared with printers manufactured by other firms). In addition, these more expensive printers are not as versatile as those made by those other firms. These versatile printers are compatible with the computer made by another manufacturer, it is certainly advisable to mix and match.

Before making commitments to purchase equipment for an initially conceived pilot project, consideration has to be given to realistic prospects for utilizing that equipment in future computer-education projects. Experience has shown that a computer that was originally purchased for use in computer-assisted instruction in one laboratory was subsequently found to be suitable on a part-time basis for developing computer literacy in another area of the school. As was suggested in chapter 2 and as will be emphasized repeatedly with specific examples in chapters 7 through 11, computers perform their assigned tasks so quickly they are underutilized for many hours of the working day. A well-planned schedule can make the most of available resources and prevent many unnecessary expenditures and over-payments.

A machine can be scheduled to perform a series of attendance-office functions in the early morning, handle an inventory problem for the supplies secretary later that morning, be utilized in the library in the early afternoon, be made available for a tutorial project in midafternoon, and then be assigned to perform a PTA mailing as the schoolday draws to a close. This multifaceted machine capability is one of the great strengths and attraction of computers. Such computer flexibility may be one of the underlying explanations for the rapid proliferation of this equipment.

Once a pilot project is under way, it is important to take advantage of any successes experienced and to advertise these successes. It is essential that the staff at large, the student body, parent groups, local school boards, and community business people are apprised of successes on a regular basis. Public relations is essential if support is to be forthcoming for expanded projects. Every avenue of communication should be employed to reach those whose support can be helpful. Word of mouth is one of the most effective broadcasting devices available. There should be no hesitation in spreading good news, and a conversation over a cup of coffee is as helpful to this objective as any other approach.

Most school administrators and supervisors have found that once the school becomes involved with computer education, additional projects for extending the overall program become quickly identifiable. Often, new projects extend to areas not considered initially. It is not uncommon for a school to direct the computer's use at one specific aspect of computer literacy, and soon after the machine arrives, have conflicts develop among staff members who insist that the equipment be used to assist with either tutorial instruction, teacher preparation of materials, or to help solve a number of administrative problems. Expansion becomes inevitable as the possibilities become clearer.

Such squabbles are among the healthiest because they reflect a faculty and staff that is learning and growing. It does, of course, cause new problems that have to be handled and resolved. Careful planning and continuing sensitivity to the needs of human beings will help to avoid many unnecessary problems from arising. What should be the uppermost objective for school administrators and supervisors is the continuing effort to create dissatisfaction with the status quo and to challenge the constructive thinking and energies of staff, faculty, and student body.

4

Assessing the Costs of Developing a School Computer Facility

Overview

One of the most difficult tasks in the entire process of establishing a viable school computer facility is the accurate assessment of costs. There is presented to the administration an overwhelming number of complex choices as to precisely what to buy. There is often little time for comparative shopping. Informational brochures and catalogs generally do little to enlighten and instead often serve to muddle the myriad of choices available. Salespersons who often are motivated by purely pecuniary interests and know little about the needs of schools tend to add to the confusion. The picture becomes hopelessly complicated. Available options become further limited by constantly contracting educational budgets. What seems to occur most often is the seeking of advice from other administrators who have already experienced the process. Because the tendency is to justify or rationalize decisions involving the expenditure of large sums of money, the advice given either may not be objective or may not be based on adequate knowledge of what the market has to offer. Too often, the purchases of others become the models used to guide our own decisions, but these models may not be appropriate. In addition, many administrators have been led to spend much more money than actually was necessary for equipment that was far too sophisticated for the computer facility they were planning or simply not competitively priced. This may be due to the trust we have in the integrity of sales personnel. Unfortunately, some individuals who represent reliable manufacturers are inexperienced, may be inadequately informed about the product they are selling, and sometimes are ignorant of the advantages and disadvantages of similar equipment manufactured by competitors. On occasion, they are less than candid in their presentations and in their responses to probing questions. Such individuals do not always serve the best interests of their companies, nor do they meet the specific needs of the prospective organizations they seek to enlist as customers. Caution is needed.

Once viable priorities have been established, specific initial projects identified, and the general direction the computer facility is to take clarified, administrators will delimit significantly the choices they will have to make. A guarded approach, proceeding slowly, is advisable. Commitments to purchase should be avoided until: (1) the process of assessing costs has

47

been completed, (2) there are sufficient funds available for purchasing necessary supplemental hardware and software, (3) adequate funding is provided for the training of supervisors, teachers, and secretaries, (4) specific areas in the school have been equipped with proper electrical wiring accommodate initial equipment as well as the equipment that may be anticipated for future growth, (5) there is assurance that adequate funds are available for a comprehensive equipment-maintenance program, and (6) specific components have been identified.

As was suggested in chapter 3, schools can begin the development of a viable computer facility based on a wide range of dollar expenditures. It is possible, though not necessarily advisable, to establish a viable remedial-reading computer laboratory for an approximate cost of five-hundred dollars. It is also possible, when budgets permit, to spend thirty-five-thousand dollars to accomplish the same goal. The differences that may be found in both reading laboratories reflect initially etablished priorities that demand differing levels of sophistication. Both laboratories, however, can accomplish some of the same essential goals. This chapter and chapter 5 will address such wide-ranging cost parameters by examining the options available in hardware and in peripheral equipment and by offering genuinely practical guidelines for ensuring that purchasing decisions result in "getting the biggest bang for the buck."

How much money is it necessary to spend, without any significant sacrifice in quality, to start a computer facility? The answer to this question cannot be provided by even the most informed computer-literacy expert. The answer cannot be provided by the most knowledgeable school administrator who may fully appreciate the particular needs of his or her own complex and who understands the extent to which purchased computer equipment is meeting those needs. The answer cannot be answered by sales representatives who are employed by manufacturers whose products vary in quality and price.

The only individuals who are able to provide a reasonable answer are those who have thoroughly and systematically analyzed the needs of the projects identified for initial development in their particular school. They can do a better job in making such assessments if they understand and use some basic parameters that have guided the thinking and decision making of administrators in a variety of comparable facilities. Once applications are tailored to specific goals and projects, the answer to this very difficult question becomes clearer. This chapter will provide an overview of costs for essential hardware and software and an inside look at the spectrum of available competitive equipment. Reasonable purchasing decisions can then be made. The following chapter will offer guidelines for securing funding and for using such monies to best advantage.

Let's explore the possible options that administrators need to consider to provide computer assistance for central administration, for supervision, for instruction with drill and practice, for instructional tutorial programs, and for developing effective programs in computer literacy (discussed in chapter 2). The differing needs of primary and secondary schools will be considered.

**Administration and Supervision: Hardware
and Software**

As was indicated in chapter 3, computer equipment in a school facility generally is shared. Based on the experiences of a large number of schools, it is highly unlikely that a computer used for administrative purposes will be utilized every hour of the schoolday. If scheduling plans are made carefully, with provision for cooperation and flexibility, that one machine is capable of assisting personnel in several offices during these hours. A useful rule of thumb is that one microcomputer equipped with commercially available programs for word processing and for data-file maintenance generally can handle the needs of five administrators during a schoolday. Similarly, one microcomputer can provide assistance for four or five supervisors during a schoolday. The assignment, however, of a microcomputer to a remedial-reading or remedial-mathematics laboratory or to a library or multimedia center, where the demand for its use is constant, may make sharing much more difficult. If the initial thrust is targeted for assisting the staff in the central administration, then the purchase of one microcomputer is indicated. If sufficient funds are available to accommodate the needs of supervisors, then the purchase of a second computer becomes possible. The special needs of other school agencies may limit the extent to which a microcomputer can be shared and priorities will have to be established. Each project can be accommodated only if adequate funding is available. The administration is strongly advised to proceed slowly so as to better ascertain the degree to which the computer will be in real demand by the various offices and agencies within the school. It is important to avoid the temptation to purchase more machines and peripheral equipment than is actually needed. This will not only preclude underutilization of expensive equipment, but it will also encourage those who have genuine need of computer assistance to seek its purchase. Too often individuals avoid becoming involved because they perceive that the costs involved for the equipment needed will be prohibitive. Sometimes, truly worthy projects are delayed too long because of such frustration.

Once equipment is brought into a school, there is a tendency for personnel to become possessive; but commitment by the administration to ensure flexible scheduling and sharing is essential if needs are to be assessed realistically and purchasing decisions are to be rational. One example will illustrate the possibilities. During a three-year period between 1976 and 1978, a New York City junior-high school, designated as a federally aided Title I educational facility, began its computer program with the introduction of only one microcomputer as a pilot project. The cost for this machine was approximately one-thousand dollars. Its only peripheral equipment was a single, comparatively inexpensive cassette recorder. The microcomputer lacked the more sophisticated data-saving disk drives, color, and a printer. Yet its careful scheduling permitted utilization during each day of those three years by approximately four-hundred-and-sixty students divided into fifteen classes in a remedial-mathematics laboratory and by another one-hundred-and-ten students divided into three classes in a computer-literacy-education program. Had the budget permitted the purchase of additional equipment, larger numbers of students could have benefited.

The central administration can begin its computer operation with one microcomputer having a minimum of 48 kilobytes of memory, possessing 48K of usable random access memory (RAM) (the computer's capacity to store approximately 48,000 characters of a single program in its memory), and preferably containing at least one and possibly two disk drives (for permanent saving of data). A quality printer is essential for the word-processing and data-file-maintenance programs that are at the heart of most administrative computing functions. Although it is possible for the central administration to function with less equipment than recommended above, we have found that such a decision inevitably results in frustration, dissatisfaction, and regret that the proper equipment had not been purchased at the outset.

Administrators sometimes are tempted to purchase a single purpose, cosmetically attractive word processor for a price ranging anywhere between eight- and fifteen-thousand dollars. They may be unaware that such a machine may require the individual using it to memorize a complex series of code keys that can be cumbersome in operation. They often are unaware that a more flexible, multifunctional microcomputer, equipped with 48K of usable RAM, double disk drive, a quality printer offering several type faces, and commercially available word-processing and data-file-maintenance programs can perform a much wider variety of administrative chores including more elaborate word-processing functions than the more expensive dedicated machine and for less than one-third the price. Administrators often are unaware that such equipment can be purchased for a total cost of approximately three-thousand dollars. The choice is clear. The demands of budget and project priorities will of course influence the choice. It is also important to become aware of precisely what limited dollars can buy.

A 48K RAM microcomputer ranges in cost from approximately six-hundred dollars to three-thousand dollars depending on the brand and a number of important factual considerations. Sound purchasing decisions must ensure that any microcomputer under consideration be adaptable to disk drives and printers, essential peripheral devices that are needed to execute successfully the greatest number of administrative functions. Certain brands of microcomputers can only accommodate highly expensive peripheral devices. Others are designed to accept a very limited selection of peripherals. For example, one popular microcomputer was not designed to operate with disk drives or printers, thereby creating significant subsequent problems for the unwary purchaser. It is of utmost importance that if a microcomputer is to be used for scheduling the programs of more than one-thousand students, it have the capability for accommodating a hard disk drive, a peripheral device capable of retaining many millions of bytes of data. If word processing is to be the principal function for which the microcomputer is to be used, then a modest disk drive will handle the work load efficiently. The administrator must know precisely how the computer is to be utilized before any purchases are made.

It is unnecessary to purchase microcomputers with audio capability, color screens, and high-resolution graphics to handle the general functions required by the central administration in most schools. The expenditure of hundreds of extra dollars for such equipment generally is unwarranted. Neither the quality of word processing nor file-data maintenance is significantly enhanced by sound or color capability. Should it become evident that specific administrative chores require sound, color, and high-resolution graphics and that the results are worth the expenditure of extra dollars, then it is advisable that the microcomputers under consideration have these features built in as part of the machine. Adding such features later on can be very expensive or impossible. If they are not a necessity, then such money, often as much as 50 percent, can be saved.

One additional point seems to be warranted. There are many factors that may influence the purchase of one microcomputer rather than another. The recommendation of a trusted colleague, the experiences with a particular machine by a user group, the prestige of a manufacturer's name, the persuasiveness of a salesperson that assures a more simple operation, and cosmetic appearance are among these factors. No matter the reason, if a particular machine is desired, it is possible to rationalize the expenditure of even an additional thousand dollars. If this is all that had to be considered, the matter is closed. The purchaser, however, may subsequently learn to his regret that the cost of the software that the microcomputer is designed to accommodate may be as much as four times higher than had another machine been purchased instead.

Word processing is accomplished most efficiently with microcomputers that allow for a minimum of sixty alphabetic characters on each line of the screen. Some computers allow for only thirty or forty characters on each line, thereby making word processing considerably more difficult. Generally, color computers permit less characters on each line than comparable noncolor machines. This is yet another factor that must be taken into account when deciding on the basic computer to be purchased.

An essential administrative computing peripheral device is the disk drive, the mechanism used for rapid permanent saving of information and data produced by the microcomputer. The available brands of disk drives are standardized structurally and will accommodate a variety of brands of diskettes. It is the commercial software programs, stored on diskettes, that are configured to run on only certain microcomputers. Disk drives range in cost from approximately one-hundred-and-fifty dollars to five-thousand dollars, depending on whether they are designed to accommodate either soft or hard disks. Disk drives that accommodate soft (flexible or floppy) diskettes are generally less expensive and range in cost from one-hundred-and-fifty dollars to six-hundred dollars. Disk drives that accommodate hard disks are generally more expensive and range in cost from one-thousand dollars to five-thousand dollars. Additional costs may be incurred if it is necessary to attach additional disk drives to the computer. A cable, ranging in cost from twenty to eighty dollars, may have to be purchased to connect the disk drive to the microcomputer if such a cable is not included in the price of the disk drive. One such cable per disk drive may be necessary but some such cables are designed to accommodate two or more disk drives. In addition, a separate power supply, ranging in cost from twenty to one-hundred-and-fifty dollars, may have to be purchased to supply each disk drive with its necessary electrical power, if the power supply is not already included in the price of the disk drive. The price depends on the specific power requirements of the disk drive. Additional hardware may be required by some computers, known as *disk-interface hardware*, ranging in cost from eighty to six-hundred dollars depending on the brand of microcomputer. The purchase may be necessary if the microcomputer is not already so equipped.

Some disk drives are capable of holding seventy-thousand bytes (characters) of information. Other disk drives can hold more than eighty-million bytes. Each brand of disk drive is individually priced. A given manufacturer of a particular brand of disk drive may offer several models of drives, each with a different price tag. It is convenient—both cosmetically and, more important, for convenience of handling—that the disk drives be part of the microcomputer's housing unit. There is much less chance of damage. As the computer continues to be used for additional functions, *outside* disk drives may be added. The various brands of disk drives are standard devices that are compatible with almost all computers. All disk drives will accommodate available diskettes that contain software programs. It is extremely important that before making firm commitments to purchase equipment determinations be made to ensure that desired software programs will run on the microcomputers under consideration for purchase, since software that runs on one model machine will be unlikely to run on another.

An alternative to disk drives is the cassette player/recorder, which may be used to store data on cassettes. Although such equipment ranges in price from eighteen to approximately two-hundred dollars, experience has shown that price is not necessarily a reflection of quality and, for most school chores, the less expensive cassette player/recorders are highly adequate.

A quality printer is another essential peripheral device that is used extensively by the central administration. Not only is it important to save data on diskettes for future reference, but also it is often necessary on a regular basis to print that data, often on quality paper, a product referred to as *hard copy*. The microcomputer causes the printer to accomplish this task automatically whenever the administration so desires. Printers range in price from approximately two-hundred dollars to four-thousand dollars. There are printers that print characters in dot-matix form (see figure 4-1), producing a quality of work that is highly satisfactory for most school-related functions.

These range in price from two-hundred dollars to four-thousand dollars. Other printers are designed to do impact printing as does the more familar standard typewriter. These range in price from six-hundred to four-thousand dollars. Other printers shoot ink onto paper as the document is created. Still other printers accomplish the task with the use of laser beams. The variety of printers is nearly endless. In the last ten years, printer technology has moved forward at a more rapid rate than has computer technology.

All manufacturers of printers ensure that their machines will be compatible with the more popular microcomputers. Some printers, not necessarily the most expensive, allow for a variety of interchangeable type faces. The purchaser, therefore, has to compare printers for price, speed and ease of operation, variety of typefaces, ability to accommodate differing qualities of paper, aesthetic qualities (amount of noise generated and appearance), quality of end product, and durability (cost of maintenance). A cable, ranging in cost from twenty to eighty dollars, may have to be purchased to attach the printer to the computer if it is not already included in the price of the printer.

There is considerable competition in peripheral hardware. Many manufacturers design and build disk drives, cassette players, printers, and other peripheral devices that fit standard microcomputers. One major computer manufacturer sells disk drives for its computers for approximately five-hundred dollars each. Competing hardware vendors sell disk drives for use with the same computer for less than two-hundred-and-fifty dollars each. It makes sense to purchase the computer from one company, and should there develop a need for additional disk drives, to purchase them from another. Regarding printers, the discrepancies are often wider. One major manu-

Sample A – This printing sample was printed on a "Daisy Wheel" style printer. The letters were struck by an impact process and are as close to quality office typewriter printing as any presently available computer print.

Sample B – This printing sample was printed on a "Dot Matrix" style printer. The letters were struck by an series of pins and are not as close to quality office typewriter printing as the sample above.

Sample C – This printing sample was printed on a "Dot Matrix" style printer with special overstriking ability. The letters were also struck by an series of pins and while the finished product is better than ordinary "Dot Matrix" print it cannot compare to the "Daisy Wheel" sample above.

Note: Three styles are displayed. First, impact print. Next, standard dot-matrix print. Finally, dot-matrix print with dots "filled in." Impact printers are slower than dot-matrix machines but produce a more business-like product.

Figure 4-1. Common Print Styles

facturer sells its most sophisticated printers for more than twenty-five-hundred dollars. A competing hardware vendor sells a comparable printer for less than one-thousand dollars. Both printers will properly interface with the same computer.

The market in computers and in peripheral equipment is in a constant state of change. Attempts to list specific pieces of equipment are futile. The names of companies and the products they manufacture seem to change quickly. Certainly, the price tags change even more quickly. To comparative shop with the least amount of effort, it is necessary to remain current. Regular attendance at computer and business shows is helpful. It is also advisable to subscribe to a number of quality computer magazines (listed in appendix B). The important thing is be alert to changes in available equipment and price lists, particularly those items that either are applicable or may become applicable to your particular computer facility.

Administrative Software

Once having decided on appropriate hardware, administrators must then confront a large menu of choices involving software. There are basically two categories of administrative software; (1) programs for word processing and (2) programs for data-file maintenance. Software, depending on the degree of sophistication, covers a significant range in price. What may be considered to be expensive by one school may not even raise an eyebrow at another. As was indicated above, it is essential to remember that commercial software is *machine dependent*. For example, a diskette containing a computer program, purchased for an Apple II microcomputer, will not run on an IBM Personal Computer. The converse is true as well. It also holds true for diskettes configured to run on specific models offered by the same manufacturer. For example, a commercial program designed to run on a Radio Shack TRS80 color computer will not run on a Radio Shack TRS80 Model III computer. It is the microcomputer, therefore, that determines the kinds of programs that can be purchased. If a selected program requires the need for sound and graphics capability, then the microcomputer must be equipped to accommodate these two features. It is important, then, to evaluate not only each microcomputer but also the software that it will accommodate.

Commercially prepared word-processing programs generally cost between sixty dollars and two-hundred dollars. Such programs have applicability for the central administration and for other supervisors. The more simple the program the less it probably will cost. The more elaborate programs are designed to provide more complex operations, resulting in opportunities for accessing many kinds of information, and will usually cost a good deal more. Each word-processing program has advantages and disadvantages. No single program offers what may be deemed ideal features. Each administrator may desire significantly different features in a program. Should available word-processing programs not meet an administrator's needs, patience is advised until some individual in the school gains adequate proficiency in writing programs. A program tailored to the specific needs of a particular project can then be designed.

Commercial word-processing programs also provide dictionary functions. The insertion of a diskette having dictionary capability permits the computer to electronically scan a large document very rapidly, identify those words that are spelled incorrectly, determine whether any of the accepted grammatical conventions are violated, isolate words that should have been capitalized, determine the number of times words have been used, and even determine if specific words used throughout the document reflect blatant sexist or racist attitudes. The computer can then provide for a print-out of errors so that modifications can be facilitated.

Data-file-maintenance programs also have applicability for the central administration and for other supervisors. Although such programs eventually may be written by individuals in the school who have acquired some degree of expertise, this software is usually purchased from a number of firms that specialize in their preparation. Data-processing software packages range in price from approximately thirty dollars to fifteen-hundred dollars. Each program serves specific needs that once again vary from school to school. Time has to be set aside for assessing the merits and limitations of each program to ensure that most of the functions offered can be utilized. A quality data-file-maintenance program can be purchased for approximately one-hundred dollars to two-hundred dollars and is generally able to provide the service required by most administrators.

Some schools that develop sophisticated computer-literacy programs encourage teachers to assign the creative "writing" of needed software programs to either entire classes as laboratory assignments or to more gifted students in order to provide additional challenges and to enrich the curriculum. Youngsters seem to enjoy the challenge of having to solve practical problems. They appreciate the confidence that is placed in them and they glory in the recognition that they receive. They are afforded an immediate opportunity to see that the results of their efforts are used and appreciated by others. Elementary and secondary-school students have designed highly serviceable administrative software tailored to the specific needs of the school. In many instances, such in-house programs help to save the school money and are often preferable to available commercial software. The more sophisticated quality software for word processing and data-file maintenance, however, often need greater expertise than can be provided by less experienced and less knowlegeable computer-literacy students. These programs, therefore, are almost always purchased from professional firms.

Computer Media

To save developed software, copies of letters, and valued data, it will be necessary to purchase supplies of diskettes and cassettes. Price is not necessarily reflective of high quality. The soft, five-and-one-quarter-inch diskette is a circular, flat, plastic sheet with a magnetic coating covering its surface. For protection, this diskette is permanently enclosed in a five-and-one-quarter-inch square plastic jacket. Such diskettes can be purchased individually or in a boxed set of ten or more and range in cost from nineteen to eighty dollars for ten. The eight-inch diskettes range in price from twenty-five to one-hundred dollars for the same number. It is advisable to choose the products of reputable firms. Hard disks generally are physically included within the disk drive in sealed units and are therefore not removable. These disks are not purchased separately. With regard to cassettes, they range in price from one to nine dollars per cassette and come stored in a plastic box. It is advisable to avoid purchasing a cassette for less than one dollar. Those costing over one dollar generally perform very satisfactorily.

Computer-Aided Instruction: Hardware and Software

Computer-aided instruction (that is, drill and practice) is heavily dependent on software. Therefore, the administration carefully must consider the nature of its planned CAI project and the software that will be needed to implement that project *before* decisions are made about specific hardware for that project. For example, as was indicated above, a program requiring sound and graphics capabilities can only be used with a computer equipped to accommodate these features. If teachers desire that the program provide for an ongoing record of student grades, then a computer with disk drives is necessary. Disk drives are also essential if the computer is to assign problems each day based on each student's performance the previous day. If a listing of accumulated grades for each student in class is desired, then a printer is necessary.

How Many Machines Are Necessary?

Once decisions have been made regarding software, the microcomputer, and compatible peripheral hardware, the next step in the process is to determine the number of machines that actually are necessary for implementing the CAI program. Sales personnel would have us believe that ideally, regardless of grade level, the optimum number is one computer per student. Teachers who have been involved with grouping of students, however, know that much good results from the process that encourages children to work in small groups. Although some problems arise, most teachers feel that the advantages outweigh the shortcomings.

In computer-aided instruction, grouping offers distinct advantages. Children in small groups generally learn much from one another. If the members of the group are assigned judiciously, the groups, in effect, become mini classes. Each group develops its own leaders and followers. Based on many years of first-hand experience with grouping in the elementary-school through the college level, the optimum number of machines needed for computer-aided instruction is:

Grades 1-3: one machine for every three students

Grades 4-8: one machine for every four or five students

Grades 9-12: one machine for every 3 students

Effective computer laboratory environments often provide for a variety of experiences. Many of these experiences do not require the use of a computer (kits, workbooks, audio-visual materials, and such). For this reason it is not always necessary or even advantageous for computer facilities to include many machines. In the lower grades, difficulties seem to arise when more than three youngsters work at assigned computer stations. In the middle school or junior-high school, students seem to work together most effectively in groups of approximately five. At the high-school level, students involved with more difficult concepts tend to work well together in smaller groups. (This may also be attributed to a heightened sensitivity when they have to reveal any lacking in knowledge or skill.) Clearly, the above recommendations regarding group size are not inviolate. There are many skilled second-grade teachers who are successful with groups composed of five students. In contrast, there are teachers in the middle school who find that no more than three students may constitute a viable group.

Tutorial Programs: Hardware and Software

Instructional tutorial programs are entirely software dependent. Presently, it is extremely rare for a school to have individuals with the expertise necessary for preparing quality in-house tutorial software. Whether the software is designed to teach mathematics or French or whether it allows students to simulate the activities of a governmental leader and through that simulation learn about politics, the tutorial computer program is almost always purchased from commercial sources. As increasing numbers of supervisors and teachers become involved with the utilization of computers on a regular basis, however, they will be able to develop quality in-house software that can be used by students in a variety of ways. As was indicated in chapter 2, programs are being written that allow students to review specific units of work, do advanced independent study in all subject areas, review for uniform or standardized examinations, or do remedial work in all subject areas.

Simulation programs are used by industry to teach people how to drive automobiles and how to fly airplanes. Some schools in their driver-education programs have already adopted industry's simulation techniques. In schools, the simulation mode is useful because the student can interact with the computer. There are simulation programs available for remedial-mathematics students who need to learn useful approaches for problem solving. Programs exist that allow students to "inject" substances into a simulated biological entity and then immediately learn the effects of the injection. In this mode, the machine allows the simulated activity, informs the user of the result, and then allows the user to modify his choice of substance to effect the desired result. Music also lends itself to this mode of tutorial instruction. Students can learn to orchestrate their own compositions. Art students can learn to draw in color by using the computer's "etch-a-sketch" mode. Students of medicine, chemistry, physics, and engineering use this mode of instruction to advantage. Such commerical programs range in price from approximately fifteen dollars for simple simulations to approximately four-hundred dollars for more complex programs.

Many other quality commercial programs are available for tutorial instruction. For example, LOGO is one such software package that includes a language and is ideally suited to tutorial instruction, particularly in the areas of logic as well as geometric and spatial relationships. There is every indication that administrators and supervisors can expect in the very near future to be inundated with quality tutorial-oriented software in all subject areas and at all levels of instruction. It is reasonable to assume that such programs will not be inexpensive but the potential instructional assistance that they offer may well make their acquisition by schools worthwhile.

**Computer-Literacy Education: Hardware
and Software**

It is anticipated that there will be significant expansion of computer-literacy education in the nation's elementary, middle, and senior-high schools. At each level, decisions will have to be made as to how much time to devote to such instruction, the degree of sophistication that is desirable, and how to make provision for such instruction in already-overcrowded curricula areas. Presently, there are no model curriculum guides available to which schools may turn. There is every assurance that, shortly, appropriate courses of study will be developed. There are no commercial software programs available presently for offering comprehensive computer-literacy education. The software that is available is concerned with only one aspect of computer literacy, namely, the computer, its construction, and its parts. This information is available in the instruction manuals provided by the manufacturers of microcomputers. Such manuals deal with the program built into the machine. They deal with the specific language (usually BASIC) understood by the computer and with which the user must become proficient if communication is to result. Once schools decide to become pedagogically involved with the teaching of computer languages, specific instructional techniques will be developed.

With regard to the other vital facets of computer-literacy education, namely, the history of computers, the positive and negative social impact of the computer revolution on society, and efforts to harness and control computers to maximize efficiency and accuracy, no commercial software is yet available. The possibilities are limited only by the extent of human creativity. Education and curriculum specialists will have to develop large-group and individual-class instructional presentations for the elementary school. In the junior-high school where student interest in the world of computers may be more extensive, more complex instructional programs need to be developed. At the senior-high-school level, a series of elective courses may be offered. Certainly, the mathematics, business-education, industrial arts, English, and social-studies departments will need to devote lessons to further the goals of computer literacy. For example, the social-studies department can offer a series of dynamic lessons as part of already-established units of work. These might include the Industrial Revolution, the U.S. labor movement, and current problems in U.S. society. The difficulty will lie in making hard decisions as to those aspects of the curriculum that may have to be deleted.

Assessing the Costs at Each Level

Computer-Literacy Education: The Elementary School

Specifically with regard to the development of computer literacy in the elementary school, a number of successful programs have been established. Experience has shown that one 16K black-and-white microcomputer (CRT) with a cassette recorder for permanent saving of programs can service ten classes of students from kindergarten through grade six. Disk drives and printers generally have been found to be unnecessary for this application. The ratio suggested above for machine to classes allows students to have a computer in their classroom for half-a-day each week. In those elementary schools that have introduced even limited computer-literacy programs, the pedagogical approach most often adopted for teaching computer languages is modeled on the teaching of foreign language and is vocabulary oriented. This approach makes the constant presence of a computer unnecessary except for those periods when youngsters are to be given the opportunity to apply learnings directly to the machine. Reading and teacher explanations are not enough. The presence of the machine is necessary if students are to learn how to program a computer. Actual time at the computer for each student is an essential element if mastery is to be accomplished. At the elementary-school level, considering the needs and attention span of the children, the ratio suggested here is viable.

Computer-Literacy Education: The
Middle or Junior-High School

In the middle school, instruction in computer literacy is somewhat intensified. The youngsters at this age are more receptive to the demands for concentration than their younger elementary-school counterparts and they expect greater in-depth instruction in computer languages. They also have expressed frustration and resentment when they are given what seems to them to be inadequate time segments with a computer. Experienced teachers have found that five or six microcomputers, either black and white or in color, each with a cassette recorder to allow for the saving of programs, supplemented with one microcomputer with disk drive and a printer, are what is necessary for meeting the needs of ten classes or approximately three-hundred students. Such provision would enable each student to work in small groups at a computer three periods each week. This machine experience is complemented with large-group instructional lectures twice or three times each week. Such scheduling will permit a well-rounded middle-school computer-literacy program to be established.

Computer Literacy Education: The
Senior-High School

As with elementary and middle schools, senior-high schools on an individual basis have devised varying qualities of computer-literacy programs. Generally, such programs are laboratory centered. Students attend large-group instruction lectures for three periods each week at which new material is presented. They are then scheduled for small-group practice sessions in a computer laboratory equipped with from five to fifteen microcomputers. Some schools make do with fewer machines while other school laboratories are equipped with as many as fifty microcomputers. At the high-school level, all microcomputers should be equipped with disk drive. A minimum of 30 percent of these machines should also be equipped with printers so that these level students may leave the laboratory with hard copy. Having a printed record of the programs that have been written with an opportunity for at-home modification elevates the quality of this aspect of computer literacy. Many teachers also recommend that at least one or two machines in a high-school computer laboratory be equipped with color capability and the capacity to generate high-resolution graphics.

   One additional observation seems to be in order. There are no hard and fast rules about establishing ratios for numbers of students per computer. Each school at each educational level needs to proceed slowly and to experiment to find that ratio that best meets the needs of its student body. Many laboratories have been successful with relatively little equipment. Others have found that additional equipment is necessary. The guidelines suggested here are useful in the planning stages of developing a computer facility. Adjustments usually become necessary.

Computer-Literacy Education: A Recap

As was indicated above, teachers at each educational level are finding it exceedingly difficult to find the time to teach the concepts and skills required by varying curricula and, often, specific courses of study. Various community interest groups persist in pressuring boards of education to provide, at the least, lessons, if not semester elective courses, to reach students on issues that are of vital concern to them. If teaching about labor movements, Black history, women's rights, and the Holocaust becomes required, and the schoolday and school year is not extended, then other areas in the curriculum have to be abbreviated or deleted. The time factor is further compromised by needs for remediation, for driver education, and for college preparation. To ask those who direct the educational destinies of the nation's youth to now provide for programs in computer-literacy education is a most sensitive undertaking. Still, there is a responsibility to alert educators to the need to make accommodation to this revolution in computer technology. We would be remiss if the nation's educators failed to provide adequate education of its youth in so vital an area. Computers are where much emphasis will be for many years to come. They are having an incredible impact on the lifestyle of the world community. They will be the focal point around which career opportunities will develop.

On the elementary-school level, some time during each school week should be allocated to computer-literacy education. Each subject area may have to yield some portion of time to accommodate this new area of instruction.

In most middle schools or junior-high schools, computer-literacy education is often approached by allowing students to opt for such exposure in lieu of classes in industrial or fine arts for one semester or year during their stay in these grades. In some schools, computer-literacy education is handled in mini elective courses scheduled for ten weeks of a school term. Many schools offer computer-literacy courses as part of the cocurricular program. Student reception has been incredibly positive.

In the senior-high school, a meaningful computer-literacy program can be organized within departments. Elective courses are ideally suited to this educational venture. At the least, each subject area should consider modifying its courses of study and calendars of lessons to accommodate the introduction and development of viable computer-literacy education. In addition, the senior-high school's cocurricular program seems ideally suited to the extension of computer-literacy education.

Cost of Supplies

Supplies for the computer include cassettes, diskettes, printer ribbons, paper, extension cords, and electrical extension cords and adapters. There is considerable competition among firms for the sale of these items. Many vendors sell cassettes and diskettes that can be used with any microcomputer (see your hardware vendor for a listing). Their prices for competing brands are generally much lower than those offered by the original manufacturers. One well-known computer manufacturer offers its brand of diskette at a price of forty dollars for a box of ten. The firm producing this brand of diskette for the computer manufacturer markets the same diskette under a different label at a price of twenty-three dollars for a box of ten. This difference in price is significant.

If a printer is used extensively, then securing quality paper is important. Most school-stationery vendors carry a full line of computer paper. Their prices are generally much lower than those of hardware vendors. If a school district or individual schools have a contract with a stationery vendor, it often becomes possible to secure paper at a significant discount. Most vendors of stationery supplies can also provide printer ribbons at reduced prices. Some manufacturers of printers offer so-called captive parts for sale (parts that can only be used in their printers). The majority of printer manufacturers, however, use standard cartridges and ribbons that are 20 to 30 percent cheaper. Comparative shopping is highly advisable.

Extension cords and adaptors (devices that allow the plug on the extension cord to fit into the electrical wall outlet) are often needed in a computer facility. Although it is important to avoid cumbersome wiring with a spaghettilike conglomeration of extension cords and three-way outlets, needs do arise occasionally for a temporary extension of electrical power. Although a computer draws approximately as much electricity as does a standard color-television set (most of them draw less than one amp for the basic computer), it is advisable to consult with the school custodian before purchasing equipment. Any needed rewiring may be very costly.

Cost of Maintenance

Too often, inadequate attention is paid to the problem of equipment maintenance. Although microcomputers and their peripheral equipment tend to break down infrequently and generally require little maintenance, occasionally they do need attention. This is particularly true of disk drives, which need periodic alignment. Maintenance costs vary from brand to brand. Generally, service contracts are based on the value of the equipment. A one-year service contract can cost between 10 and 20 percent of the overall purchase cost of the equipment. Equipment costing five-thousand dollars can require a maintenance contract costing between five-hundred and one-thousand dollars each year. A computer can be purchased for less than the cost of maintenance on some machines. In addition, maintenance on large equipment such as minicomputers can cost more than the purchase of many smaller microcomputers that are much more functional and require less maintenance. Administrators often find that service contracts are far too expensive to be managed within limited budgets, but this is one consideration that cannot be overlooked.

Cost of Security

The administration must also investigate the need for adequate security precautions. It is recommended that all computers and peripheral equipment be secured in a window-free room and with special security-bar locks. The microcomputer, without peripheral equipment, costs between five-hundred and two-thousand dollars. It weighs about as much as a standard electric typewriter and is therefore easily victim to theft. The expression "computers have legs" cannot be taken lightly.

Cost of Personnel Training

Lastly, administrators will have to consider some temporary costs involving personnel during the period of training. Coverages will have to be made or temporary substitutes hired. CAI activity usually requires little teacher training. Teachers only need a few hours to learn how to turn the computer on and off and how to run the appropriate CAI program. Many hardware and software vendors will provide teachers with the necessary training at the school site. Software configured to handle administrative chores often is packaged with a simple manual of operations requiring only a few hours of training. Most tutorial programs are designed so that they are self-explanatory. To handle computer-literacy education proficiently at the elementary and middle-school levels, it has been estimated that a minimum of fifty hours of training is required. There has been a significant increase in the number of computer workshops sponsored by school districts. In addition, particularly at the high-school level, teachers should consider enrolling in college-level computer-science courses that afford opportunities for time at a computer under the guidance of computer specialists. If this option is adopted we recommend courses in computer education not computer science be taken.

Cost of Class Scheduling

There is also a cost factor related to class size. Computer classes are sometimes designed to accommodate smaller numbers of students and therefore additional teacher time may have to be allocated. In many schools, computer classes are structured in such a way as to schedule only fifteen or twenty students in each class. This is not necessary, as many administrators have found that viable computer classes can function effectively with thirty or more students. Careful scheduling can minimize the problem. Actual computer-class-size ratios need not be significantly different from other subject classes. Industrial-arts and home-economics teachers can be assigned to teach computer classes as well as classes in their own fields. This allows administrators to utilize teachers who normally have a lower student-teacher ratio in their subjects for computer classes and thereby improve their overall school coverage.

The Cost of Inaction

The establishment of a viable computer facility will be costly. The initial expenditure is determined by budget and by project priorities. The administration can continue to function with traditional equipment and traditional utilization of personnel. Supervisors can continue to function as they have throughout the years. Teachers can continue to function with textbooks, chalk, and a chalkboard. Students can receive an education without any computer-assisted instruction and without computer-assisted tutorial programs. The educational process can survive for a time without the implementation of computer-literacy programs. It is, however, difficult to conceive that education in the United States would revert to the philosophies, programs, and approaches associated with the nineteenth and first half of the twentieth centuries. Schools without programs in physical education, industrial arts, music, and the fine arts would be unthinkable. Schools without audio-visual and laboratory equipment would be unthinkable. How then can educational leaders deny the handwriting on the wall? How can they face youngsters and their parents and deny a future that will require computer literacy? The time is now.

5 Funding an Effective Computer Facility: Securing and Utilizing Funds Effectively

As was pointed out in chapter 4, a viable computer facility can be funded for less than one-thousand dollars. Such a facility would utilize one black-and-white cassette-based microcomputer. It would service many school needs. One such machine would provide an effective introduction to the world of computers for many students. Many youngsters would derive educational benefit as a result of a computer's availability. Each year, should budgets permit, additional projects and equipment could then be introduced.

To assist superintendents and principals who may be considering more ambitious programs on any of the three educational levels, the following cost guidelines may be useful:

Cost Guidelines: The Elementary School

The needs of the administrative and supervisory staff can be met for a cost ranging between twenty-five-hundred and three-thousand dollars. This money would provide a 48K RAM black-and-white CRT microcomputer with disk drives, a quality printer, supplies (for example, diskettes, extension cords, and adapters), and maintenance.

A program in CAI for ten to fifteen classes could be introduced at a cost ranging between eight-hundred and sixteen-hundred dollars. This money would provide one or two cassette-based CRT microcomputers (with black-and-white CRT screens), supplies (for example, cassettes and such), and maintenance.

A laboratory-based tutorial program for five classes could be established for a cost ranging between two-thousand and six-thousand dollars, depending on the sophistication of the software selected. This money would provide equipment ranging in complexity from several cassette-based black-and-white CRT microcomputers to one or more cassette-based black-and-white or color machines with disk drives, a quality printer, supplies, and maintenance. Because tutorial instruction is software-dependent and the choice of software varies from school to school, it is impossible to determine in advance whether there will be need for color or black-and-white CRT screens, diskettes or cassettes, a dot-matrix printer, or other accessories.

A laboratory-based computer-literacy program could service the needs of ten classes for a cost ranging between sixteen-hundred and thirty-two-hundred dollars. This money would provide two cassette-based black-and-white CRT microcomputers, supplies, and maintenance.

Cost Guidelines: The Middle School

The needs of the administrative and supervisory staff can be met for a cost ranging between twenty-five-hundred and three-thousand dollars. This money would provide a 48K RAM black-and-white CRT microcomputer with disk drives, a quality printer, supplies (for example, diskettes, extension cords, and adapters), and maintenance.

A program in CAI for ten classes could be established for a cost ranging between five-thousand and seven-thousand dollars. This money would provide five cassette-based black-and-white CRT microcomputers (with screens), one or two black-and-white CRT microcomputers with disk drives, one or two printers, supplies (for example, cassettes, diskettes, and so forth), and maintenance.

A laboratory-based tutorial program could be established for a cost ranging between thirty-five-hundred dollars and fifteen-thousand dollars, depending on the sophistication of the programs selected. This money would provide four black-and-white or color cassette-based CRT microcomputers, two or three black-and-white or color CRT microcomputers with disk drives, two quality printers, supplies, and maintenance.

A laboratory-based computer-literacy program could service the needs of ten classes for a cost ranging between five-thousand dollars and seven-thousand dollars. This money would provide one or two black-and-white CRT microcomputers with disk drives, five black-and-white cassette-based CRT microcomputers, one or two quality printers, supplies, and maintenance.

Cost Guidelines: The Senior-High School

The needs of the administrative and supervisory staff, in a school with more than two-thousand students, can be met for a cost ranging between six-thousand and ten-thousand dollars. This money would provide one or two 48K RAM black-and-white CRT microcomputers with disk drives, one hard disk drive, two quality printers, supplies (for example, diskettes, extension cords, adapters, and such), and maintenance.

A program in CAI for ten classes could be introduced for a cost ranging between twenty-thousand and thirty-thousand dollars. This money would provide between ten and fifteen black-and-white CRT microcomputers with disk drives, three printers, supplies (for example, diskettes and so on), and maintenance.

A tutorial program based in the school's library or multimedia center could be established for a cost ranging between thirty-five-hundred dollars and nine-thousand dollars, depending on the sophistication of the programs selected. This money would provide between four and ten black-and-white cassette-based CRT microcomputers, two or three black-and-white CRT microcomputers with disk drives, two quality printers, supplies, and maintenance. If the software that is selected requires sound or color graphics, then the cost of the equipment will probably approach the upper limits suggested here.

A laboratory-based computer-literacy program could service the needs of ten classes for a cost ranging between twenty-thousand dollars and thirty-thousand dollars. This money would provide between ten and twenty black-and-white CRT microcomputers with disk drives, five to ten black-and-white cassette-based CRT microcomputers, one or two quality printers, supplies (for example, cassettes, diskettes, extension cords, and adapters), and maintenance.

It is apparent that it takes imagination and much effort to secure the funds necessary for establishing a computer facility. Traditionally, the support of education throughout the United States has been left to state and local governments. The 1957 Soviet Union's successful launching of Sputnik, however, forced the federal government to reevaluate its role. That the United States had fallen behind in the space race was viewed as a threat to national security and to U.S. prestige abroad. The quality of education in the United States had to be improved.

The U.S. Congress enacted legislation that was to allocate federal funds to state and local governments for the development of educational programs. Initially targeted at upgrading the teaching of science, mathematics, and foreign language, federally sponsored programs soon encompassed all the major subject areas. Many large corporations sent specialists to help teachers in summer institutes learn to use classroom equipment more effectively. Corporations also began to underwrite the establishment of research foundations. Publishers provided relevant books and articles. Colleges and universities granted graduate credit for completion of courses in institutes teachers attended to meet upgraded state-certification requirements. Local school boards accepted such credit toward salary increments and differentials. This was a national effort.

In recent years, however, with the economy plagued by inflation, unemployment, and a disappointing annual gross national product, there has been a pronounced retrenchment with regard to support of educational programs. An unfortunate misconception now prevails, namely that sources of funding for educational programs no longer exists. This is not the case.

Currently, there are five principal sources of funding for educational programs. There are (1) local-school-district funding, (2) local business or community grants, (3) private-foundation grants, (4) state grants to educational institutions, and (5) federal grants to education. School administrators have continued to utilize each of these sources. It is useful to explore the considerations that have served to convince each of them to continue to make contributions. Similar approaches may be used for securing the means to establish computer facilities.

Local-School-District Funding

The attitudes, policies, and practices of each local school board vary. It is almost impossible, therefore, to suggest any uniform approach for securing funds. Money is available but more limited in supply. Therefore, priorities have to be established. In recent years, innovative school boards have shown a willingness to fund computer projects that are targeted at remediation, enrichment of curriculum, and assistance for handicapped children. It is helpful to gain insight into the thinking of local school boards to discern changing attitudes toward priorities that they have supported in the past. A campaign can then be mounted to secure funding for computers. Such an effort must be rooted in sound educational principles that meet responsibilities to the future. The approaches addressed in chapter 3 apply. The desire to establish a computer facility must be widely publicized. Educational objectives need to be clearly identified. Costs must be carefully estimated. Long- and short-range plans need to be formulated. The reasons for the computer program envisioned must be presented clearly and enthusiastically. Each member of the school board must be educated to see that further delay in bringing the world of computers into the schools may have an adverse effect on the appropriateness and quality of the educational program. Money is available but it has to be channeled toward programs that will continue to be meaningful.

Grants by Local Business and Community Groups

Because their self-interest is directly linked to the quality of educational programs offered in the schools, local-business and community groups continue to be among the most reliable sources of funding. They recognize clearly that the schools are the training centers of the future labor force. If the educational program becomes more comprehensive, affording youngsters the opportunity to learn about and become skilled in the use of equipment used regularly in industry, then any subsequent need for upgrading training will be minimal. In addition, the publicity accorded local business firms and community groups when they help to underwrite educational programs, generally results in increased customer loyalty and favorable public relations. As indicated in chapter 2, business and community leaders, once made aware of educational needs, somehow find a way to donate time, money, equipment, supplies, and assistance. Over the years, whenever schools have had difficulties in funding projects, whether for team uniforms, athletic equipment, or textbooks, business and community leaders rarely have evaded responsibility. Politicians are also members of the community and often their children are students in local schools. Their assistance can help resolve difficulties. Various service organizations and lodges take an active interest in the educational programs offered by the schools. They have been another major source of funding. Fund-raising dinner dances and raffles often will provide some of the money needed. The energy and creativity of the student body should not be discounted. Young people, when convinced of the worthiness of a program, will assert themselves in an all-out effort to raise funds and to secure equipment and supplies. The generosity of local colleges and universities should also not be discounted. These institutions are often willing to donate equipment that they no longer need. They encourage their specialists to assist with training programs and with resolving technical difficulties. The resources are available. They need to be tapped.

Private-Foundation Grants

There are more than twenty-two-thousand private foundations in the United States. Each foundation can be the source of grants. Private foundations are often willing to assist educators who are in need of seed money necessary for establishing a worthy project. Each foundation tends to channel its funds toward a limited number of specific programs. Some have interest only in agricultural projects. Others seem to favor assisting in the education of minorities. There are a number of books available in the public libraries that offer information as to those foundations that have traditionally been willing to help underwrite educational projects. Most helpful should be *The Foundations Directory* and the *National Data Book* published by the Foundation Center in New York City. These volumes provide specific information about the history and philosophy of each foundation. They also indicate the nature of grants awarded by each over the years. They may be reached at:

The Foundations Center
888 7th Avenue
New York, New York 10106

Colleges and universities have specialists known as *grants officers*, who may provide direction toward enlisting the assistance of sympathetic foundations. It is useful to prepare one comprehensive proposal (see the suggested proposal guidelines that follow and to submit it to each foundation that might give it consideration. Although the success ratio of grants to requests can be improved significantly, nothing can be gained without an effort. Foundations will not provide grants unless they know about your specific needs and unless they are approached for assistance. Private foundations have funded many worthy educational projects.

Specific Guidelines

It is useful to enlist the assistance of professional grant writers who reside in the community. Such individuals know exactly how to proceed and will save time and energy. As indicated above, the full-time grants officer employed by virtually every university can provide immeasurable assistance. Many of the nation's larger school districts also employ full-time specialists whose singular function is to write proposals that will result in funding. The experience, expertise, and services of such individuals should be sought. It is also useful to contact other individual schools and communities that may have specific guidelines to offer on how to influence private foundations favorably.

State Grants to Educational Institutions

Each of the fifty state departments of education serves in a dual capacity. It is the office that may dispense state grants to local-community educators for the purpose of improving education. It is also the office through which federal funds for education allocated to the state may be funneled to local communities. Each of these departments makes regular mailings to superintendents of schools and principals with specific information regarding the availability of grants.

The grants that may be made available to local-community educators vary from state to state. Based on past performance, the general areas most often given favorable consideration have been related to remediation, improving the quality of educational programs for handicapped children, enrichment of curriculum for gifted children, and furthering the process of integration. State education departments in the Midwest have shown favor to agricultural programs. Their counterparts in some northern states have given assistance for upgrading vocational training in the industrial arts.

Each state department of education makes available to local-community educators informational brochures and *filing packets* that describe specifically the various types of grants currently being given consideration and the deadlines for filing. It is advisable to write for all information available and to request placement on future mailing lists. It can then be determined which grants may be most appropriate for assisting with the establishment of a computer facility.

Many local-community school boards insist on monitoring such activity and generally wish to be apprised of any intention to request specific state grants. State grants will not be awarded to any individual school district or to any individual school without the specific approval of appropriate local-community school-board officials. It is advisable, therefore, that school administrators make known their interest in applying for outside funding. A series of conferences may be anticipated at which there will be much discussion about the need for and the specific use of such funds. It is essential that the support of responsible officials be secured if efforts to gain special state funding are to be successful.

Federal Grants to Education

The federal government continues to offer a large variety of grants to educational institutions. Federal funds are available to assist not only with the general gamut of educational programs but with more delimited projects as well. The application for a federal grant to assist with the introduction of computer education may receive favorable consideration. Grants are available from many federal agencies. The federal government each working day publishes the *Federal Register*. This publication provides, in addition to a potpourri of data, information about current funding sources and regulations issued by the U.S. Department of Education. Because the subscription cost is significant, only major libraries generally receive this publication. In past years, favorable consideration was accorded such educational programs as remediation, improving the quality of education for handicapped children, enriching the curricula and quality of education for gifted children, developing upgraded programs in occupational education, and furthering the process of integration. Each of these seems an ideal area for introducing comprehensive computer-education projects.

It seems that the possibilities for securing federal grants change not only from year to year but even from semester to semester. It is strongly recommended that letters be written on official school stationery and sent to all of the federal agencies currently in existence. Such letters should request the most recent information about the availability of federal grants and specific guidelines for writing proposals. Once such information is received, follow-up letters should request all appropriate *submission kits* that may result in federal grants for the development of a computer-education facility.

Suggested Guidelines for Writing
Successful Proposals

Over the years some individuals have been more successful than others in securing state and federal grants. Analysis reveals that these proposal writers employed specific techniques that significantly improved the chances for receiving the funds needed for school projects.

1. Proposals must be specific and to the point. For example, if a funding agency is willing to grant funding to further articulation between elementary and middle or junior-high schools for improving the quality of educational programs for handicapped children, it should be clear to the agency that the proposal is specifically targeted at this objective. If it appears to the individual reviewing the proposal that the school's principal objective is the purchasing of computers and that improved articulation is secondary, the chances are that the proposal will be rejected.

2. Proposals should meet the funding agency's specific guidelines delineating the form and length of the document to be submitted. Many proposals have been rejected because one or more paragraphs did not fit into the designated space.

3. The figures used in the proposal should reflect an accurate assessment of need. Numbers must be totaled correctly. One of the major reasons for proposal rejection is incorrect arithmetic.

4. Proposals should indicate accurately the size of the target population to be served as well as the nature of that population. A funding agency is more likely to fund a request for money if a grant of $2,000 will serve 1,000 children for each of ten years (that is, 1,000 children multiplied by ten years equals 10,000 children; $2,000 divided by 10,000 children equals twenty cents per child served) rather than a second request that is to cost $1,500 and will serve 2,000 children for one year (that is, $1,500 divided by 2,000 children equals seventy-five cents per child served). Whereas the first proposal will cost the agency an additional $500 the expenditure will be almost four times as effective and will serve many more children. The funding agency is looking for "more bang for their buck."

5. It is advisable to seek assistance in writing proposals from those who have already succeeded. Such individuals as college grants officers, experienced school-board officials, able administrators, and representatives of local public-television and radio stations should be consulted.

6. Among other things funding agencies generally will request information about the following: spending limited resources efficiently, duration of the program after the funding terminates, title of program, amount of funds requested, period of time involved, size and nature of target population, selection criteria for target population, major performance objectives, description of procedures and operation of the program, staff-selection

criteria and resumes, activities, per-capita cost, training and material, and equipment needs.

It is important to reiterate three vital points made in chapter 4 with regard to purchasing equipment efficiently. (1) Careful planning should permit flexible scheduling so that the sharing of each microcomputer results in its fullest utilization. Because microcomputers are multidimensional and can be programmed to perform many function, the needs of many administrators and supervisors can be serviced with a single machine. (2) The utilization of microcomputers to assist the secretarial staff will result in the saving of considerable amounts of money. Individual secretary productivity will be increased. Peak loads during the school year, requiring the expenditure of money to hire additional secretarial and paraprofessional assistance will be reduced. Repetitive time-consuming tasks are costly and inefficient. The real savings realized by the use of computers quickly pay for the investment in such equipment. (3) Large sums of money can be saved by comparative shopping and by mix-and-match purchasing. Purchasing a microcomputer from a hardware manufacturer and peripheral devices (that is, disk drives and printers) and supplies from other vendors can easily save between 30 and 50 percent on those devices and supplies. And as was indicated earlier, it is often possible to purchase superior and completely compatible products for much less money. It has often been suggested that computer manufacturers make relatively little profit from the sale of machines but a great deal more profit from the sale of peripherals and supplies. This is one acceptable explanation for the extensive competition in the sale of these products.

Valuable Sources of Information

Appendix B lists the names of selected computer magazines. According to an article in the 4 October 1982 issue of *Newsweek*, "A Byte and a Bonanza" by William D. Marbach, William J. Cook, and John Taylor, "microcomputer journals now boast 1.5 million in circulation and about 5 million readers." A subscription to some of these publications will provide access to the names of vendors who offer microcomputers, peripheral devices, and supplies. Periodically, experts who write for these publications evaluate the quality and performance of the latest in equipment. These magazines also offer the names of computer clubs that meet regularly at locations throughout the nation. These publications also provide information about the periodic scheduling in communities throughout the nation of a variety of computer and office-equipment shows that exhibit the most recent developments in hardware, software, and supplies. Attendance at such shows offers invaluable education as to the functions that each manufacturer's hardware can perform and the kinds of commercial software that has become available and may be most useful in solving particular problems. At these shows there is opportunity for first-hand contact with the representatives of vendors. These approaches assist with decision making.

Fear of Equipment Becoming Outdated

Fears seem to persist that by the time expensive equipment is purchased and ready to operate additional funds will have to be expended to ensure that the computer is up-to-date. There is also the belief that the school's limited purchasing power is best served by waiting for manufacturers to produce improved products with less-expensive price tags. Such thinking is akin to waiting for better color-television sets to appear for a lower price. Of course it is in the nature of progress for improvements to be made, for new applications to develop, and perhaps for prices to eventually drop. It is possible to wait forever, but resolutions to problems will have to wait as well. The quality of the hardware and software that is currently available offers sufficient incentive to make the necessary investment as soon as possible. The functions that computers can now perform will serve a school's needs for many years and will repay the investment many times over. Word-processing and data-file-maintenance programs will reduce the costs of hiring additional personnel and will permit a more modern, productive approach for handling volumes of school data. There is little reason to believe that emerging equipment over the next decade will be so much improved that waiting is justified. A new machine in an even smaller housing unit with increased memory capacity or chips that permit faster operation may be able to operate more rapidly but only marginally more proficiently in doing school-related tasks. The equipment available in today's market will be able to do the job now and for many years to come. You are well advised to take time in making decisions and to buy what is needed to handle the projects you have identified. You are also advised to get started. If, eventually, new equipment offers additional growth opportunities, the administrators will then be in a better position to recognize them and be more likely to be able to afford them.

Personnel Involvement

Whenever possible, knowledgeable members of the staff should encouraged to participate in the process of purchasing equipment. Not only is their thinking of value but it is they who will be using the equipment. Those who play a role in decision making usually feel a vested interest in making a plan work. Resentments are inevitable when others, often less informed, make decisions that result in personnel working with equipment that may not be the best for the projects identified. Staff retraining generally requires very little released school time. One or two morning or afternoon sessions will usually suffice if the projects involve computer assistance with administrative problems, supervisory programs, CAI, or tutorial instruction.

Training of staff to implement a computer-literacy-education program will involve much more time. Many communities throughout the nation have handled the problem successfully by (1) central-district or citywide-funded programs, (2) intraschool inservice courses taught by previously trained members of the staff, and (3) college-level computer-training programs.

Central-district or citywide programs for training of personnel in computer literacy have usually been arranged by hiring outside computer-education experts and by providing the necessary thirty to sixty hours of released time for key personnel in each school, including at least one supervisor from a pilot school. Such experts teach the fundamentals of computer literacy including the skill of program writing. Successful central-district programs permit trainees to spend approximately 50 percent of course time at the computer. Of course, if a district or city does not yet own computers, this approach to training cannot be effective.

Intraschool training programs can be effective only if at least one member of the faculty has received adequate previous training. As new members of the staff become adept, they should be utilized to train others. Trained back-up personnel, supervisors, teachers, and secretaries are essential, so that the entire project does not become dependent on only a few individuals. High-school or college students, parents, local business people, and visiting teachers from other school districts, who have acquired expertise in using computers, should also be encouraged to assist in the training of staff. Lastly, college professors are often hired to provide inservice training.

College or university programs offer a third possibility for training staff in computer literacy. Interested individuals usually have been willing to take appropriate college-level courses at their own expense, particularly when success is viewed as a means to advancement. Incentives by the administration can be helpful in motivating such study. If an individual is assured that there will be opportunities to teach projected training courses, that individual will undertake the necessary preparation. A word of caution seems warranted. Many college-level computer-literacy courses are engineering oriented and are not necessarily the most effective means to acquire educational computing skills. Because not too long ago, computers were primarily understood and used by engineers, most computer experts in the nation are engineers. Their tendency is to emphasize mathematics and, as a result, the kind of skills needed for educational computing are neglected. It is helpful to look for courses having such titles as "Computers for Teachers" or "Computers in School Administration." Perhaps such courses will offer effective approaches and materials that are practical and can be utilized by school personnel.

Equipment Necessary for Computer-Literacy Training

The training center must have computers available if staff training is to be effective. The computers should be the same brand and model as those that will be used by the staff in school offices and classrooms. Each brand and model has its own unique peculiarities. Some of the keys on each brand of machine are designed to perform different functions, and much in the training process is negated if the trainees learn on one computer and then try to apply their skills on machines foreign to their experience. Ideally, of course, trainees would learn on the machines they eventually would be operating.

Experience has shown that training is most effective when there is one microcomputer for each group of two or three staff members. Successful training programs have also been implemented with a less desirable ratio of one machine for every sixteen staff members. Quality instruction, however, is much more difficult and trainees experience more frustration with the poorer ratios.

Anticipating the Inevitable Questions

1. *Why are computers needed in our schools?*
Computers are labor-saving devices. Their utilization permits greater efficiency and increased productivity. If managed wisely, these include administrative as well as academic activities. Budget allocations have continued to contract and there are fewer staff members to handle the work load. Computers can do the tedious, repetitive, unsatisfying chores and permit each individual to do more creative work. Computers are part of our nation's lifestyle and we cannot avoid much longer making them part of the lifestyle of our schools.

2. *If budget allocations are limited, then how can we afford to purchase such expensive equipment?*
Computer utilization will result in savings. There will no longer be as great a need to hire supplementary personnel during peak periods. Saving of space will result. It will no longer be necessary to store multiple copies of

materials we produce. Magnetic diskettes and cassettes will store the data. Computers will easily pay for themselves in just a few years of use.

3. *Why should youngsters be encouraged to play computer games in school when they already watch too much television at home?*
In school, students will use computers for remedial work and for advanced study. Computer-literacy courses will prepare them for the future when almost every profession and occupation will demand computer knowledge and skill. Computers will assist the staff with reducing burdensome paper-work. Teachers can use student love of computer games to motivate learning, to develop better coordination, and to involve youngsters in meaningful cocurricular activities. Students enjoy working with computers and school attendance improves.

4. *Can we wait until next year?*
Each year we wait will result in denying ourselves, our students, their parents, and the community, the right to become an active part of the future. A worldwide revolution in computers is taking place. Denying the fact is to look backwards. We have an obligation and responsibility as educators to make the educational process relevant and meaningful. The future is now.

6

Setting Up Your Computer Facility

A Brief Review Before We Proceed

Before moving into the considerations and techniques involved in setting up a viable school computer facility, it is appropriate at this point to review several of the major concepts and premises that have thus far been offered.

Computers are affecting the way we live and the way we think. The word *computer* is socially powerful. When viewed, either alone or in context with other words, it usually has the effect of causing a pause in activity and thought. It is one of those unique words that will in the future be used to measure the development of civilization. Computers are continuing to have an impact on every major area of industrial endeavor. It is inevitable that schools throughout the nation will begin to make fuller use of the multiple services that computers can provide.

It is important, when planning to come to terms with the computer revolution, that school administrators and supervisors accept a comprehensive definition of *computer literacy* that includes (1) providing for an understanding of the term, *computer,* its basic parts and their relationships, and the means by which human beings can communicate with computers; (2) ensuring that there is an awareness of the history of computers and their evolution; (3) coming to grips with the positive and negative impact that computers are having on society; and (4) taking the steps necessary for introducing computer education in the schools so that these machines may be controlled with quality programs that permit the achievement of established objectives proficiently and accurately. It is important that vocabulary be extended to include those words and expressions that are associated with computers.

In schools, computers can be utilized effectively by the administration for word processing and data-file maintenance. The process of supervision can also be given significant assistance by computers in word processing and data-file maintenance. Classroom teachers can draw on computer assistance for instruction, particularly with drill and practice. On a larger scale, computers can be utilized for assisting with tutorial programs for remedial and advanced work and for review. A school's entire education program can be upgraded and made more meaningful if there is provision for computer literacy.

It is essential to motivate and involve school personnel, students, and the community at the earliest possible time in plans for establishing a school

81

computer facility. Interested individuals with the potential to succeed need to be identified, trained, and given the opportunity to participate in the planning of the facility, in the identification of appropriate projects, and in the implementation of programs.

A carefully selected committee composed of administrators, supervisors, teachers, students, and parents should be organized to identify and evaluate equipment that might be potentially appropriate for projects envisioned and to assess costs. Needed commercial software should be isolated from the great volume that is regularly available. Such analysis will affect directly the decision as to the specific brand and model of microcomputer that will be needed. Proper peripheral equipment will then be more easily identified. The concept of *mix and match* must be entertained at each stage of decision making so that limited budgets have their maximum impact.

There needs to be an organized program for securing the funds necessary for putting the envisioned computer facility into operation. Once the facility begins to function, it is essential that a committee be established to write those proposals that are necessary to secure additional supplementary funding so that the facility may continue to be expanded.

Setting Priorities

The setting of clear priorities is probably the singular most difficult task for administrators and supervisors. Hard decisions have to be made and no two schools are the same. Each school plant has its strengths and weaknesses. The personnel in each school has its own identity. Personalities, backgrounds, values, educational philosophy, and approaches to the process of education differ not only from school to school but within each school as well. Student bodies differ as do communities. The needs of each school, therefore, are truly different, and these needs are constantly changing and evolving. It is essential to identify specific needs. It is necessary at the outset to identify those supervisors, teachers, and secretaries who will be directly involved in implementing programs and in using computers for specific projects. It is essential to know how much money is available for the introduction of computers. It is essential to identify specifically the equipment that will be needed to launch the facility.

Those charged with the responsibility for making decisions related to the establishment of a school computer facility need first to address budgetary considerations. The amount of money available will affect directly the decision as to the brand, quality, and quantity of equipment to be purchased. A generous budget with which to set a school computer facility into operation affords a wider range of choices. A more limited budget imposes restrictions. Now on to the business of setting up a viable school computer facility.

Getting Started: Word Processing versus
Data-File Maintenance

There is no reason that both functions cannot be undertaken. The real problem is to apportion time with careful deliberation so that the personnel using the equipment can be assured of a block of time to carry out the completion of assigned projects. Time will have to be divided between word-processing functions and data-file-maintenance projects. It is important to identify precisely the specific projects to which computers will be assigned.

As a word processor, the computer can be used for preparing letters, notices, bulletins, lists, conference agendum and minutes, and organizational reports. In this capacity, computers can assist with projects in pupil-personnel services, in the school treasurer's office, and in the program office for student scheduling. It can help to reduce the mass of paperwork generated by the dean's office, the medical room, the transportation office, the attendance office, and the lunch-program office. The frequency with which such materials are prepared will determine the time allotment to word-processing functions.

With regard to data-file-maintenance projects, it will have to be determined whether priority is to be given to payroll, inventory, student and teacher profiles, various reports, student schedules, or the college office. Projects involving data-file maintenance can require large segments of time. Once again, time allocations will depend on the frequency that such data files have to be supplemented with additional data, on the frequency that information has to be accessed from each file, and on the number of reports that need to be generated from each file. Much depends on the attention given to scheduling the sharing of available computers. Smoothness of operation can be increased by locating equipment as centrally as possible among the personnel involved.

If a microcomputer is to be shared among several selected supervisors, then arrangements will have to be worked out so that maximum utilization of equipment involved is affected. If there are adequate funds for purchasing additional computers, then additional decisions will have to be made as to where their most effective utilization can be realized. As was discussed in chapter 2, supervisors can ease many burdens by using computers for word processing and for projects involving data-file maintenance.

Computer-Aided Instruction versus Tutorial Programs

Both of these areas are worthy of consideration. It is essentially a question of setting priorities. Computer-aided instruction may be targeted for either reading and mathematics laboratories or for selected individual classrooms, the latter to serve as a base of operations for sharing by teachers on a grade or in a department. If, however, the establishment of either a centralized or departmental tutorial program is needed, the school library or multimedia center can serve as an effective base of operations. A school may eventually wish to make both programs available to its student body.

When Should Computer-Literacy Education Be Introduced?

There should be little reason to postpone the initiation of a meaningful computer-literacy educational program. If budgetary allocations are restrictive, students can still be introduced to computers and to the interrelationships of their parts. They can learn about the evolution of computers. They can try to understand the potential blessings and the hidden dangers that involvement with computers can bring for society. If budgets permit the purchase of adequate numbers of computers, then students will be afforded the opportunity for hands-on experience and can be taught to program these machines.

A comprehensive or limited computer-literacy educational program can be undertaken. A series of difficult decisions will have to be made. Administrators will need to determine if such a literacy program should be conducted centrally from a specially organized computer laboratory whose capacity for instruction may permit the education of a limited number of youngsters. If the computer laboratory is to be utilized primarily for instructing youngsters in how to write computer programs, then a series of sequential elective courses for those interested may be the direction the project will take.

With imagination, however, many more classes of students may receive such instruction. To accomplish such extended student scheduling, it will become necessary to enlist the aid of school personnel. In the elementary school, many supervisors have found it to be necessary for teachers to develop an experimental curriculum for each grade. Appropriate lessons will have to be planned for each of the four aspects of computer literacy so that the real needs of each student age group can be met.

In the middle or junior-high school, teachers in the science department may be called upon to prepare a series of lessons directed toward the history of computers and their evolution. The industrial-arts department can prepare lessons dealing with the computer as an entity as well as its parts and their interrelationships. The foreign-language department can undertake the task of providing students with an understanding of the various computer languages that enable human beings to communicate with computers. The social-studies department can develop a series of in-depth lessons that permit students to consider and evaluate the favorable and unfavorable impact that computers are having on society. Informed, motivated people will have to write such lessons and their knowledge should not be underestimated.

In the senior-high school, by the very nature of its organization and the maturity of its student body, more sophisticated and comprehensive approaches can be attempted. A greater number of in-depth, more intense lessons can be sustained by each department. The talents of teachers in the business-education department can be tapped to explore projected job opportunities. The English department can teach résumé writing and provide for the reading and discussion of novels dealing with the revolution in technology and its impact on the lifestyle of society. The fine-arts department can explore the world of high-resolution graphics and the industrial-arts department can demonstrate the art of computer printing. The guidance department can arrange a series of seminars focusing on the planning of careers. There are opportunities for using large-group instruction to advantage to reach large numbers of students. There are opportunities for developing quality elective courses that can make computer literacy a reality.

**Should Instruction in Computer Programming
Be Emphasized?**

Although students are enticed by computers and crave opportunities for hands-on experience, it is important that each phase of computer literacy be given attention. Certainly it is important that instruction in programming be given its due, but it is also important that the other aspects of computer literacy are not neglected. Computer languages come and go but the social impact of computers is here to stay. If we concentrate on the teaching of a computer language, the skill may be useless five years later. If on the other hand we give students an appreciation for the power and durability of computer activity, we give them something they can use forever.

**Can a School Staff Handle the Development
of a Meaningful Computer Facility?**

Each school has the capacity for establishing a first-rate computer facility. Special talents can be helpful but are not required. Intelligence, interest, motivation, and the desire to help initiate needed changes in the educational process are the basic ingredients that are required. With proper training, a school should have the quality people necessary for establishing a meaningful, comprehensive program in computer education.

Should Day-School Computer Equipment Be Made Available for Programs in Adult Education?

Because breakage or damage is feared, there is a tendency to overprotect expensive equipment. The current breed of microcomputers, however, are quite hardy. There should be little hesitation to share the equipment with the adult community. There must be provision, however, for ensuring that the equipment will be treated intelligently and that security will not be sacrificed. Many senior-high schools serve as centers for adult education. The same equipment, if used by trained professionals, can be a strong force in extending computer-literacy education to the community at large. Using day-school personnel to teach night courses is a good way to help protect valuable equipment.

Should Initial Emphasis Be on Administrative Needs or on Upgrading the Instructional Process?

Each administrator will have to determine specifically where the greatest impact may be realized. Can the needs of the administration be met without neglecting the quality of educational programs that are offered to the student body? Are there available individuals on the staff whose receptivity to the introduction of computer education will serve as a positive force? Which departments or grades, if given the opportunity to develop quality projects with computers, will make the most of that opportunity? Though the administrator may make what seem to be the best choices available, experimentation and ongoing evaluation will be guiding factors in making adjustments in the projects undertaken.

How Can a Computer Facility Be Made Secure?

It is essential that the matter of security is not treated lightly. Computers and their peripheral equipment must be made secure with police-type locks installed in metal doors. Windows should be fortified with strong, locked metal screens and bars. Floors above the first floor should be given priority whenever possible. It may be necessary to fasten computers, printers, disk drives, and cassette player/recorders to furniture. These precautions may restrict movement and mobility, but in some school plants choices may be severely limited. Generally, it is good practice to keep the movement of equipment from place to place to a minimum. If the choice is available, it is better to move staff to equipment than to have the equipment do the moving. If the transporting of equipment from one part of the plant to another becomes necessary on a regular basis, then it is recommended that sturdy metal carts large enough to accommodate the microcomputer and its peripheral devices, preferably with a lip around the perimeter to prevent sliding, be purchased. Such carts range in cost from thirty-five to approximately one-hundred dollars.

How Much Space Is Required?

Microcomputers are about the width, depth, and weight of an IBM Selectric typewriter. The only variance of any significance is the additional height necessitated by the screen. If a large number of microcomputers are to be centrally located in a laboratory environment, then an area the size of a large classroom is suggested. If only one or two microcomputers are to be utilized with disk drives or a cassette player/recorder and a printer, then the average office should accommodate them. The area should be large enough to permit personnel to walk around comfortably. It should not be so small that interested personnel are discouraged from visiting, touching, and becoming familiar with the equipment. Should shelves be desired, there should be adequate wall space. There also should be enough floor space to accommodate desks, tables, file cabinets, and storage cabinets.

Where Should Microcomputers Be Located?

Whenever possible, computers should be located centrally so that personnel who are sharing the equipment may have ready access. Maximum utilization of equipment may thereby be realized. Computers must not be located near a window where they are in direct sunlight. The reflection of light on the microcomputer's screen causes difficulty for personnel operating the equipment and direct sun may cause the computer's internal parts to overheat. Vision is affected adversely and the operator may experience fatigue. Good standard lighting, properly placed is advised. It does not matter how far the back of the microcomputer is from the wall. The presence of dust, even some chalk dust, may cause the operator discomfort, but there will be little adverse effects on the computer. A regular vacuuming compensates for most regular classroom dust conditions. An air-pure room is unnecessary. Printers and other mechanical peripheral devices (that is, disk drives and cassette player/recorders) often are subject to dust and dirt damage. It is advantageous to locate the computer as close to a wall outlet as possible. Extension cords may be necessary but the fewer the better. It is important to keep the power cord and any extension cords away from careless feet. Not only can people trip over them but also, should power be turned off inadvertently, many hours of effort and much valuable work may be lost.

How Essential Is Evaluation of Electrical Wiring?

It is essential that the school's custodian be consulted at the outset to determine if a room's power requirements are adequate and if safe circuiting is present. A circuit is a collection of outlets connected to a single circuit breaker or fuse. A microcomputer should not be plugged into the same electrical circuit that contains either a refrigerator or another device with a motor. If, for example, the microcomputer is placed on the same circuit with a refrigerator, and that appliance is equipped with a motor that turns itself on and off, the data stored in the computer's memory, often representing many hours of concentrated energy, can be lost. An informed custodian can offer best advice as to which circuits are safe. Generally, the operation of a waxing machine in the corridors adjacent to the room in which the computer is located, should have no adverse effect on the fuctioning of a computer unless it is on the same electric line.

Generally, most rooms have sufficient electrical-power capacity to accommodate a microcomputer. The power cord carries approximately one-hundred-and-ten volts, between one and three amps, ranges in length from three to six feet, and is much like the kind found on television sets. Periodically, the power cord should be checked for wear and fraying even though power cords are usually quite sturdy in construction. Often, the power cord is equipped with a three-pronged plug that must be connected to an outlet that generally accepts only a two-pronged plug. An adapter, easily available in a hardware store, is an inexpensive device that permits the interconnection of two such incompatible pieces of equipment. It cannot be stressed too often that power cords must be kept away from the feet of operators and visitors.

In a centrally located computer laboratory, it is necessary to connect the power cords of many machines to many outlets. Inexpensive multiple outlet strips ranging in price from ten to forty dollars are available. These multiple outlet strips are devices that have a plug at one end that fits into a standard wall outlet and multiple receptacles at the other end, often containing a built-in fuse that permits the various power cords to be connected. The advantage of such a device is that the microcomputers, the disk drives, and the printer may be plugged into a single outlet. Another alternative is to plug many microcomputers into a central console that permits the operation and control of disk drives from one central source. A good rule of thumb is the least amount of wiring, the safer the facility.

Are Special Office Furniture and Equipment Necessary?

It is not necessary to purchase special office furniture and equipment. Standard office furniture already present is most adequate for meeting the needs of computer equipment. Whatever furniture is appropriate for working with an electric typewriter is appropriate for working with a microcomputer. A sturdy table that is able to accommodate the width and depth of an electric typewriter is adequate for holding a microcomputer. If office personnel are accustomed to having tables available for collating the materials that are produced, such surfaces may continue to be necessary until the advantages offered by a computerized system makes them obsolete. Chairs and desks normally used in an office need not be replaced. Desk drawers, however, should be equipped with locks that function efficiently. If budgets permit and if aesthetics are important, there are many vendors that sell specially designed, functional, eye-pleasing, and often expensive computer furniture. Regular stationary vendors can be called upon for locating furniture suppliers if they do not carry what you need themselves. There are computer desks, computer chairs, computer tables, computer lamps, computer filing cabinets, computer fans, and computer rugs. Good overhead standard lighting by fluorescent lamps is highly adequate as long as the lamps do not reflect directly on the screen.

Are File and Storage Cabinets Preferable to Shelves?

File cabinets will continue to be necessary. They can serve either for storage of hard copy, the storage of diskettes or cassettes, or for the storage of quality paper for the printer. Metal storage cabinets equipped with sturdy locks can be useful for the storage of disk drives, cassette player/recorders, diskettes, and cassettes. Metal file and storage cabinets, with functioning locks, offer the necessary security. They make equipment and software less accessible. They provide a dust-free environment for diskettes and cassettes. A word of caution is advisable. Because diskettes are made of plastic and are coated with a magnetic surface, they must be kept at a respectable distance from magnets (or devices containing magnets such as stereo speakers, electric typewriters, radios, and such). The rule of thumb is a distance of one foot. In addition, diskettes must not be stored near sources of either excessive heat or cold. The rule of thumb is that if human beings can withstand the heat or cold of a given storage location, then the diskette can also. The same applies for cassettes. Storage cabinets are also useful for holding diskette storage systems such as mini-cassette storage trays with or without lids. Vendors also make available *head-cleaning diskettes,* which sometimes are useful.

Shelves, on the other hand, offer accessibility. They can hold software packages, manuals, magazines, and books. It is advisable to have available a good standard dictionary and a thesaurus. Because materials are displayed in the open, they are vulnerable. There are uses for both shelves and for file and storage cabinets.

It is helpful if a walk-in storage closet is available for overnight security of the microcomputer, the disk drives, the cassette player/recorder, the printer, and the screen (if it is not built into the microcomputer).

Office supplies that will be needed regularly are ribbons for the printer, labels, vinyl binders, computer paper, log books, and a wheel-type index file.

How Are Log Books Organized Most Effectively?

A standard looseleaf notebook with reinforcements on the holes of each page can be used just as well as commercially printed logbooks. Both permit the development of an index for quickly locating data that has been produced and saved on either cassette or diskette. It is essential that such data be easily identifiable for subsequent accessing. It is also possible to use a diskette as an electronic logbook for the same purpose. Some people prefer a wheel-type index file known under various brand names. Preferences vary. Experience will determine which serves the particular needs of each individual best.

The logbook may be organized alphabetically, sequentially, or topically. The logbook should provide for (1) the title of the program, (2) the number of the diskette or cassette on which the program may be found, (3) the date that the program was prepared and saved, and (4) a description of the program.

How Sturdy Is a Microcomputer?

The modern table-model microcomputer is designed to withstand a considerable amount of abuse. As with most office equipment, some computers are built to withstand more punishment than are others. These machines, if the power is left on and not interfered with, can remain in operation nonstop for approximately three years. Even then, the only effect would be that the screen would darken. At times, youngsters—out of curiosity, mischievousness, or for no other reason than a desire to test the teacher's assurance that microcomputers are built to take punishment—type very firmly on the keyboard, and some have even inserted gum, candy wrappers, pencil erasers, and other small objects into the disk drives or into the computer's innards. On occasion, liquids have been spilled accidentally. No matter. Though inconvenient, the current breed of microcomputer is easily repairable and the service costs are relatively small.

Some manufacturers locate their service facilities in a central location. Others provide a wide geographic network of service centers. This fact should be a major consideration when evaluating the merits of one machine in comparison to others.

An ordinary fan may be used to keep the flow of air moving if room temperatures rise over eighty degrees. Special computer fans are sold but are not necessarily more efficient than others. Room filters help in offices where smoking is persistent.

Which Microcomputer Is Preferable for School Use?

Aesthetics should be a secondary priority when deciding on a microcomputer for use in schools. A soundly constructed microcomputer with keyboard, screen, and disk drives contained within the housing structure is preferable. When these components are separate and externally located, the chance of damage is increased. If budgetary considerations, however, mandate the initial purchase of a less expensive machine, without disk drives, then a cassette player/recorder can still serve adequately for most school projects. As the microcomputer is assigned increasingly sophisticated projects, it will eventually require the addition of externally located disk drives. Located at the back of a microcomputer is a series of input-output ports much like those at the back of stereo receivers and tape decks. These receptacles are designed to accept the connection by cable of disk drives, cassette player/recorders, printers, keyboards, screens, and telephone modems. The latter are interfacing devices that permit a telephone to be connected to a computer.

How Much Distance Should There Be between a Microcomputer and Its Peripheral Equipment?

Preferably, the microcomputer's components should be contained within its housing structure. If, however, the components are externally located and are connected to the microcomputer, then they should be located as close together as possible. The individuals using the microcomputer will find this arrangement more convenient than having the various parts located at different points in the room. There will also be less chance of having many cables connected via a series of extension cords, thereby creating increased possibilities for either damage to the equipment by people tripping over wires or by having hours of work erased by a power cord becoming disconnected that results in the termination of electric current.

If peripheral equipment is not contained within the microcomputer, then surfaces with adequate area will need to be used for support. It is helpful to know in advance how much surface area will be required.

Disk drives range in size from two inches (width) by six inches (height) by eight inches (depth) to five inches (width) by nine inches (height) by twelve inches (depth). For some disk drives, a separate power supply may be required to provide the electrical power necessary for operation. Additional equipment, known as disk-interface hardware, may be required if the microcomputer lacks this component. On some models the interface mounts inside the regular cabinet while on others a separate box is needed for this purpose.

Printers range in size. Small-dot-matrix printers are approximately twelve inches (width) by three inches (height) by twelve inches (depth). The dimensions of impact printers range from fifteen inches (width) by eight inches (height) by twelve inches (depth) to thirty inches (width) by twelve inches (height) by eighteen inches (depth). A familiar standard of comparison is the IBM Selectric-II typewriter, which is twenty inches (width) by eight inches (height) by sixteen inches (depth). A cable may be needed to attach the printer to the microcomputer. In evaluating printers, noise factor is a major consideration.

Access jacks for cassette player/recorders must have adequate diameter apertures so that they will be compatible with the microcomputer's cable. If the diameter of the apertures is too large or too small, adapters will be required.

Which Computer Language Offers the Most Flexibility?

BASIC (Beginners All Purpose Symbolic Instruction Code), an English-like language, is the most flexible of the many computer languages available. It is composed of approximately fifty words, which have definitive spellings and are used in a prescribed manner for different purposes. It is a small but powerful language that enables human beings to make the microcomputer function in a prescribed manner. Other languages are FORTRAN (used primarily by mathematicians and scientists), COBOL (designed with a business orientation for storing large amounts of data), PASCAL (a general language), LOGO (a game- and spacial-relations-oriented language), FORTH, and C to name just a few of the more than one hundred languages. Another computer language that is currently gaining popularity is PL/1 (used for advanced computer programming). It is also available for some microcomputers. There is little, however, that cannot be accomplished expeditiously with BASIC. This is the language that offers a school maximum flexibility. Before energy is devoted to the mastering of other languages, it is strongly recommended that personnel and students acquire facility with BASIC.

Are There Special Considerations for Proper Maintenance of Equipment?

Modern table-model microcomputers are generally quite reliable and need little servicing. They break down rarely. Therefore expensive service contracts are not usually cost efficient and are not recommended. When service is required for microcomputers, it is generally performed away from the school plant at designated repair facilities. When evaluating the merits of each brand of microcomputer, it is advisable to make inquiry as to whether loaner machines can be provided either gratis or at a negligible cost during such periods of service. It is also recommended that equipment be inspected periodically. Cables and wiring should be checked for wear and fraying. When necessary, they should be replaced. The keyboard cannot avoid becoming soiled, thereby requiring periodic cleaning. A brush attached to the nozzle of a vacuum clearner should be used for periodic dusting of equipment. Tables holding the microcomputer and its peripheral equipment should also be inspected periodically.

How Can Staff Members Best Familiarize Themselves with the School's Microcomputers?

The tendency is to protect expensive equipment. People are often cautioned to look but not touch. This is unfortunate because many individuals initially have a natural inclination to want to learn about new equipment. The attitude of overprotection by the administration, however, serves to reinforce either overt or latent fear of computers. As many as 30 percent of computer users continue to be afraid of the machines they operate even after they have learned how to use them proficiently. The key to changing attitudes and behavior is to open the doors, to reassure personnel, to demonstrate the operation of equipment, and to invite people to look and to touch. The rule should be: use but don't abuse. Familiarity breeds confidence. Confidence encourages people to become involved. It is recommended that faculty conferences be held in small groups so that demonstrations can be presented. Individuals on the staff should be encouraged to visit offices where computers are in operation so that opportunities are provided for hands-on experience.

How Much Staff Training Is Necessary?

Workshops, inservice courses, and college courses are recommended so that proficiency may be achieved. To be able to use the microcomputer as a word processor, however, involves very little training for an experienced secretary. To be able to use commercial programs, almost no training at all is required. The individual need only be familiar with the parts of a microcomputer and be able to read and follow instructions that appear on a screen. To be able to use disk drives, cassette player/recorders, and printers takes somewhat more intensive instruction. To be able to type in such programs as those that are discussed in chapters 7 and 11, the user need only carefully follow the instructions that appear in appendix D.

How Can Public Relations Be Strengthened
by the Presence of Computers?

At every opportunity staff, students, parents, and members of the community need to be educated. They need to be reminded of the responsibility and obligation to teach youngsters those skills that are necessary for functioning in a technologically oriented society. They must be reassured that computers offer no threat but rather liberation from daily drudgery and repetitiveness. They must be encouraged to accept that the use of computers will provide opportunities for creative productivity and for the learning of new skills that can make each working day more of a joy. They must be reminded that ways need to be found to restore the dignity of doing meaningful work.

Faculty, departmental, grade, committee, individual, and parent-teacher conferences offer excellent opportunities for communicating the thrust of such messages. The student body should be aroused through such vehicles as elective courses, articles in school newspapers and magazines, and contests. Parents should be informed at conferences and at the meetings of community organizations. The programs in adult education should be expanded to provide for meaningful computer literacy. Parent and student volunteers should be recruited to assist the less able but more needy youngsters with computer-assisted tutorial programs based in the school's library or multimedia center. Advertising success with projects is vital. Press coverage, whenever possible, should be exploited to the fullest. Every avenue of communication should be utilized to share the successes that are experienced.

Which Pitfalls Should Be Avoided?

Criteria should be established for the careful selection of individuals on the staff for involvement with initial projects. Time and care must be devoted to the evaluation of all appropriate equipment under consideration for purchase. Staff, student body, and community must be involved in the planning of the computer facility. Attention must be given to properly preparing the various school offices for receiving and setting up purchased microcomputers, peripheral equipment, software, and supplies.

Lack of attention to these key phases can lead to frustration and disappointment. Decisions should not be based on emotion, personal relationships, or heresay. All decisions should be rooted in the singular objective of providing the best chance for making the computer facility succeed.

**Evaluating the Effectiveness
of Computer Performance**

There should be a periodic monitoring of the impact that computers are having on the administration, on supervision, on instruction, and on the extension of computer literacy for staff, student body, and community. Appropriate ongoing conferences should consider problems that develop and seek cooperation in their resolution. There should be no hesitation in calling for expert assistance whenever necessary. Evaluation should be in terms of (1) specific educational objectives, (2) unexpected returns on the investment of money, time, and energy, (3) the extent to which the staff has made necessary adjustments to newly introduced technology, (4) degree of receptivity to computer assistance, (5) new components selected to supplement initial equipment, (6) development of additional more sophisticated projects, (7) numbers of staff members who continue to become involved, (8) the role of administrators and supervisors in guiding the success of the computer facility, (9) use of reliable and valid questionnaires to be completed by staff, student body, and parents, (10) impartial evaluation by professional experts, (11) providing for recommendations with which to improve the overall facility and specific projects, and (12) utilizing data-based evaluation (for example, improvements in student reading and math scores, growth in independent study courses and tutorial programs, saving in storage space, saving in secretary time).

If the approaches suggested here are given careful consideration and implemented, a school computer facility has every chance of succeeding and of providing a new dimension in the educational process and environment.

7 Administration: Resolving Selected Problems

Once a school's computer facility has been established and is ready to begin functioning, it is only natural that there should be some measure of apprehension as theoretical computer-assisted solutions to administrative problems are put to the test. This chapter will demonstrate, with a selection of several of the more common administrative problems, how computers can be utilized to modernize and facilitate their handling. It will become apparent that increased speed of operation will result, that accuracy and cosmetics in the preparation of documents will improve significantly, that modification of documents will be made easier, that large amounts of data can be accessed at the touch of a key, and that additional time will become available to school personnel for other projects.

Word Processing

As described in chapters 2 and 6, the utilization of a microcomputer for word processing can facilitate the preparation, modification, and saving (on either diskettes or cassettes) of a wide variety of documents such as letters, bulletins, and notices; weekly, semester, and annual calendars; conference agendum and minutes; teacher and supervisor evaluation reports; annual performance objectives; reports; proctoring schedules for standardized examinations; organization sheets identifying classes, teachers, and rooms; and a countless variety of lists involving transportation, lunch programs, confidential medical-office listings of students with special problems, attendance-office records, and student-admissions and discharges files.

It is strongly recommended that a quality commercial word-processing program be purchased so that the computer can be assigned the variety of clerical tasks described above. Commercial word-processing programs range in cost from fifty dollars to six-hundred dollars. The wide range in cost reflects several factors. Some brands of microcomputers can accommodate only one or two particular word-processing programs. Had other commercial programs been written for these machines, the price of the software available would be significantly less since competition would have created a healthier marketplace. As was indicated in chapter 4, it is essential to determine in advance of purchase, the cost of available software for the microcomputer under consideration. The second factor affecting the cost of word-processing programs is the complexity of operations that the program affords. For example, an attractive feature of one particular program may be its capacity to have the computer automatically change every occurrence of a specific word to another. In specific application, a letter directed to a Mr. Smith may contain that gentleman's name a number of times. Should it be desired that the same letter now be sent to a Mr. Jones, the word-processing program may provide for the automatic replacement of one name with another. Another sophisticated word-processing program may provide an attractive feature that allows for the separate typing of the same letter to fifty different individuals. It is therefore advisable that the word-processing program to be considered contain those features that are necessary for the completion of most projects.

A commercial word-processing program comes supplied on a diskette or cassette. Since most offices purchase and use diskette-based machines our illustrations in this area will all involve diskette-based programs. If cassette-based machines are selected the same general descriptions apply. Because the expense involved in its purchase is significant, the word-processing diskette should be copied electronically by the computer onto many blank diskettes by using what computer programmers call a *back-up program*. These newly prepared copies of the word-processing diskette may then be used for the preparation of all documents involving words, as the repository on which such documents are saved or stored for future use, and as the source for accessing particular information in the future. The specific procedure for copying software varies. Each brand of microcomputer requires that a precise set of instructions be followed when preparing back-up diskettes.

To begin utilizing the microcomputer as a word processor, a diskette containing the word-processing program should be inserted into the main disk drive. The word-processing program is then *loaded* from the diskette into the microcomputer's memory. The loading procedure is different for each brand of microcomputer. It is advisable, therefore, to consult the manual of instructions provided by the manufacturer for the specific procedure to be followed. The entire operation takes just seconds to complete. The microcomputer is now ready for word processing in the preparation of documents.

Upon completion of each document and after it has been saved on diskette, immediate attention must be given to its specific identification by labeling the diskette and its protective jacket with the document title and then recording this information in a log. This procedure ensures ease and precision in *locating* a document in the future. Suggested procedures were described in chapter 6.

It is essential that any word-processed document or data file be saved electronically on at least two back-up diskettes. The individual preparing the document on the word processor should cultivate a procedural habit used by professional programmers. Typing should stop at approximately each fifteen-minute interval so that the material completed to that point can be saved on at least two diskettes. The *saving process* consumes under half-a-minute in time but the time and energy expended in the preparation of the document will have been safeguarded and the document itself will have been preserved. Once again, because the procedure for saving data differs with each brand of microcomputer and word-processing program, the manual of instructions should be consulted.

Once hard copy of the completed document is printed and filed away and one of the diskettes has been stored safely for future reference, the back-up diskette, if desired, can be wiped clean electronically and subsequently used again for the preparation of other documents. It should be noted that many individuals, based on experience, prefer to save completed documents on two or more diskettes rather than on only one diskette. They also prefer storing each of these diskettes in separate places. Those individuals who regularly work with computers have learned through hard experience to respect what the computer can accomplish but also never to trust in computers or to trust circumstances. Too often, because of any one of a variety of reasons, and not necessarily due to the carelessness of the individual preparing the document, the document has been lost. One case in particular will illustrate the reason for caution. A diskette containing a number of saved documents was inadvertently left lying on a desk. A coworker stopped by to chat and without thinking moved a magnetized paper clip receptacle too close to the diskette. The diskette was wiped clean because of the proximity of the small magnet to the diskette. Hours of work had to be prepared anew from hard copy that had fortunately been printed. Had the document been saved on a second diskette, all that would have been necessary was the preparation of a copy, taking only a few seconds. Professional computer programmers are not paranoid when they distrust magnetically stored information. They are merely cautious.

All word-processing programs provide a *typing mode* and an *edit mode*. In the typing mode, the microcomputer is used generally as is an electric typewriter. Utilization of the microcomputer as a word processor, however permits each character typed to be displayed on its screen. Before the content of the document is finalized and hard copy is printed, each character, word, sentence, and paragraph may be modified or replaced. The pressing of one or more keys permits ready editing. In this mode, material already typed may be deleted, modified, or replaced by inserting new characters, words, sentences, or paragraphs. These changes are accomplished quickly and easily. In addition, words, sentences, and paragraphs may be transposed, or even moved, immediately and automatically from one location in the document to another location with precisely the same speed and ease of operation. As this transposition or movement of copy is taking place, the microcomputer immediately and automatically rearranges the proper spacing of the balance of the document.

The document can be proofread on the screen and additional modifications effected before hard copy is printed. Once printed, the administrator has the option of either using it as is or modifying it once again. Retyping the entire document is no longer necessary. The computer, acting as a word processor, then electronically directs the printer to produce hard copy automatically, providing for centering, proper spacing, and the specific number of lines per page.

Data-File Maintenance

As was indicated in chapter 2, a school's administration can utilize the microcomputer to assist with a variety of problems in data-file maintenance. During the school year, it is often necessary for the administration to secure many kinds of information from personnel in a number of offices: supervisor in charge of administration, supervisor in charge of pupil-personnel services, treasurer, payroll secretary, supplies secretary, coordinator of transportation services, coordinator of lunch-room services, dean's office, medical office, and attendance office. Much of this information represents a systematic accumulation of data by individuals in these offices either on a daily basis or periodically. This information may serve as a key factor in decision making or may comprise the basis of subsequent cumulative reports.

Such data-based information, compiled on a cumulative basis and stored permanently on diskettes, creates a series of data banks or data files. Because the process is ongoing and requires the entering and saving of large varieties and large masses of information, human beings find it difficult and time consuming, particularly during peak periods, to maintain such files the traditional way. Microcomputers are designed to perform intricate data-file maintenance and to provide, instantaneously, varieties of information at the touch of a key. The microcomputer is ideally suited to assist the administration with many of the tasks its personnel must perform throughout the school year.

The College-Advisory Office:
Diagnosis of a Problem

In almost every senior-high school, the guidance department provides a wide variety of pupil-personnel services. Among these is the maintenance of a college-advisory office, generally coordinated by a qualified guidance counselor, grade advisor, or teacher. It is useful to explore one of the many problems faced by this office. Because of budgetary limitations, schools generally can afford the assignment of only one individual to tend to the needs of hundreds of graduating seniors each year. Sometimes this individual is provided with the assistance of a full-time secretary, part-time assistance by teachers on building assignment, and part-time volunteer assistance by students and parents. The problem is exacerbated by increasing numbers of students in the junior class who seem to have begun the process of identifying and evaluating the nation's twenty-four-hundred four-year colleges at a much earlier stage than in previous years.

Time is needed to meet with and counsel students who, because of different personal problems and academic needs, require individual attention. Each youngster seems to have an inexhaustable supply of questions to which they feel they are entitled to answers. The schoolday simply does not provide adequate time for meeting this professional responsibility. The stream of youngsters seems endless and incessant. In addition, it is necessary for the college-office coordinator to oversee the dissemination of general information, the distribution, processing, and collection of city-and state-university college applications, the preparation and processing of applications for private colleges, the securing and processing of appropriate letters of recommendation, the generation of certified high-school transcripts, the overwhelming task of preparing envelopes and mailings, the coordinating of informational college nights, the maintenance of informational bulletin boards, the securing of college bulletins, the arranging for speakers, the dissemination of information related to financial assistance, the interviewing and counseling of parents, and many other related activities.

Generally the standards for admission to city and state universities are clear cut and the choices that students have to consider and make are limited. The process is largely automatic. Problems arise, however, when students have to consider the many ramifications related to the selection of and application to the nation's private four-year colleges. Once readily available on request, college catalogs are no longer easy to acquire. High printing and mailing costs and repeated school requests for replacement catalogs have necessitated that colleges reconsider policies related to catalog distribution to senior-high schools. When college catalogs are available, the information they contain may no longer be current. Reduced frequency of printing schedules makes it almost impossible for college administrators to keep catalog data that is relevant.

Several very fine guides to colleges are published and updated each year. These books, however, are expensive for many youngsters. Limited expense budgets make it difficult for the college office to purchase the number of copies necessary for the many students seeking to use them. School libraries are also able to afford the purchase of few, if any, of these guidebooks each year.

The cost of making application to college has risen significantly. Because youngsters are uncertain as to the wisest choice of college and experience frustration when trying to evaluate their chances for acceptance to the various private colleges under consideration, they tend to cover all bases by actually overapplying. If a school does not limit the number of applications per student and the individual counseling necessary is unavailable, the tendency is to apply to many more colleges than is actually needed. This results in excessive costs that many parents and most schools can really not afford. Time and energy are wasted in processing applications and related documents. The cost of telephone calls and postage continues to increase.

Two other factors need to be considered. Just as colleges and universities prefer a faculty that reflects a wide national geographic distribution, there seems to be a tendency to select the incoming freshman class from as wide a geographic and ethnic base as possible. This may lead to a limited number of students being accepted from each senior-high school. The ability to pay without seeking financial assistance is yet another factor in the process of selecting an incoming class. In reality, youngsters must measure their chances for acceptance by comparing their credentials with those of other students seeking admission. Students must be concerned with competition from students in other geographic areas and with competition from students in their own school.

Before students can give consideration to other important tangential criteria for acceptance such as nature and level of high-school courses completed, performance in advanced placement courses and on achievement tests, rank in class, cocurricular activities, the quality of essays written for the application, relative strength of letters of recommendation, and the personal interview, it must be determined if their statistical academic credentials are "in the ballpark" for admission.

For each college and university considered, the student must evaluate chances for admission based on a cumulative three-year academic average and on verbal and mathematics scores achieved on national aptitude examinations such as the SATs and ACTs. This is an extremely difficult process without proper, informed, professional counseling. It becomes even more difficult when recent trends in admission policies are almost impossible to discern. Unless a youngster has some reliable statistical data base to guide decision making, the process of identifying colleges where there are reasonable chances for acceptance becomes expensive, compromised with wishful thinking, and one of blind chance. Frustration and disillusionment often result.

Reducing the Impact of the Problem

The utilization of a microcomputer provides the school administration with a proven viable approach for reducing the impact of this problem. Students will be able to narrow the field significantly and focus on a number of colleges at which they stand a reasonable chance for acceptance. A microcomputer equipped with a good commercial data-management program (available commercially for nearly every brand of machine) provides each student with access to a reasonably current data-file bank for each college to which candidates in the previous year's graduating class have applied. This *electronic college directory* will enable students each year to compare their specific academic credentials, namely cumulative three-year academic average, verbal and math scores on the SAT examination, and verbal and math scores on the ACT examination, with those of applicants in the previous year's senior class. Such comparisons provide the school's current crop of students with specific, relevant data as to how selected colleges acted on the previous year's applications. Students are thereby assisted with narrowing the number of colleges to which they should consider making application. A major bottleneck will be removed for students, their parents and the school's college office.

In order for an electronic college directory to be developed, specific information is needed. Once accumulated, this data needs to be entered into the computer's memory bank and stored permanently on diskettes. The process is repeated each year, permitting students in each subsequent senior class the advantage of being able to use this information as the basis for informed decision making.

The first step is to secure appropriate information and data. Students should be apprised of the reasons for the college office accumulating such information and data. They should be assured that the names of applicants will not be identified. The college office should require that an informational three-by-five-inch index card be completed and submitted with every college application to be processed. Either preprinted or blank index cards may be used. A clearly worded instruction sheet is strongly recommended. Block printing increases chances for legibility. The following information should be requested:

Last name: first name: middle initial: — official class:

Name of college or university:

Overall three-year high-school academic average:

SAT: date:	verbal score:	math score:
ACT: date:	verbal score:	math score:
Acceptance ( )	Rejection ( )	Wait-listed ( )

All index cards are filed alphabetically by name of applicant. As students receive notification from each college, it is required that they report to the college office and indicate on each index card submitted, the action taken by that college or university. By the middle of the spring semester, virtually every college will have made its decisions and notified applicants. The completed index cards are then rearranged alphabetically by name of college or university.

The secretary assigned to the college office then utilizes the commercial program suggested in this chapter, which is configured to accept data from the index cards. The secretary, a student volunteer, or a parent volunteer can begin the process of transferring the data from each index card into the memory of a computer that has now been equipped with the program. The program will call for the information included on the sample index card shown here. Once all entries have been completed, the information is permanently stored on diskette.

A library of twenty diskettes will store permanently this data representing the experiences of the previous year's graduates who applied to some of the nation's most popular colleges. Each diskette is configured to store data for ten colleges, each side of the diskette holding the data of five colleges. This number is arbitrary and may be adjusted to serve the particular needs of each school. The twenty diskettes provide a statistical picture of recent decision making by two-hundred selected colleges and universities.

An alphabetically arranged index is posted to identify the number of the diskette on which each college file is stored. In addition, the program on diskettes used by students has been configured to ensure that the correct diskette has been selected for examining data appropriate for a specific college under consideration.

It should be noted that such a college directory can be developed and maintained on separate sheets of paper for each college in oversized looseleaf notebooks. Such notebooks, however, are quite cumbersome, difficult to handle, and difficult to maintain. A library of twenty diskettes can store a quantity of data that would require thousands of sheets of paper. Such notebooks are easily damaged when constantly handled by large numbers of students, and the information contained on each page is often lost. The diskette is permanent and is much easier to use.

The electronic college directory is now ready for use. A student enters the college office with a list of colleges under consideration. The index listing each college for which data is available is consulted. The appropriate diskette number is identified, the diskette secured, and inserted into the computer. The file (that is, the name of the college) is then loaded from the diskette on which it has been stored into the memory of the computer. Once again, the computer's manual of instructions should be consulted as to specific procedures for loading a program from a diskette into the computer's memory.

The student responds to a series of programmed instructions displayed on the screen. The student will be asked to type in the name of the college or university under consideration. The program will double-check that the proper diskette has been selected and that the name of the school indicated is in fact the college whose data has been requested for examination. The computer's screen will then display the cumulative statistical data reflecting the experiences of students in the previous graduating class who had applied to that particular college.

The student can now compare his or her statistical academic credentials with those of other individuals who had applied previously. The computer's screen will reveal all statistical data stored in the college's file. A detailed and careful evaluation can result. The student may then repeat the process with diskettes containing data on other colleges under consideration.

The School Treasurer's Office: Diagnosis of a Problem

A school receives and disburses significant sums of money each year. The school treasurer (teacher or secretary), conscientious, well organized, and accurate, assumes responsibility for protecting the administration's fiscal integrity by monitoring and recording all financial activities involving receipt of income and the allocation and disbursement of funds.

Regularly, monies are received from a wide variety of sources. Receipts must be issued, information recorded, and deposits made. Requests for allocation of funds by intraschool personnel must be processed, approved, and the amounts disbursed recorded in checkbooks, accounting ledgers, and journals. Bills received from vendors must be checked against invoices to ensure that items ordered were received. Again an accurate written record must be maintained in a checkbook, accounting ledgers, and a journal. These documents must provide for the identification of the individual or office involved in the transaction, the vendor, the date, and the amount paid. If more than one checking account is maintained, accounting procedures are made more difficult. Each month, checkbook, accounting ledgers, and journal must be trial balanced and reconciled with bank statements.

Painstaking problems arise when a vendor claims that a bill has not been paid. The treasurer must determine (1) if the bill was in fact paid and (2) the date that the check was drawn. Similarly, should school personnel claim that items previously ordered have not been received, the treasurer must determine (1) if the bill for the item was paid and (2) the date that the check was drawn. In either case, the claim necessitates a great deal of physical cross-checking and the expenditure of much time because easy accessibility of information is lacking. Voluminous numbers of invoices must be handled and checked. Accounting ledgers and journals must be perused.

Check stubs and canceled checks must be examined. The problem is further compounded because more than one school office may have made purchases from the same vendor. The treasurer may also be handicapped by not knowing precisely how far back to go in checking information so that the problem may be resolved quickly. It is conceivable that costly errors may occur. It is also difficult to access information without resorting to time-consuming research.

Resolving the Problem

The computerized *treasury program,* offered in appendix E, is configured to encompass the major activities with which the school treasurer is most likely to be concerned. This program should be typed into the computer and permanently saved on diskette in accordance with the specific instructions provided in appendix D. The program may then be loaded into the computer at any time so that it can be used by the administration to alleviate the intensity of the many demanding tasks required of the treasurer. The treasurer merely follows the program by providing the information requested. The treasurer is then able to record and permanently store all data electronically and to subsequently access instantaneously all or any segment of that data.

Rather than hand-record pertinent information in one or more repositories, entries are made electronically either once a day, more frequently, or at the treasurer's convenience. Provision is made for the recording and permanent storing of information related to each transaction: (1) the teacher responsible for the transaction, (2) the school agency or account responsible for the transaction, (3) the date of the transaction, (4) the name of the vendor involved in the transaction, (5) the number of the check issued for the transaction, and (6) the amount involved in the transaction.

The process involves identifying the file with a descriptive name for future reference. The treasurer then has a variety of options: (1) Records such as those described in the above paragraph may be added to the file. (2) Records in the file may be modified. (3) The file may be instantaneously searched electronically via amount of transaction, date of transaction, check number, person responsible, school agency responsible, or name of vendor. (4) Records in the file may be deleted. (5) A listing of all transactions in data sequence may be printed on the screen. (6) A listing of all transactions in date sequence may be printed on hard copy.

The treasurer, at the touch of a key, may secure instantaneously, the total amounts of all checks issued, the total amount of all bills incurred, a listing of all transactions made by individuals, a listing of all transactions made by a school agency, and a listing of all transactions involving vendors.

In addition, the computer can be configured to generate lists of checks to be issued and to prepare the envelopes for mailing. Large varieties of information become immediately available to the administration. The process of informed decision making is thereby strengthened.

The Supplies Secretary: Diagnosis of a Problem

It is necessary for the administration to maintain a current inventory of all textbooks, supplies, and equipment. Thousands of items may be involved. To be able to reorder replacement items, it is important that as supplies are distributed and used and requests made for replacement appropriations, the inventory reflect accurately what is needed. Generally, a teacher, paraprofessional, or supplies clerk is assigned the responsibility for maintaining an up-to-date record of materials on the shelf. A record of software (for example, chalk, paper, chalkboard erasers, marking books, and such) is not easy to maintain but manageable ballpark figures are available to the administration. Inventories of textbooks are usually maintained by supervisors in charge of grades or departments. Expensive hardware, however, presents a problem. Each typewriter, mimeograph machine, spirit-duplicating machine, photocopy machine, adding machine, calculator, microcomputer, film projector, filmstrip projector, slide projector, overhead projector, opaque projector, cassette player/recorder, and microscope must be identified and immediately located. The problem is compounded as hardware is moved from place to place within a school plant. It is difficult for any individual assigned the task to keep track of precisely what equipment is available in the school. Often, it seems that the school's administration tends to be a half-step behind the reliable tracking of equipment.

Resolving the Problem

The computerized inventory program offered in appendix E is configured to resolve one of the major problems concerning the supplies secretary. This program should be typed into the computer and permanently saved on diskette in accordance with the specific instructions provided in appendix E. The program may then be loaded into the computer at any time so that it can be used by the administration to resolve one of the more demanding tasks required of the secretary. The secretary then merely follows the program by providing the information requested. The secretary is then able to record and permanently store all data related to hardware and equipment electronically and to subsequently access instantaneously all or any segment of that data. Rather than hand-record pertinent information, entries are made electronically either once a day, more frequently, or at the secretary's convenience.

Provision is made for the recording and permanent storing of information related to each piece of hardware or equipment: (1) the name of the piece of hardware or equipment, (2) its serial number, (3) the individual to whom it has been assigned, and (4) the school agency or office in which the hardware or equipment is located. The process involves identifying the file with a descriptive name for future reference. The secretary then has a variety of options: (1) Records such as those described above may be added to the file. (2) Records in the file may be modified. (3) The file may be instantaneously searched electronically via the item, the serial number, the name of the individual to whom the item has been assigned, or the office to which the item has been assigned. (4) Records in the file may be deleted. (5) A listing of all items may be printed on the screen. (6) A listing of all items may be printed on hard copy.

The secretary, at the touch of a key, may secure instantaneously specific information regarding any piece of hardware or equipment by name of item, by name of individual to whom the item has been assigned, and by location of area in which the item has been assigned. Information becomes immediately available to the administration. The process of informed decision making is thereby strengthened.

It should be noted that another major problem faced by the secretary in charge of supplies maintenance is the acquisition of information necessary for completing monthly reports on massive numbers of telephone calls, generally involving thousands of dollars in charges. A record of each bill for local calls, long-distance calls, basic-equipment service charges, overcalls, other charges including those for directory assistance, and deductions for third-party calls must be maintained. The secretary must complete detailed reports requiring information as to (1) date of call, (2) telephone number called, (3) name of individual making call, (4) purpose of call, (5) name of party called, and (6) name of individual authorizing call. The total amount may not exceed the amount provided by the annual budget allocation. It is obvious that the utilization of a computerized program would provide much needed relief for the individual assigned the responsibility for accumulating such voluminous information.

The Need for a Staff Profile: Diagnosis of a Problem

Each year the administration or the various offices to which it delegates responsibilities are required to submit various types of detailed reports. The payroll secretary, for example, expends considerable time and energy compiling information for teacher record cards, for cumulative absence reserves, for personnel reports, and for staff-evaluation reports. The work is tedious, repetitive, and demanding. Concentration and accuracy are required because large sums of money are ultimately involved.

Resolving the Problem

A computerized *teacher-data program,* offered in appendix E, is configured to accumulate staff-related data with which the school's administration is most likely to be concerned. Once again, this program should be typed into the computer and permanently saved on diskette in accordance with the specific instructions provided in appendix D. The program may then be loaded into the computer at any time so that it can be used by the administration to access pertinent information that may be necessary for the generation of a variety of reports. The individual using the program merely follows its instructions by providing the specific information requested. Individuals such as the payroll secretary are then able to record and permanently store all such data electronically and to subsequently access instantaneously all or any segment of that data.

Rather than hand-record pertinent information in one or more repositories, entries are made electronically either once a day, more frequently, or at the convenience of the individual or individuals involved. Provision is made for the recording and permanent storing of information related to: (1) name of staff member, (2) address of staff member, (3) telephone number, (4) file number of staff member, (5) staff member's social-security number, (6) license level, (7) subject of license, (8) subject taught, (9) status—tenure or probation, (10) date of appointment, (11) seniority date, (12) leave status, and (13) any five other relevant kinds of data required by individual schools.

The process involves identifying the file with a descriptive name for future reference. The responsible individual (such as the payroll secretary) then has a variety of options: (1) Records such as those described in the preceding paragraph may be added to the file. (2) Records in the file may be modified. (3) The file may be instantaneously searched electronically for specific kinds of information. (4) Records in the file may be deleted. (5) A listing of specific information may be printed on the screen. (6) A listing of specific information may be printed on hard copy.

The administration, at the touch of a key, may secure instantaneously information and data that may be needed for the completion of reports. In addition, the computer can be configured to generate time cards, staff-evaluation reports, staff record cards, personnel reports, and other documents used by the administration. Large varieties of information become immediately available to the administration. The level of informed decision making is thereby raised. Work loads are reduced. Staff members are free for assignment to other needed tasks. Tedious, repetitive chores are eliminated. Accuracy is increased. Increased productivity becomes possible.

The Need for a Student Profile: Diagnosis of a Problem

Throughout the school year the administration has need for large varieties of information related to the student body. The secretaries responsible for making reports on student admissions and discharges need specific kinds of information. The guidance department (pupil-personnel services) requires other information about each youngster such as race, ethnic background, current reading and mathematics scores on standardized examinations, language limitations, and perhaps even specific emotional or physical handicaps. The attendance office may require many kinds of personal data. To make proper referrals to outside agencies or to provide information necessary for affecting suspensions, the administration may require information related to student behavior. The secretary in charge of processing working papers for students may be in need of other kinds of data. Bits and pieces of information may reside in many different offices. It is clear that a confidential, electronic, computerized student-body profile would provide large varieties of information and make such data accessible instantaneously.

Resolving the Problem

A computerized *student-data program,* offered in appendix E, is configured to accumulate data related to the student body with which the school's administration is most likely to be concerned. Once again, this program should be typed into the computer and permanently saved on diskette in accordance with the specific instructions provided in appendix D. The program may then be loaded into the computer at any time so that it can be used by the administration to access pertinent information that may be necessary for the generation of a variety of reports. The individuals using the program merely follow its instructions by providing the specific information requested. Individuals are then able to record and permanently store all such data electronically and to subsequently access instantaneously all or any segment of that data.

Rather than hand-record pertinent information in one or more repositories, entries are made electronically whenever necessary at the convenience of the school agency involved. Provision is made for the recording and permanent storing of information related to: (1) name of student, (2) address of student, (3) telephone number, (4) name of parent, (5) home contact or emergency telephone number, (6) most current reading-test date, (7) most current reading-test score, (8) most current mathematics-test date, (9) most current mathematics-test score, (10) name of previous school, (11) sex, (12) race, and (13) any five other relevant kinds of data required by individual schools such as dean's record of offenses, need for free lunch, need for free transportation, language disability, emotional or physical handicap, and so on.

The process involves identifying the file with a descriptive name for future reference. The responsible individual then has a variety of options: (1) Information such as that described in the preceding paragraph may be added to the file. (2) Information in the file may be deleted. (3) Information in the file may be modified. (4) The file may be instantaneously searched electronically for specific kinds of information. (5) A listing of specific information may be printed on the screen. (6) A listing of specific information may be printed on hard copy. (7) Data may be ordered sequentially. (8) A particular element may be changed in many records. (9) Attendance functions may be performed (including generation of regular postal cards). (10) Class lists may be printed out.

The administration, at the touch of a key, may secure instantaneously wide varieties of information and data that may be needed for the completion of a variety of reports. The process of informed decision making is thereby enriched. Work loads are reduced. Staff members are free for assignment to other needed tasks. Tedious, repetitive chores are eliminated. Accuracy is increased. Increased productivity becomes possible. Most important, the administration is better able to service the many needs of its student body.

Computerized data-file maintenance is a powerful tool for the administration. It provides accuracy, speed in accessing needed information, opportunities for easier generation of reports, and above all the means to serve the student body and staff more effectively.

8 Supervision: Resolving Selected Problems

Principal Supervisory Functions

It is generally agreed that the principal purpose of supervision is to improve the quality of instruction. Toward that end, the supervisory process involves attention to a wide variety of tasks. Supervisors work with the teaching staff to develop or adapt courses of study to meet the needs, interests, and abilities of the student body. Supervisors have the responsibility for ensuring the availability of textbooks, supplementary resource materials, audio-visual hardware and software, and basic office equipment such as typewriters, spirit-duplicator, mimeograph, and photocopy machines. Supervisors are expected to upgrade teacher proficiency. This involves judgments in assigning teachers to classes, assisting with the improvement of lesson planning, and assessing the quality of teacher performance in the classroom. Supervisors are also expected to upgrade the quality of teacher-made examinations so that student performance may improve on these and on periodically administered standardized examinations.

Selected Current Supervisory Problems

The supervisory process often depends to a very large extent on the availability of extremely large quantities of paper, on the creative efforts by teachers to use that paper for the development of materials needed to further the instructional process, and on the ability to store such materials for subsequent reference and utilization. As educational budgets contract, the availability of paper becomes severely restricted, the creative efforts of teachers impeded, and the instructional process adversely affected. Because paper is basic to the educational process and the unit cost of paper even in large quantities has become exorbitant, efforts by supervisors and teachers to improve the quality of instruction are hindered. In many communities, teachers voluntarily contribute money, so that paper and needed supplementary supplies may continue to be available. The saving of paper becomes an important priority.

Another fundamental element in the supervisory process is time. Even when paper and supplies are available, and human creativity and energy are used to best educational advantage, time is needed to prepare, proofread,

113

modify, duplicate, and collate teacher-made materials. Many tasks are repetitious, tedious, and extremely time consuming. Eventually, even the most highly motivated and professionally dedicated individuals, faced with the reality and frustration of having to battle for needed paper and supplies so that they can do their job, become weary when year after year they are confronted with having to devote so much time to the preparation of these materials. Large segments of time and much space are then also needed to file and store these materials.

These factors promote a climate of apprehension and guilt. There is the overt, ever-present anxiety of not having adequate amounts of paper and the materials that this paper permits to be generated. There is the latent guilt of not having either the time or the inclination to continue the ongoing process of preparing these needed materials. As a result, there is a tendency to overproduce what is actually needed to meet the educational needs of a specific number of students in a given year. Too often, the number of copies of courses of study, calendars of lessons, assignment sheets, readings, documents, bibliography, examinations, and other materials are far in excess of what is actually needed. These materials must then be stored either on shelves or in file cabinets and it becomes an almost impossible task to efficiently handle the volume of paper involved.

Ironically, the needs of the study body seem to change from year to year. Materials prepared in a previous year no longer seem as appropriate or useful. As professional growth continues, teachers change as well. New materials either surface or it is found that they can more effectively serve the needs of changing lesson plans. Examinations once regarded as valid and reliable devices for assessing student achievement are reevaluated and are often found lacking. The length and content of units of work change, requiring the preparation of new examinations to measure student mastery of content. Bibliography, often annotated for student use, becomes outdated quickly as student interests change and as new, more stimulating books appear. The preparation of revisions in bibliography require paper, creative effort, and much time. Such projects often go undone until staff can no longer tolerate the material. Much waste results unintentionally. Paper and materials are discarded. Precious blocks of time might have been spent more productively achieving other worthwhile objectives. Time spent in going through file cabinets to determine specifically which materials to save and which to discard might be allocated to the many other endeavors "that we just never seem to have time to get to."

Utilizing the Microcomputer in Supervision

The availability and utilization of a microcomputer can help to resolve many of the problems described. As with the variety of administrative problems dealt with in chapter 7, the process of supervision can be assisted significantly in areas requiring word processing and electronic data-file management. In this chapter approaches for using a computer to handle a sampling of some of the more pressing problems faced by supervisors will be explored. It is appropriate to reemphasize a point made earlier in chapters 4 and 6 that, by careful planning and scheduling, one microcomputer may be shared by several supervisors, thereby serving to resolve a number of similar problems on a more extensive school-wide basis.

Management by Objectives

Supervisors throughout the nation are expected to implement procedures under an umbrella term, *management by objectives.* This necessitates the annual preparation by each supervisor of a document, often involving at least a dozen legal-size pages. This document requires the expression of specific annual performance objectives, goals, strategies for their achievement, a data base on which to construct such worthwhile objectives, targeted completion dates, and an indication of the personnel responsible. The preparation of this document annually requires multiple copies, is tedious, may necessitate ongoing modification, requires periodic evaluation of the extent to which each objective and goal has been achieved, and necessitates storage of this document in limited space in file cabinets. The microcomputer used as a word processor would permit the preparation and modification of the document, the printing of either one or more hard copies of the document, the permanent storage of the document on diskette, and the opportunity to subsequently access all or a portion of the document whenever needed. Significant paper, time, and storage space would be saved by this electronic process. Supervisors need only prepare the document on the computer, save it permanently on diskette, and print only the number of copies required. Whenever needed in the future, the appropriate diskette is identified, the document loaded into the computer's memory, and the specific number of copies desired printed on paper. Limited, valuable file-cabinet space need not be taken for storage of multiple copies of this massive, annually prepared document.

Courses of Study

In junior- and senior-high schools, supervisors are often expected to prepare comprehensive courses of study for each of the required and elective course offered. These massive documents require an almost standardized format: course title, rationale, objectives (specific knowledge, vocabulary, attitudes, appreciations, and skills), course format, titles of textbooks, appropriate resource materials, appropriate audio-visual materials, activities, speakers, unit topics, calendars of lessons, criteria for student and teacher selection, methods for evaluation, and anticipated course limitations. Such a document for each course offered consumes many pieces of paper. Modification of portions of the course becomes necessary as an ongoing procedure. Duplication of the course of study consumes voluminous amounts of paper. These multiple copies of the course of study must be stored. Experience has shown that many courses, particularly elective courses, undergo change or lose appeal for students as interests change. Much paper, creative energy, and time has been expended. The utilization of the microcomputer as a word processor permits the preparation of the course of study, subsequent modification of the document at any time, permanent storage of the document on diskette, the printing of a specific number of copies needed, and instantaneous future accessing of the document. Paper, materials, time, creative human energy, and limited storage space are saved.

Calendars of Lessons

As was indicated in the preceding paragraph, supervisors, particularly in the junior- and senior-high school, are often expected to oversee the preparation of calendars of lessons for each course of study. Each such calendar is a massive document requiring many pages of text material. Each calendar divides the course of study into units of work. Each such unit of work is then subdivided into topics suggested for coverage by the teacher. Under each topic heading there is usually a listing of important specific concepts, events, terminology, vocabulary, skills, and appreciations that are suggested for teacher coverage. These topics constitute a suggested guide of lessons for teacher preparation. Of course, lessons may be added, deleted, modified, or their sequence rearranged. Following such a calendar helps to structure the term's work, tends to assure some degree of uniformity by all teachers presenting the same course of study, ensures that teachers cover important, preidentified concepts without wandering too far astray of the course of study, and provides students with the preparation necessary for them to score well on standardized examinations. Each year, however, as courses of study are evaluated and revised, it becomes necessary to revise calendars of lessons as well. Often the sequencing of lessons is changed as particular lessons are deleted, others modified, and new ones added. The retyping and duplication of many such massive documents each year is onerous, wasteful of paper, materials, time, and human energy. Because of the tremendous amount of work involved, calendars, in reality, are revised only periodically. The use of the microcomputer as a word processor permits the preparation of the document, modification and revisions to be made during the process of preparation, the permanent storage of the document on a diskette or cassette, and the printing of a reasonable number of copies for distribution to teachers. Periodically, as evaluation and revision of the course of study takes place, the document is retrieved from the diskette or cassette, loaded into the computer's memory, modifications made with ease, the newly revised document saved once again on magnetic media, and limited numbers of copies printed and distributed. What is usually regarded as a monumental task is handled with routine ease by the microcomputer. Paper, materials, time, creative human energy, and storage space are thereby saved.

Student Assignment Sheets

In a similar manner, teachers in the junior- and senior-high school can either prepare individual assignment sheets or cooperate in the preparation of uniform assignment sheets for students. Such documents provide for textbook pages to be read and a series of objective and subjective questions created. By using the microcomputer as a word processor and saving such documents on magnetic media, subsequent revisions are easily and efficiently handled without wasting paper, materials, time, and creative human energy.

Resource Materials

In developing and maintaining files of resource materials, the microcomputer used as a word processor can be an invaluable tool. Specific readings and original documents, selected by teachers for use in the presentation of lessons, need only be typed once, saved permanently on diskette, and the specific number of copies needed, printed on paper. Each term or year, as needed, the document may be retrieved and a specific number of copies printed again. Paper, materials, time, creative energy, and limited storage space are not wasted. Once again, the instructional process is well served.

Bibliographies

In the junior- and senior-high school particularly, either teachers individually or departments collectively periodically attempt the monumental task of preparing bibliographies for required and elective courses. To assist students in the tentative selection of appropriate books for supplementary reading, attempts are made to annotate each bibliography. This results in the preparation and duplication of voluminous amounts of paper. Because the mere task of collating so much paper is overwhelming, class sets of forty copies are generally prepared. The storage problem for each teacher and for the supervisor becomes evident. Each year as new books are published, each listing prepared the previous year should be adjusted to accommodate the additional books. Because it is an almost endless, impossible task, it is neglected. Utilization of the microcomputer as a word processor permits the supervisor to resolve the impasse and bring the situation under manageable parameters. The typing of the bibliography for each course is done once, but on the microcomputer. Each document is then saved permanently on diskette and a specific number of class sets printed. Each year, as selected books are to be deleted and new ones added to the annotated listing, the document is retrieved from the diskette, loaded into the computer, modifications made, the document saved permanently on diskette, and the document printed for a specific number of class sets. The process is repeated, as needed, each school year. Paper, materials, time, creative energy, and limited space in filing cabinets are saved.

Examinations

Each year, supervisors oversee the preparation of teacher-made unit examinations and standardized uniform and final examinations. Generally, individual teachers expend much time and energy in the preparation of periodically administered unit examinations. Because the work involved is extensive, class sets of forty copies of such examinations are duplicated. When administering these examinations, teachers require that students write answers on separately provided answer sheets. Such examinations are then stored in file cabinets and used again the following year. Too often, however, teachers find that individual questions were either unclear or ambiguous. Changes in the subsequent selection of content the following year result in the disqualification of other questions. Eventually, the unit examination has to be prepared again. Similarly, standardized uniform quarterly, midterm, and final examinations undergo the same process. Many questions are retained but many others require modification, replacement, and rearrangement within the entire sequence of questions. The paper, materials, time, creative human energy, and secure storage facilities, present supervisors and teachers with genuinely significant problems. The use of the microcomputer as a word processor, however, helps to resolve these problems. Examinations are typed on the computer, proofread, modified, saved permanently on diskette, and the specific number of copies needed printed on paper (or printed once on a spirit-duplicator stencil and dittoed repeatedly). As needs arise each year, the examination is retrieved from the diskette, loaded into the computer's memory, modifications made, saved again on diskette, and new copies printed out. Examinations are evaluated, revised, and kept current. Paper, materials, time, creative human energy, and secure storage space saved.

Examination-Questions Data Bank

The construction of valid, reliable, unambiguous questions for either teacher-made unit examinations or for standardized uniform examinations is difficult, involved, and time consuming. Examinations should be balanced both in the selection of content and in the kinds of questions included. Individuals who construct examinations must constantly be aware of the purpose of the question. The question may be designed to test for recall, facts, understanding of concepts, inductive reasoning, deductive reasoning, the application of knowledge, interpretation of information, vocabulary mastery, or understanding of cartoons, charts, and graphs. Each teacher brings to bear a particular degree of expertise in writing questions and constructing examinations that are balanced, fair, clear, and in fact test what they are designed to test. Supervisors can assist in this process by culling from teacher-prepared unit examinations and from standardized examinations quality questions and by adding additional supplementary questions. Such questions are arranged by units within courses of study. Each year additional questions may be added to the file. In this way, a quality question data bank can be developed, saved permanently on diskette, and made available to the teaching staff. Computer programs can be easily written that would allow each teacher to visualize a number of questions on the computer screen, to select those desired, and to print out an examination composed of those questions selected (along with an answer key). Different questions can be selected to construct different examinations for each class or the sequencing of the same questions can be rearranged so that the examination appears to be different. The possibilities seem to be endless. Once again, paper, time, creative human energy, and storage space are saved. More reliable examinations result and the process of instruction is upgraded.

Lesson Plans

Many supervisors feel that an important key to upgrading the quality of instruction is the preparation of a viable, challenging, carefully conceived, and effectively implemented lesson plan. Lesson plans should reflect currency both in content and in the status of the teacher's professional growth. The lesson's aim, the motivation on which the lesson's presentation rides, the pivotal questions on which the lesson is structured, the summary questions, and the application should reflect the best in a teacher's arsenal at a given moment in the teacher's development as a skilled classroom craftsman. To assist teachers, the supervisor using a microcomputer, can develop a file of quality lesson plans in each subject area. During preparation periods, teachers can select an appropriate diskette containing model lesson plans for a specific unit of work in a specific course of study, load the file into the computer's memory in seconds, and have such lessons appear on the screen for evaluation and consideration. A copy of any desired lesson plans may then be printed on paper. The teacher may then modify the plan to suit his or her personality, academic background, and particular preferences as well as the needs of the students in each class. Furthermore, the supervisor can use such a file of lesson plans as the basis for teacher training. Small-group seminars can be conducted at which teachers critique printed copies of these model lesson plans. Demonstration lessons, designed to show how such model lesson plans may be implemented can be followed by seminars during which the plan and the implementation of the plan are critiqued.

Materials for Per-Diem Substitute Teachers

Supervisors have the responsibility for ensuring that coverage of classes by per-diem substitute teachers results in meaningful education for students. Often, it is difficult to ascertain in advance the specific lesson that students in a subject class expect to receive from their regular teacher who is absent. Even if such a lesson plan were available, the per-diem substitute in most probability will have been trained in an entirely different academic discipline and will be unable to implement the lesson. The familiar study-hall classroom session that produces little of meaning can be avoided with the use of a microcomputer. Each teacher submits a series of *enrichment lesson plans* dealing with values, current issues, or problems in U.S. society related to the subject area of the absent teacher. These plans are grouped, typed into the computer, and saved on diskette. At the appearance of a per-diem substitute, it can be quickly and easily ascertained as to the specific kind of lesson that the substitute teacher can handle most effectively based on the needs of the class and the strengths of the substitute teacher. The appropriate diskette is selected, enrichment lesson plans loaded into the memory of the computer, and displayed on the screen for evaluation and selection. The teacher selects one or two lesson plans and these are printed on paper. The teacher is thereby armed with one or two viable, quality lesson plans with which to approach students in subject classes so that meaningful instruction may take place. Attempts to store large quantities of such lesson plans in the traditional manner eventually result in a depletion of files and the abandonment of the project. Per-diem substitutes are then left to their own devices and valuable instructional time is wasted. Storing such enrichment lesson plans on diskette forces the substitute teacher to engage in a process of evaluation and selection. Single copies of such plans are printed out. There is a minimum waste of paper. The teacher's day in the classroom becomes meaningful for the teacher and for the students in each class.

Observation Reports

The most frequently used devices for assessing a teacher's effectiveness are the supervisor's classroom visit, the postlesson conference, and the written observation report. The written observation report, describing the presentation's strengths and weaknesses, reflecting the conclusions mutually arrived at during the postlesson conference, and providing recommendations for improvement, allows the teacher to carry away a written account of the lesson. This can be of genuine assistance in the teacher's professional development. A copy of the observation report is stored by the supervisor for future reference as a device to measure the teacher's growth. Eventually, each teacher's file expands to a point where it becomes difficult to manage. To ease the storage problems caused by large numbers of multiple-page reports accumulated over many years, the supervisor can utilize the microcomputer as a word processor. Generally, the observation report is written, proofread, and then modified to eliminate errors. The process is extremely time consuming and the retyped reports often contain new typographical errors. Using the microcomputer as a word processor, the observation report can be written, proofread, and modified without having to retype the entire document. A library of diskettes, one for each teacher, can be set up to accommodate the cumulative savings of each observation report. At subsequent postlesson conferences, the teacher's diskette is inserted into the computer's disk drives, the file loaded into the memory of the computer, and selected previous observation reports can be visualized on the screen. These may then be used as a basis for measuring the teacher's progress. Each teacher's file of observation reports is thereby permanently stored on a single diskette. Paper and space are saved.

Computerized Teacher-Profile Data Bank

Supervisors strive to use both objective and subjective criteria in evaluating the ability and effectiveness of each teacher. Such assessments influence decision making in the assignment and rotation of classes. Supervisors generally make decisions based on expressed teacher preferences and on an assessment of teacher effectiveness in presenting subjects on a particular grade and with meeting the needs of children with differing levels of academic ability. To better ensure that the greatest number of factors affecting decision making has been given proper consideration, a teacher-profile data bank is useful. With minor adjustments, the teacher-profile-data-bank program suggested for use by the administration and described in chapter 7 can be of significant help to supervisors. The entire teacher profile is of course useful. The code provided in this program can be used for identifying either specific college courses completed or experiential activities engaged in by each teacher. Modification of each teacher's profile on a continuing basis requires a minimum of effort. Such information can be particularly helpful when considering teachers for particular class assignments or for roles as faculty advisors in cocurricular activities. The code can also be used to identify the number of days absent and the number of times late of each teacher annually. This information is helpful in determining teacher assignments. The code can also be used to identify specific administration or departmental assignments performed by each teacher. Such information can be helpful when evaluating a teacher's cumulative experience in consideration of either promotion to higher license or recommendation for participation in such programs as institutes or workshops. This information, once stored permanently on diskette, can be retained, modified, deleted, or subsequently readded. As teachers leave a school, return for assignment, or move to new responsibilities, their record is always available and instantly accessible.

Computerized Inventory: Hardware and Software

Supervisors are responsible for maintaining an up-to-date inventory of equipment. Hardware and software are expensive and limited educational budgets preclude easy replacement. Schools make available such hardware as microcomputers, photocopy machines, cassette-copying machines, mimeograph machines, spirit-duplicator machines, calculators, adding machines, microscopes, phonographs, cassette player/recorders, film, filmstrip, and filmloop projectors, overhead and opaque projectors, and a variety of other tools. Schools also make available a large variety of noncomputer software such as maps, globes, charts, graphs, films, filmstrips, filmloops, and phonograph records. Periodic audits require identification of each piece of equipment and its location in the school. With minor adjustments, the inventory program suggested for use by the administration and described in chapter 7, can be utilized to catalog and to maintain a current inventory of the school or department's hardware and software. Such information, accessible at the touch of a key, provides instantaneous data for deciding on the appropriateness of placing orders for additional equipment. The code in the inventory program provides opportunity for identifying manufacturers, vendors, catalog number, and price of equipment.

The supervisor can, at the touch of a key, add, modify, or delete records. A search of the file for specific information can be made by item, serial number, individual responsible, or room location.

*Computerized Inventory: Textbooks Issued
to Teachers*

A school or department makes available to teachers and students thousands of different textbooks, each costing large sums of money. With minor adjustments, the inventory program suggested for use by the administration and described in chapter 7 and in the preceding paragraph in this chapter can be adapted for maintaining an up-to-date textbook inventory. Teachers generally follow a procedure of retaining a receipt for each textbook issued to students. In addition to personal information, the receipt states the title of the textbook, the serial number, and the penalty in case of loss. Teachers then hold students to account at the end of the term or year for either the return of the textbook or payment of penalty. The supervisor, using a microcomputer, can easily maintain an electronic inventory of all textbooks issued to each teacher. The supervisor can enter the name of the teacher, the title of each textbook issued, the number of textbooks issued, and the subject class receiving the textbook. The code included in the program permits identification of the total number of each version of each title issued, the number of textbooks outstanding, and the number of book receipts returned. This procedure permits the supervisor, at the touch of a key, to determine instantaneously, the extent to which each teacher has been exercising responsibility for ensuring either the return of textbooks or the payment of penalty for losses incurred.

Conclusion

It is evident that the process of supervision will be upgraded significantly by the utilization of the microcomputer for word processing and for data-file management. Paper, materials, time, creative human energy, and limited storage space can be saved. The improvement of instruction will result.

9

Classroom Instruction: Drill and Practice

Overview

The microcomputer can be a potent tool for improving the level of student achievement. The success of the instructional process in many subject areas often depends on rote learning. A planned unit of work involves a series of lessons, homework assignments, and activities designed to teach and reinforce selected knowledge and skills. Assignments often involve memorization and rote learning. In many subject areas, the success of teacher instruction often depends on students having mastered basic information. In language arts, mastery of vocabulary definitions, spelling, and correct usage are among many skills fundamental to student progress. The ability to discern the main idea in a paragraph is basic to reading comprehension. In mathematics, the memorization of basic number facts directly affects the teacher's efforts to develop concepts and to strengthen the student's ability to deal with problem solving. In foreign language, the mastery of vocabulary and verb conjugation is the foundation for other learnings. In social studies, mastery and spelling of vocabulary, terms, names, and places are essential for comprehension of content and for the development of concepts. Some degree of memorization is necessary if students are to understand the essence of each of the twenty-six amendments to the Constitution of the United States. The biological and physical sciences require significant memorization of terminology. A course in driver education also requires students to memorize important information. Although the understanding and appreciation of concepts are essentials of meaningful education, rote learning continues to play an important role in the instructional process.

The most dedicated teacher often faces genuine frustration and a sense of helplessness in trying to assist many youngsters. A body of content and skills is taught. During classroom sessions, teachers attempt to identify those students who have difficulty understanding concepts and mastering skills. Homework assignments, quizzes, and examinations are used to identify specific weaknesses. Teachers face a myriad of difficult problems when trying to provide remedial assistance. High student-to-teacher ratio often hinders efforts to make individualized remedial instruction possible. Students with emotional and other problems often contribute to the dissipation of teacher energy. Students who have been identified as having learning disabilities require individualized instruction, which makes additional demands on teacher time. The demands of expanded curricula usually prevent the teacher from reteaching specific lessons to those youngsters who need additional help. Teachers strive to complete courses of study and are pressured to find time for remedial assistance for those children who learn at a slower rate. The pressures on the teacher are endless. The causes are genuine and valid, but the resolution of the problem continues to plague educators.

Years ago the family structure was a positive force in the education of children. Students who were asked to memorize a body of information went home, studied, and then sought the assistance of a parent or an older sibling. The request, "listen to me," was common. Spelling words, reciting multiplication tables, the regurgitation of dates, French verb conjugations, or products associated with a particular country involved a rehearsal process in which a youngster had the active, interested assistance of some individual in the home. Today, it seems that the time needed to sit down with a child in order to ensure reasonable mastery of content is too often limited. Broken homes, the one-parent home, the presence of many siblings, the lack of a quiet place in which to study, and the attractiveness of television or computerized games affect adversely the youngster's efforts to master a body of content. As a result frustration and dejection often sets in. A negative self-image develops. Youngsters who anticipate failure fear going to school. Fear of being wrong is reinforced. The threat to ego blocks attempts to reach the child. The reticence of the insecure child becomes more pronounced. Self-confidence is drained. Such youngsters are terrorized by the prospect of being laughed at by peers and ridiculed or chastized by teachers. A teacher's look, an inflection in tone, or a gesture may damage a child. When precious moments are found to extend assistance, the well-meaning teacher's plea, "Who needs help?" often fails to reach students who have learned to expect failure and who have become turned off.

Computer-aided instruction has proven to be a breakthrough in the instruction process. Teachers who have learned how to harness the microcomputer have come to respect it as an invaluable tool for providing much-needed drill and practice for those children in need of remedial assistance. CAI is not designed for use with every child. Improperly used, CAI can have negative impact quickly. It can be viewed as a means for keeping students unproductively busy. Teachers must be highly selective and judicious in identifying those youngsters who might benefit academically from regular assigned sessions with computer-aided instruction. To cite an observation by Stephen White, director of Special Projects at the Alfred P. Sloan Foundation, the computer "is more or less indifferent to the purposes for which it is being used." Used properly, the computer can provide meaningful assistance in the form of drill and practice for some students. Students who have failed to achieve minimum standards of achievement previously and who have been exposed to a quality CAI program need only be reevaluated by other educational yardsticks to determine if real learning has in fact taken place. In the September 1982 issue of *T.H.E. Journal*, former California governor, Edmund G. Brown, Jr., observes that just as the United States was the world's first to offer free public education, it must now make the commitment to bring computer-literacy education into all of the nation's schools.

Educators can no longer afford to disregard the computer as an innovative and nontraditional device for reaching students in need of special assistance. In an address on 27 September 1982, U.S. Secretary of Education Terrel H. Bell astutely pointed out: "Those of us born before the Pac-Man generation have to candidly admit that we sometimes approach today's informational technology with a little trepidation. Maybe it is just because our children outscore us when we play their video games. Maybe it's because those of us who have spent the majority of our lives with television cannot yet adjust to a flickering screen that requires user interaction. Whatever the cause, it is the persistent notion that computers are still 'magic machines' beyond our ken that we must rid ourselves of—if we are to meet our responsibilities as educators."

What is it about computers (and most particularly school-based computers) that has captured the imagination of our youth? Some observers express the view that by allowing children to experience a sense of being in control of a situation, computers strike a responsive chord. Others feel that children experience satisfaction when interacting with computers. In a fast-moving society in which personal relationships are often superficial, this reason for the computer's attraction should not be dismissed. Others are convinced it is the immediate recognition of achievement and approval expressed with sound and high-resolution graphics that entices our youth. All such explanations seem plausible. The bottom line is that computers appeal to and have a hold on our youth. Computers are tireless and will perform until the child decides enough is enough.

The traditional situation is reversed because it is the child who dismisses the computer. The computer does not criticize. It is regarded as a kind of personal coach in a one-on-one situation that seems to satisfy deep-felt needs. It encourages positive achievement. The sense of failure, negative self-image, and negative attitudes toward learning are not reinforced. Instead, children seem to thrive on the educational challenges provided by the computer. Even youngsters with learning disabilities and physical handicaps have had positive learning experiences as a result of computer-aided instruction. One anecdote will perhaps illustrate the magic spell that computers weave for youngsters. A teacher in charge of a mathematics computer laboratory in a New York City Title I junior-high school was assisted each day by a group of volunteer students, who were identified as among the brightest youngsters in the school. Their scores on standardized reading and mathematics tests were on a par with those of the city's finest students (five and more years above grade level). These were superbright youngsters who were completing advanced courses in mathematics and who were to attend nationally recognized high schools. Each day these students assisted the teacher in setting up the mathematics laboratory so that youngsters in need of remedial assistance could utilize the school's computers for programs in drill and practice. Each day, these Arista students arrived early, requested the key to the laboratory, and proceeded to ready equipment for those students who were expected. The teacher was impressed with their enthusiasm. He was also astounded to find these academically gifted children sitting at computers each day for extensive periods prior to the start of classes, doing the most simple kinds of arithmetic drill and practice problems. Plausible reasons for such a waste of time could not easily be discerned. Gentle probing, however, elicited the surprising explanation that these youngsters simply enjoyed watching the graphics display of a little person on the screen who kept nodding approval each time a correct answer was provided. Perhaps it is this need for approval from some entity, even an inhuman device, that explains the compelling hold the computer has on our youth. In his address on 27 September 1982, Secretary Bell pointed out that "the so-called information revolution, driven by rapid advances in communication and computer technology, is profoundly affecting American education. It is changing the nature of what needs to be learned, who needs to learn it, who will provide it, and how it will be provided and paid for." It is essential that we harness the microcomputer and learn how to use it effectively. By taking advantage of its appeal, we can utilize its vast potential for helping youngsters to learn. The concept of individualizing instruction takes on new meaning.

Minimum Computer-Aided-Instruction
Equipment Requirements

In the elementary school, ideally, each classroom engaging in computer-aided instruction should be equipped full time with a minimum of two or three microcomputers to provide a meaningful program. When budgetary considerations dictate making available only one microcomputer to a classroom, or when several teachers must share a single machine, a meaningful, viable program in CAI cannot be implemented. Under such restrictive conditions, a microcomputer can still be used for drill and practice, but on a much more limited basis, with only those children most in need. Careful scheduling allows each teacher to plan a series of computer lessons and activities every third or fourth day for these youngsters. Lessons may be presented to the entire class and the machine can be used selectively with some children for CAI, for remedial or advanced tutorial instruction, and for learning how to write programs. A contingency schedule should allow another class to use the microcomputer should a teacher whose turn it is to have the machine be absent from school. This alternative is preferable to having the computer sit idle in a corner of a room for the entire day.

In the junior-high school, a meaningful CAI program is implemented most effectively in a laboratory environment. A minimum of four or five microcomputers are required so that every student in each class has access to hands-on experience at least once a week. Small-group activity (four or five students in each group) has proved useful in many CAI-equipped junior-high schools. In the senior-high school, CAI programs have been implemented successfully with a minimum of four or five microcomputers located either in a centralized computer laboratory or in more specialized reading and mathematics laboratories. In addition, the placement of one or more microcomputers in a senior-high school's library or multimedia center permits effective servicing of individual students with computer-assisted instruction, tutorial, or independent-study programs.

However, until teachers in all subject areas become computer literate, the regular use of computer equipment will continue to be limited. Michael W. Kirst, professor of education at Stanford University, in his article, "How To Improve Schools Without Spending More Money", in the September 1982 issue of *Phi Delta Kappan*, expresses the view that whereas computers may be found in many of the nation's schools, they "generally remain isolated from the rest of the curriculum." He urges that computer-literacy education be incorporated into the curriculum in every school. In addition, he feels that classroom teachers should be given the opportunity to participate actively in the selection of programs for their classes and for individual students so that the computer's maximum potential may be realized.

In chapter 2 it was pointed out that there are two approaches to computer-aided instruction. In one, the computer generates a series of questions without storing a record of either the student's correct or incorrect answers. It merely informs the student if the answer to each question is right or wrong. For example, one program instructs the student to type in the answers to a series of multiplication questions. The student is thereby allowed to practice basic number facts. As the student types in a response to each question, the computer informs the student if the answer is correct or incorrect. The second approach to CAI involves drill and practice with a file-management feature. The computer maintains a record of student scores on each question. Teachers can then analyze the results and identify specific skill areas in which individual students showed weakness and need additional drill and practice. The computer can then generate new questions and create supplementary assignments based on those questions that were incorrectly answered. Many schools throughout the nation have experienced considerable success with such programs.

It has been found that some schools use computers exclusively for CAI. This reveals the lack of a comprehensive computer-literacy-education program. It is obvious that attention has not been given to training either the staff or the student body in how to write computer programs. As a result, teachers are not able to write CAI programs for the students in their own classes. Such schools, therefore, must rely entirely upon commercially purchased software.

Commercial Computer-Aided-Instruction Software

Commercial CAI software can be extremely helpful. Generally, such software is packaged attractively. It can also be expensive. Some schools spend more money on software than on hardware. Commercial CAI software is designed to accomplish specific goals based on specific learnings. These are not likely to be identical with the goals or learnings that a teacher may have selected for students to achieve. The use of such programs regularly results in frustration to students and teachers. Such frustration is exacerbated because teachers who are saddled with inappropriate software usually are those who were not invited to participate in the decision-making process at the time of purchase. They also find that they cannot change the curriculum or what the software is configured to practice, particularly when the latter is inappropriate for their classes. If they wish to use the computer for CAI, they have no choice but to use software that was selected by others.

In the 13 September 1982 issue of *Education U.S.A.*, the question is raised as to whether software content will be controlled by educators or programmers. Estella Gahala, director of curriculum and instruction at the Lyons Township High School District in LaGrange, Illinois, expresses the view that school personnel should become involved in the process of the review and evaluation of computer software. Julie McGee, microcomputer project director in Lyons Township claims that "schools which purchase software rely largely on word-of-mouth about good or bad products." Experience has convinced her that periodicals often do not provide objective reviews of commerical software.

Even when reading specialists are brought in to develop, view, evaluate, or recommend commercial computer software, one vital element is still lacking, namely, the classroom teacher. Only the teacher knows precisely whether a particular commercial program will meet the specific needs of the children in a class. If, for example, a commercially purchased program has been designed to practice fifty individual skills, there is little likelihood that these include attention to the specific skills that a teacher may have identified as important for students to master. Usually a classroom teacher's input is not sought until after the software has already been purchased and delivered.

This is not to indicate that commercial software doesn't have its place. When written by groups of educators who truly understand how to get computers to do specifically what they want them to, quality commercial CAI software can improve most school curricula. Some of the best quality programs have been produced by a cottage industry developed by teachers who have purchased microcomputers and who have been writing commerical CAI software in their own homes, while other fine software has been generated by some of the better school-textbook companies.

According to the 22 November 1982 *Newsweek*, a unique agency, the Minnesota Educational Computing Consortium (MECC), established in 1973, brings together curriculum-development experts and programmers to write computer software that will meet the goals of teachers and the needs of students. Some of the nation's major publishers and commercial software companies now regularly couple talented, expert classroom teachers with professional programmers. Together this combination has produced high-quality CAI software.

Those who create software must be able to write challenging programs with questions that are reliable, valid, and unambiguous, These are used to assist students in measuring their comprehension of a topic. They are used to test recall, concepts, skills, and the ability to apply knowledge to the process of inductive or deductive reasoning. The most successful CAI software is that that includes the element of interactive programs such as those youngsters have become accustomed to at home and in game arcades. If a teacher's needs, however, include the management functions described earlier in this chapter, then generally, commercial publishers are the only available source of appropriate software.

The best sources of information about commercial software still seem to be magazines and user groups. As was indicated earlier, however, some individuals such as Julie McGee of Lyons Township do not subscribe to the idea that objective reviews can be found in periodicals. In fairness, however, no reviewer can determine for any school district whether the software reviewed is appropriate for all students in a particular community. User groups, however, can serve as a more reliable source of software-evaluation information. An educational user group is a group of professionally trained teachers who meet periodically to discuss the availability of hardware and software, to evaluate their quality and appropriateness for use in schools, and to explore mutual problems and techniques for the most effective utilization of software. User groups and magazines can be valuable resources for identifying software houses and the variety of products they make available. Some of the more experienced computer-user groups even arrange for members to demonstrate sample software. The sharing of ideas by members of user groups is desirable with the important qualification that others do not select the software that a school is to purchase. It is advisable to attend the meetings of such user groups, to listen carefully to opinions expressed, to examine the software in operation closely, and to seek additional qualifying information. The bottom line requires evaluation by each school, preferably on site, with as much input by teachers as possible before decisions are made to expend limited funds for purchase of software.

The Advantages of On-Site Evaluation

Commercial software cannot be evaluated properly in a vacuum. The only way to determine if a specific piece of software will meet the needs of a school is to test it in the classroom with the students for whom it is intended. This is not always a viable choice for administrators. It is not sufficient for teachers to test the software themselves or to test the software with students. The opinions of other colleagues are valid for evaluating the appropriateness of software for their own classes but not for the students of other teachers. Each teacher should be encouraged to participate actively in the process of software selection, evaluation, and the purchase decision.

One example will suffice. A New York City high school received a grant of $20,000 for the purpose of developing a computer program to enhance the school's career-education curriculum. Software and hardware were ordered. The software purchased included business-oriented software as well as mathematics- and English-content software. When the software arrived, it became apparent to the supervisors of the English and mathematics departments that the software content was inconsistent with the instructional goals of both departments. Because of the pressures and the time limitations involved in writing and preparing the original proposal, neither department had been consulted. The decision to purchase the software was made without such consultation. As a result, the software has continued to sit, unused, in cartons in a storage closet. The $20,000 investment was wasted.

Many commercial software vendors will permit approval examination. It is essential that schools try before they buy. Still other software houses have sales representatives who will gladly visit a school and demonstrate their firm's software on the school premises in front of teachers and supervisors or in the classroom with the students for whom the software is intended. In still other cases, software may be borrowed from other school districts or schools within the district and tested before commitment to purchase is made. It is important not to buy blindly. Again, try before you buy.

It is advisable, if at all possible, that school representatives attend computer shows, conferences, and publisher demonstrations. Usually, these are organized around coffee hours, teas, or wine-and-cheese sessions. The atmosphere is pleasant and professional and the software can be viewed by teachers and supervisors. This environment is fine for excluding clearly unsuitable software and aiding the staff in targeting in on some of the more likely software candidates. Then the software under consideration may be viewed in the classrooms where it is to be used. There is a much better chance for educated, objective evaluation to occur. If none of the aforementioned is possible, then supervisors and administrators have no recourse but to rely on the judgment of user groups, word-of-mouth recommendations, and magazine-review evaluations.

Most commercially written software, with or without file-management features, is designed to run in a modular fashion with each module consuming approximately thirty minutes of classroom time. Commercial CAI software without the management feature ranges in price from twenty dollars to approximately two-hundred dollars. Commercial CAI software that includes a management feature ranges in price from approximately one-hundred-and-fifty dollars to one-thousand dollars. The primary reasons for such a wide range in price can be attributed to the difficulties involved in creating and producing the software, to the varying complexities of the software's function, and to the differing demands imposed by different microcomputers on which the software is configured to run. For many schools, the expense involved in the purchase of software is considerable.

Caveat emptor continues to apply. The guidelines are be cautious, look and listen, and test the program with those for whom it is intended. Then, only after objective evaluation by teachers and supervisors, should a decision be made.

In-House Development of Computer-Aided-Instruction Software

The other popular way for a school to obtain CAI software is through in-house development by students, teachers, and supervisors who have attained at least a minimal level of programming competence. Unlike commercial software, which is written to accommodate the general needs of a broad-based population, in-house software is created by individuals who write programs to accommodate the specific needs of an individual, class, or school. The words used by in-house software authors are those of individuals who know a specific group of children, understand their dialects, provide for their language limitations, and design a program to help these children accomplish a specific, limited learning goal. In-house software is inexpensive, its cost generally is limited to the programmer's time and the price of a blank cassette or diskette. In times of budgetary contraction, this factor cannot be dismissed lightly. In-house software generally does not have colorful high-resolution graphics or elaborate sound. It is designed to accomplish a specific function in as simple, direct, and concise a manner as possible.

Many professionals assume incorrectly that programs with elaborate color-graphics displays or five-voice stereo sound are more effective than the simpler in-house teacher- or student-made programs. Laboratory classroom environments created by the authors of this book have consistently confirmed that wherever possible, given the choice, the preference is for the simpler, teacher-made programs designed to meet the specific needs of that teacher's students. Chapter 11 is devoted to computer literacy and offers an understanding as to how this fundamental concept relates directly to the writing of meaningful computer programs.

Sample Computer-Aided-Instruction Software

To illustrate our preference for in-house software, seven teacher-made programs or extracts from more elaborate programs have been selected for discussion in this chapter. The program listings are offered in appendix F with specific modification instructions so that they may be adapted by teachers for use with the four most popular microcomputers.

Program 1: STATES

Should a teacher find that some students require individual practice in recalling the names of state capitals, the program, STATES, will be of assistance. The program is written to allow the student to practice identifying up to ten correctly spelled capital cities. The program is deliberately configured to give each child the option to practice fewer than the ten capitals provided. This approach has proved less of a threat and has been received favorably by youngsters. As self-confidence grows, the child seems willing to undertake naming additional cities. A sample question is: "What is the capital of Colorado?" Each question offers the child three chances. If on the third try the child continues to enter inaccurate information, the correct answer is provided. The program's format can be modified easily to provide for practicing the recall of all fifty state capitals by the addition of more data. By changing the terminology, this simple program can allow for practicing the recall of national capitals, national leaders, continental location of mountain ranges, and so on. This simply written program has proved of value to many teachers (and there are no elaborate graphics or sound routines employed in the programming).

Program 2: ANTON

Should a teacher find that some students require additional practice in learning a selection of antonyms, the program, ANTON, can be of assistance. As in the previous program, each child is given the option to practice fewer than the ten pairs of words provided by the program. A sample question is: "What is the antonym of HELLO?" The child is given three chances to provide the correct answer. In a few instances, should the child enter the correct antonym but misspell it, the computer has been configured to provide the gentle admonition, "You are almost correct. The correct answer is goodbye." The child can then repeat running the program until all ten pairs of words have been mastered. The program's format can be modified easily to provide for additional antonyms by supplementing the pairs of words in the data. In addition, by modifying the terminology used throughout the program, the teacher can adapt the program for the practicing of synonyms or homonyms. Although seemingly simple in configuration, the program can lend real assistance to the teacher.

Program 3: SPELL

Should a teacher find that some students require additional practice in spelling a list of assigned words, the program, SPELL, should prove helpful. The program is configured to give each child the option of practicing fewer than the ten words provided in the format. A sample question is: "Which is the correct spelling, food or fude?" For each word to be practiced, the child is given two possible choices. By requiring that the word be typed out, the program encourages each child to think about the proper spelling before keyboard characters are struck. The child is given three opportunities to spell each word correctly. The reward, "Well done, Betsy!", goes a long way toward bolstering self-confidence. The program can be modified easily either to provide a third choice in each question or to provide additional words for mastery.

Program 4: SUM

Should a teacher find that some students may require additional practice with finding the sum of two numbers, the program, SUM, is useful. As in the previous programs, configuration allows each child the option of practicing fewer than the ten examples provided in the format. A sample question is: "What is the sum of 6 and 9?" The child is given three chances to enter the correct answer. A simple modification of the program would allow for a variety of compliments when the child provides the correct answer. It would take a minimum adjustment to allow the screen to display, "Great!" or "Grand Slam Home Run!" Similarly, the program can be configured to display several different phrases for informing the child that the answer is wrong. Easily displayed on the screen could be, "Good try. Take another crack at it." Furthermore, the program can be readily adapted to provide for practice or subtraction, multiplication, or division.

Program 5: CHANGE

Should a teacher find that some students require additional practice in learning how to make change, the program, CHANGE, can be useful. Each child has the option of selecting fewer than the ten problems provided. A sample question is: "How much change would you receive if you had $10.00 and purchased groceries for $5.55?" The child has three chances to enter the correct answer. The program can be expanded to provide for additional examples. It can also be modified to provide for two- or three-step problems.

Program 6: TEMP

Should a teacher find that some students require additional practice in learning how to read a thermometer, the program, TEMP, should be helpful. This extract demonstrates how the computer's screen can be utilized to display a reasonable facsimile of a thermometer with an easily readable scale. A sample question is: "Which number appears at point A?" The child is asked to select one of three choices displayed on the screen. Because there are only three choices, the child needs only two chances to discern the correct answer. The program, however, is configured to provide a third opportunity for answering correctly so that the child can be rewarded with the compliment, "Well done!" If the child enters the wrong answer, the thermometer is displayed again so that the answer may be reconsidered. The program can easily be expanded by including additional thermometer readings.

Program 7: MAINIDEA

Should a teacher find that some students require additional practice in the reading comprehension skill of finding the main idea of a paragraph, the program, MAINIDEA, can be used to advantage. In this extract, a paragraph is displayed on the screen. The child is given the chance to select one of three sentences that best represents the paragraph's main idea. If an incorrect choice is selected, the paragraph is redisplayed and the child again is afforded an opportunity to make a selection. The teacher can use this sample as a model for creating additional programs using paragraphs appropriate to any child's reading level. The program can also be adapted to allow for the practice of selecting the main idea of a story.

To illustrate the flexibility of an in-house approach, an actual classroom example is in order. One teacher, in order to motivate selected students to practice map skills, deliberately designed a series of programs that catered to her student's interests. She wrote four separate programs related to sports, using each in succession, and deliberately whetting the appetites of particular youngsters. The first program provided twenty questions that challenged the child to identify a variety of terms associated with one of five major sports. The second program, modeled precisely on the first, provided another twenty questions that challenged the child to identify one of five sports with which a variety of athletes were associated. The third program, modeled precisely on the first two, provided another twenty questions that challenged a child to identify the city with which a team was associated. The fourth program, modeled precisely on the others, provided still another twenty questions that challenged a child to identify the state in which a team played. Eventually, after completing the four programs, successfully, the student was challenged to identify those states on an outline map in which each of the teams played. The options open to a computer-literate teacher are nearly endless. Imagination and creativity are the only real limitations.

In an address on 15 September 1982, U.S. Secretary of Education T.H. Bell assessed the computer's potential in education: "In the education profession, we are finding an opportunity, at long last, to use machines to do part of the teaching. This is going to make learning more exciting and stimulating and make teachers more effective than ever before. . . . It's more than just the computer. It's the laser and the video disc and what's happening up there in the satellite area. It's a very profound change that's taking place. . . . It has such implications for education and our teaching methodology." On 16 September 1982, the secretary made the point even more forcefully: "As a nation we have moved full force into the computer age. Today, more and more administrators and teachers are using new technology as a teaching tool. Our students will hereafter have a better introduction to the world of work when they emerge from school systems that have exposed them to the computers and its role in today's world."

10 Computer Tutorial Instruction: An Overview of Problems

Computer tutorial instruction can play a meaningful role in the instructional process. It is specifically designed to teach a body of content not previously taught or presented by a teacher—unlike computer-aided instruction, which is designed to provide students with opportunities for drill, practice, and reinforcement of skills and concepts previously presented by the teacher. The idea that computers are able to provide several types of tutorial instruction, even within acknowledged limitations, raises significant questions: Can a machine actually teach? How effectively can computers perform pedagogical tasks that have been traditionally the domain of trained, skilled human beings? To what extent is it desirable that computer programs be designed for purposes of instruction? Should computer tutorial programs be designed for mass instruction or for more limited segments of the student community? Is it in the best interest of the national community to encourage any kind of personalized educational interaction between human beings and machines? How widespread is the use of computer tutorial instruction? How much more proficient can computer tutorial programs become? Should professional teachers feel threatened by the possibility that computer tutorial instruction may gain increased respectability and acceptance?

Such questions and their implications need to be discussed by our nation's educational leaders. The answers, however, will continue to be elusive because the direction that computer tutorial instruction will take is still largely undefined. Although presently in its infancy, this mode of instruction continues to be developed and refined. It is inconceivable, therefore, that the implications of such questions can be minimized or ignored. Because educational decisions of some consequence may have to be made in the near future, it is important to understand the present parameters and the relative advantages and disadvantages offered by computer-tutorial-instructional programs.

Limitations of Computer Tutorial Instruction

Computer tutorial instruction poses no perceivable threat to the professional teaching community. Machines cannot teach in the traditional sense. Made of plastic, silicon, and metal, computers cannot assume those human characteristics and traits indispensable to real teaching. They cannot offer learning experiences that result from a student's continuous exposure to and interaction with a living individual. No matter how sophisticatedly computer programs try to simulate the human presence, they cannot offer nuances, inflections in tone, a smile, an encouraging look. They cannot generate human warmth. They cannot recognize a smile, a frown, a look of perplexity on a child's face. Machines cannot know of or understand about family problems, illness, the death of a loved one, an imminent divorce. They cannot possess the capacity to sense that a child may not be receptive to the introduction of new material on a given day.

Attempts to introduce, develop, and clinch concepts are often inadequate. Issues cannot be discussed. The process of developing skills in critical reasoning is extremely difficult if not impossible. Computers cannot provide adequately for shadings. Because computers are capable of only limited anticipation of student reactions and responses, their utilization precludes an environment of interaction and socialization and the kind of give-and-take in which individuals can learn from one another. Machines cannot fulfill the need of human beings for social involvement.

The lack of these dimensions significantly limits the effectiveness of computers in the role of teacher. Unless in the foreseeable future, computers can be programmed to understand the vagaries of human behavior, they will never be able to *teach* in the generally accepted definition of the word. They cannot take on the innumerable intangible qualities that human beings possess.

At best, computers can do a fair job of lecturing, can tirelessly provide students with a series of questions to test mastery of a body of content, can evaluate the accuracy and inaccuracy of responses and assign new material based upon those responses, and though limited, if selectively and judiciously used, can be a positive adjunct to the instructional process in specific situations.

Targets of Computer Tutorial Instruction

Computer tutorial instruction is designed to assist those students who, regardless of reasons, have missed units of work that the teacher cannot present again. Such instruction can be of assistance to youngsters who have transferred from another class or school and are responsible for mastering specific units of work. Such instruction can be helpful to students who have experienced difficulty in mastering material presented by the teacher. Computer tutorial instruction can be of immeasurable use to handicapped students who may have to proceed at individualized, slower rates of learning. This mode of instruction may be utilized effectively by students engaged in independent-study courses. It may also be of assistance should the only text-books available either be outdated or lack important areas of content. Although computer tutorial instruction may be lacking in a number of important educational dimensions, its utilization seems preferable to the alternative of having nothing to offer in such situations as those just described.

Criteria for Selection of Computer Tutorial Software

A quality computer tutorial program avoids lecturing or telling. It is self-contained and does not utilize spirit-duplicated or mimeographed materials, flash cards, or audio-visual equipment. Rather than attempting to teach, first-rate programs are configured to provide students with opportunities to learn. Although there are many different types of computer tutorial programs, the two principal categories are general question-and-answer-type programs and simulation programs. Each strives for maximum interaction between computer and student. The general-type programs attempt to capture the essence of the teacher-student relationship in the classroom and emphasize the interchange of information. Those programs utilizing simulation attempt to maximize opportunities for the student to become involved in role-play situations and to thereby assume as active a role as possible in the learning process.

Both may use high-resolution graphics, color, and sound when appropriate. Graphics have been effective in helping to breakdown barriers between computers and students because, for a variety of psychological reasons, they are not perceived as threats to ego; tend to enhance clarification of visual information such as maps, charts, and geometric shapes; and are effective devices for communicating approval and disappointment.

General Computer Tutorial Instruction

A quality general-type computer tutorial program strives to emulate the kinds of presentations usually made by the classroom teacher and generally involves the interchange of information. Information, content, and issues are introduced by the computer. Questions are asked. Student responses are entered, analyzed, and evaluated. Additional questions are then posed and, based on specific responses, the program is configured to send students off in new directions. As students demonstrate academic growth by entering acceptable answers, the machine is programmed to change its patterns of questioning by moving to other content areas and by modifying its scheme of introducing new information to evaluate forthcoming student responses. In this mode students are usually automatically directed to different subroutines (parts of the program) according to their responses.

There are many areas in which students would experience significant difficulties in mastering units of work without ongoing teacher assistance. Expecting youngsters to read and comprehend materials generally covered inadequately in textbooks usually results in student frustration and feelings of inadequacy. This is best illustrated by example: One computer tutorial program in social studies focuses on the study of the Constitution of the United States. Asking even the most able students to read this document on their own and understand the language and concepts it contains is unrealistic. It is unlikely that youngsters will be able to grapple successfully with the Fourteenth Amendment, the elastic clause, checks and balances, or the very sophisticated electoral college. This computer tutorial program initially provides for the display of the Oath of Office and the Preamble to the Constitution. Questions are then posed about specialized vocabulary, concepts, and the main ideas that are emphasized. Students are introduced to the organization of the document, namely articles, sections, clauses, and amendments. The twenty-six amendments, including the Bill of Rights are summarized and explained. Vocabulary and concepts are clarified. Intermittently, a number of short questions are put to the student to test understanding and mastery. Unlike the approaches taken in most textbooks, quality computer tutorial programs avoid making assumptions that students bring with them an adequate apperceptive base and are able to comprehend such sophisticated concepts as constitution, written constitution, power, writs, self-incrimination, double jeopardy, null and void, judicial review, bills of attainder, ex post facto, and the implications of each. Concepts such as division of power, separation of power, delegated power, residual power, concurrent power, implied powers, powers prohibited to the federal government and to the states are explored in depth. At intervals, questions are again put to the student, which are designed to strengthen self-confidence that such material has in fact been understood and mastered. Attention is given to the powers of the president, the powers of each branch of Congress, and the unique powers of the Supreme Court. The program is configured to encourage students to take notes, to exercise the option for reexamining material already presented, to take time out to study the principal vocabulary and concepts emphasized, and then to try a limited number of test questions before proceeding to the next phase of the unit. By providing frequent opportunities for students to ascertain the extent to which vocabulary and concepts have been understood, mastered, and internalized, the computer tutorial program minimizes the threat of not being able to succeed. When students are satisfied that they have indeed mastered the material, they are encouraged to ask their teacher to administer an examination on the unit of work. The successful performance by the student is the true test of the effectiveness of the computer tutorial program.

Similarly, other units of work lend themselves well to computer tutorial instruction. It would be extremely difficult for many students to undertake the study of the flow of U.S. foreign policy from colonial times through the present. Again, textbooks too often provide inadequate attention to vocabulary and basic concepts. Too many assumptions are made. In such a unit on foreign policy, a quality computer tutorial program may provide for vocabulary extension with emphasis on clarifying such terms as policy, domestic policy, foreign policy, national security, and national interest. The significant factors affecting the making of foreign policy can be explored: party platforms, lobbies, interest groups, national values and goals. Changes in foreign policy from one administration to another may be examined. For example, the evolution of U.S. foreign policy from isolationism to total international involvement may be presented effectively by well-written programs that allow for a measure of interaction between computer and student. The tutorial-programmed computer can never replace a good teacher but in situations where the teacher cannot supply the necessary individualization, a well-programmed computer can be a good second best.

Computer tutorial instruction may also be provided for the study of such recent units of work as the United Nations, the cold war, the Korean police action, the Vietnam conflict, and the tensions in the Middle East, Afghanistan, Poland, and Latin America. In other subject areas such as English, computer tutorial instruction can be effective for the presentation of supplementary selections of poetry, for an analysis of selected short stories, or for strengthening student skills in written expression. Each subject area can identify units of work that can be presented effectively via computer tutorial instruction. Supervisors and teachers in each school and in each academic area can best determine which specific units lend themselves to this type of instruction and which are most acutely needed.

Computer tutorial programs can be configured to provide a wide variety of subroutines depending on needs. One subroutine may refer students to a textbook page so that specific content may be read, understood, and learned. Another subroutine may have the computer generate a new collection of questions to probe additional learnings. After determining that students have learned minimal general information, the program then might probe the extent to which additional specific information and concepts have been understood. Still another subroutine could provide for the original question to be reasked either with identical wording or in a new form. Another subroutine, generally used in situations where student responses reflect lack of adequate mastery of a body of content, displays a chart, graph, map, or other visual aid and then either repeats the initial question or asks other related questions. This type of subroutine is designed to assist students who have failed to grasp specific concepts. By displaying such audio-visual aids, the student is permitted to extract information from a chart or graph and then is better able to answer the questions posed by the computer.

Managed and Unmanaged Computer Tutorial Instruction

This general form of computer tutorial instruction is generally packaged in two versions, managed and unmanaged. Unmanaged programs are generally configured as those described in the preceding paragraph. Such programs enable the student to be a primary force in his or her own educational development. Managed tutorial instruction includes a feature for saving student responses and generating new instructional patterns based on student responses. For example, a student may have completed a series of questions the previous day, and as a result of the incorrect responses made, was to have been offered a display of a map. For whatever the reason, the student might have had to terminte the session at that point. The *managed* computer, on resuming the next day's session, would offer the student a review of the previous day's work and then follow it with the map visualization just as though there had been no interruption of the previous day's instruction. Thus the computer is configured to remember the particular point at which each student terminates a session and may thus provide individualized continuous instructional programs over any number of days. The managed-computer program, in addition to saving the student's actual responses, can also be programmed to maintain an accurate count of the answers that were right and wrong.

Other Strengths of Managed Tutorial Instruction

In well-designed managed tutorial programs, management functions preclude the possibility of students gaining information about the successes or failures of classmates. Management functions, however, may permit teachers regularly to extract specifically needed kinds of information from computer files. For example, the teacher may wish to know the number of attempts needed by each student to select the correct answer, the number of correct and/or incorrect answers selected by each student for either each unit of work or during an entire day. The teacher may wish to identify the specific type of supplementary material accessed by each student and the frequency of each such access. For example, the teacher may wish to know the total number of times all students asked to see a graph and also the number of times each student requested the visualization of that graph. The computer has the capacity to keep track of the number of times that visual material is accessed. Well-managed programs are able to generate percentage scores for each student, percentile scores showing relative student strength within a class, and can even pinpoint topics or areas of general weakness or strength for the entire class.

Unmanaged and managed programs are available commercially for a large variety of topics in most subject areas in black and white or in color, with or without sound. Unmanaged programs generally range in cost from thirty dollars to three-hundred dollars. Managed programs generally range in cost from one-hundred dollars to one-thousand dollars. It is strongly recommended that computer tutorial programs be purchased commercially from reliable companies, preferably after previewing and trying them out on the students for whom they are intended. It is possible for teachers and supervisors to write computer tutorial programs to provide for the needs of their students. There is much better chance of success if skilled programmers lend assistance to any such project. A great deal of skill is needed for writing meaningful tutorial programs that can be used to advantage by students. If such skill is not readily available, it is preferable that educators purchase needed programs rather than expend valuable time and energy in attempting to create programs that will probably not work effectively, if at all. The primary publishing firms are your best source for this kind of educational software.

Simulation-Type Computer Tutorial Instruction

The second major type of computer tutorial instruction is that of *simulation*. In the social, biological, and physical sciences, simulation is among the most popular approaches to computer tutorial instruction. Simulation involves the student in role-play situations. The 15 September 1982 edition of *Education Daily* cites a report to Congress in which it is pointed out that in one good-quality software program, "students can learn about lake ecology by playing the part of a rainbow trout." In one very popular social-science computer-tutorial simulation program, students are asked to play the role of a government leader. The form of government may be a republic, a monarchy, or a dictatorship. Students are provided with a series of national statistical parameters: overall population and ethnic make-up, size of the military force, the amount of grain generated per acre annually, warehouse capacity, and so on. Students are then asked to allocate newly produced resources for the coming year. They must make a variety of decisions involving such factors as the amount of money to be spent on grain with which to feed the people, the number of soldiers to be hired, and the penalties to be imposed by the nation's criminal-justice system in dealing with those individuals who violate the law. The computer is configured to calculate the projected results based on each student's decisions and to advise the student of the newly developed status in light of those decisions. Clearly, if the student elected to sponsor too small a military force and allocated too little money for food, the population is likely to revolt, overthrow the government, and oust the nation's leaders. If, on the other hand, the student makes intelligent, rational, choices, the nation should grow and prosper and government leaders should enjoy the support of the people. This type of computer simulation allows students to role play, to make important decisions, and to learn the projected outcome of such decisions. In some of the more sophisticated simulation programs, the student may pose a number of questions about some of the more relevant facts, such as the current size of the military force, the amount of money left at a particular point in development, the amount of grain that has been eaten by vermin. Programs may be configured either to allow students to type in original questions or to make selections in multiple-choice offerings. Generally, such questions are limited in even the most sophisticated simulation programs.

Questions related to in-depth concepts are generally not permitted. In cases where the program has not anticipated or provided for possible student questions, standardized answers are provided, such as, "I am unable to access the information you request." Such simulation software can develop student appreciation for concepts like supply and demand or the interrelationship between a poorly fed population and revolution. Shadings, however, are absent because the computer is only a machine and has been preprogrammed to handle a limited number of situations.

Another favorite social-science computer-tutorial simulation allows students to assume the role of General Robert E. Lee during the Civil War. Again, the computer advises the general of the parameters of each battle his armies are about to fight. The student-general is requested to allocate resources and make judgments before each battle. Decisions have to be made about whether or not to attempt an assault, whether to strengthen defenses to the north or south of the battlefield, evaluating the extent to which one flank or another is most vulnerable, whether additional ammunition or food is to be purchased for the coming month, and whether it is more expedient to increase the pay of the soldiers or to spend the money for additional supplies. The computer automatically compares the student-general's allocations with those made by generals during the war. It then advises the student of the results of the battles based on decisions made and compares them with the results that actually occurred. It is possible for a student who really understands the needs of the Confederate Army at each battle to win the Civil War for the South by making better allocations of resources than did the real generals during the war. The process has a domino effect. The computer is able to evaluate the impact of each set of allocations at any given battle and apply the results to the impact on each succeeding battle. For these reasons, students are fascinated by the opportunity to role play and give each decision sober consideration.

In industry, computers are used to simulate all the conditions that may be found in the cockpit of an aircraft. These include visual-screen readouts of all gauges, a view from the plane's front window, and even such physical experiences as bumping (accomplished by the attachment of the computer to a chair equipped with a motor), which allows the screen to simulate a lifelike situation. The computer then allows the student to make decisions based upon what the student sees and feels. The student is immediately apprised of the results of decisions made and actions taken. If the student fails to notice a low oil gauge or dangerous pressure, the computer has been programmed to stall the plane or cause it to crash. If the student raised the plane off the ground too quickly on takeoff, the computer has been programmed to show that the aircraft stalled and crashed. As in a real airplane, the student has the same control as would the pilot during a stall and is given the opportunity to pull the plane out of the dive. Such simulation-type programs take into account the number of passengers aboard, the weight of baggage carried, the distribution of baggage in compartments, variable weather conditions, and so on. Airlines have found that simulation is an effective way to train pilots. They also have found that such computer-controlled training results in less wear and tear on expensive equipment. As a result, simulation has become an institutionalized part of the training of many commercial and military pilots.

Another popular computer-simulation program is used in many medical schools. Students are presented with a series of symptoms and options. The computer asks the student to elect laboratory tests and an appropriate treatment mode. It then advises the student of the outcome of each such decision. The student may be admonished: "The patient died as a result of the medication you selected and prescribed. Had you selected another (specific) medicine, the result would have been. . . ." The most sophisticated simulation programs can be configured to permit students to make adjustments so that disasters may be avoided.

There are still other types of tutorial instruction available. These include programs that are virtually nonverbal and allow for student exploration of geometric shapes. In programs like LOGO, students can move lines around, draw curves, construct angles, create geometric shapes, and develop an understanding of the relationships among geometric shapes without having to read any instructions. Other programs such as the language interpreters and compilers called PILOT and BASIC allow students to experiment with analyses of logical patterns by programming (see chapter 11). Such computer programs help students to learn how to logically order data, put things in proper sequence, and analyze logical patterns.

Clearly, computer tutorial instruction has a place in the instructional process. It is important that supervisors and administrators develop an appreciation for the potential that this mode of instruction offers. Certainly, it may not be appropriate for every school or department. In those situations, however, where some students may need assistance with mastering limited bodies of content and teachers and adequate materials are not available, individualized computer tutorial instruction may serve effectively. It is worthwhile for supervisors and administrators to become aware of the variety of commercial tutorial programs that are available so that should a school decide to offer this mode of instruction, even on a limited basis, priorities can be established and the most effective programs selected for purchase.

11 Computer Literacy

It is the contention of many school administrators and supervisors that computer literacy is the single most important facet of computer education. As educators become better informed about the complexities involved and the choices available in trying to establish a viable computer-education program, conviction increases that a comprehensive computer-literacy program is essential if students are to be prepared adequately.

One Definition of Computer Literacy

Computer literacy, as it is generally defined, involves the construction of a curriculum that provides students with the fullest possible spectrum of information about computers. As was discussed in chapters 1 and 2, for students to comprehend fully the power and capabilities of a modern computer, such a comprehensive curriculum must include: (1) the history of the evolution of computers; (2) an understanding of the term *computer*, its component parts, their interrelationships, and the means by which computers communicate with human beings; (3) an objective evaluation of the positive and negative impact of computers on society; and (4) reducing fear of computers and learning how to control them proficiently and accurately with quality programming.

The use of computers *solely* for drill and practice (CAI), common in many schools, does students a disservice. In like manner, using the computer only for instruction in programming, deprives students of opportunities for sequential exploration of the other components in the comprehensive definition of computer literacy outlined above. Increasing numbers of administrators are taking the position that it is essential to provide instruction in each of the four fundamental components of computer literacy if a meaningful, comprehensive program is to be developed and implemented. For example, the 21 April 1982 issue of *The Chronicle of Higher Education* points out that Hamline University intends to make computer literacy a graduation requirement. It is interesting, according to the *Chronicle,* by way of comparison with the definition offered above, that the definition of computer literacy at Hamline University closely parallels the definition we offer. Other colleges, secondary, and elementary schools have also begun to develop computer-literacy curricula based on these four essential components.

A Synopsis of Computer Evolution

If instruction in this aspect of computer literacy is to be provided in our schools, there must be understanding by administrators and supervisors of the major plateaus in the development of computers. The earliest computing devices developed by human beings were manually operated calculators. These were simple machines that aided the user in performing elementary calculations in addition, subtraction, multiplication, and division. The abacus, in use over two-thousand years ago, was such a device. By sliding counters such as beads up and down along a series of rods or in a series of grooves, this instrument permitted the user to perform a wide variety of calculations. As proficiency increased, the eye of the uninitiated observer was challenged to follow the rapid movement of the operator's fingers as the tiny disks were manipulated. This instrument became a forerunner of the high-speed switches that are found in modern computers.

The next major constructive development in calculating devices was the invention of the punchcard during the nineteenth century. As originally used, this device permitted the automatic weaving of intricate patterns by loom operators. It became the forerunner of the modern computer punchcard.

Many other inventions and ideas were generated during this two-thousand-year period and contributed in a variety of ways to the evolution of the modern computer. Among the most significant were the discovery of electricity, the invention of vacuum tubes, and the evolution of integrated circuit chips.

At the same time that these advances were taking place, social needs applied constant pressure for the continuous development of high-speed information-processing equipment. The ultimate goal seemed to be the development of a machine that (1) operated at the highest possible speed, (2) contained within it the largest possible amount of information-storage space, and (3) made the accessing of information as easy as possible. These are the three primary elements that have guided scientists and engineers in their quest to develop the modern high-speed computer. These factors are still the basis for pushing the development of computer technology forward. The search continues for the development of machines with larger memory capacities that are capable of operating at higher speeds and with which communication can be achieved in even simpler forms.

There is every reason to believe that within the next ten years, communication with a computer will be accomplished orally and in a human language such as English. Like the computer, "Hal," in the classic film, *2001: A Space Odyssey,* people will talk to computers and computers will respond with speech that is fully understandable. In the early 1960s, available computer memory in a large, expensive computer had the capacity for holding approximately sixteen thousand alphabetic characters. At present, the modern, comparatively smaller, much less expensive microcomputer has a storage capacity measured in millions of characters. It is highly conceivable that by the early 1990s, small computers capable of storing billions of characters will be readily available and inexpensive. Such machines will allow communication with languages significantly more complex than computer languages currently in use. Instead of BASIC, FORTRAN, and COBOL, communication with computers will be in English, French, German, Russian, Chinese, or even more likely in the form of a yet-to-be-developed international language.

Machines cannot speak these languages today for two principal reasons. The *interpreters* built into evey computer, which are necessary devices for the translation of presently used languages into a numeric language that the computer can understand, would be so large that they would require more memory than is available in the present capacities of the modern microcomputer. For example, the translation of a complex language such as English that utilizes thousands upon thousands of words requires a large memory capacity that is just not available. By comparison, the translation of a much simpler computer language such as BASIC, which utilizes only about fifty words, requires much less memory. Furthermore for audio communication, sound must also be converted into data, once again requiring large amounts of additional memory that the current models of microcomputers do not possess.

Modern technology now makes available integrated circuit chips, which replaced their transistor predecessors, which in turn replaced vacuum tubes, which in turn replaced mechanical switches. Each of these improvements were part of the evolution process and each provided greater speed of operation and significantly more compactness of the computer. As the number of switches that can be contained in a given space increases, the memory-storage capacity of the computer increases.

The modern integrated circuit chip continues to be improved upon each day. Competition among companies on a worldwide basis is producing faster and more compact integrated circuits. A single chip can now hold one million "bits" of computer information. Approximately every three years, the storage capacity of a chip has continued to double. As the chip continues to become more compact, significantly more information will be able to be stored on a single chip. Developments in microtechnology have been so incredibly rapid that only the most vivid imagination can attempt to project what will be possible by the end of this decade.

The Computer and Its Component Parts

The modern computer is a machine that is constructed from a collection of plastic, silicon, and metal parts. The fundamental building block of a computer is the integrated circuit chip. Each chip, manufactured with ultramodern microtechnology tools, is composed of plastic, silicon, and metal parts, has wires emanating from it that are electrical contacts, assumes the shape of small rectangular prisms, and ranges in size from one-fourth to three inches in length, one-fourth to one inch in width, and approximately one-fourth of an inch in height. Each integrated circuit contains many component parts. An analogy may be made to an old-time radio or television set, which was composed of hundreds of tubes, resistors, capacitors, coils, and other electronic devices. These many parts took up a great deal of space and generated much heat. In modern radios and television sets, all of these parts can be housed in a single integrated circuit chip. It is now possible to house 200,000 separate electronic parts in one chip, one-quarter of an inch square. It is interesting that the U.S. Department of Defense has recently contracted for the manufacture of just such a chip for classified military purposes. The electrical contacts emanating from each chip serve to connect them to other chips. Chips are mounted on boards. Such collections of boards, each holding a number of chips, are the components that are usually enclosed in a solidly constructed unit known as a computer. It is interesting to note that most electronic devices (television sets, radios, and such) are also made up of such parts.

All computers essentially have the same fundamental design. At the center of a computer is a device known as the central processing unit (CPU). This central processing unit is the "brains" of the computer. Its singular purpose is to assume the role of a traffic officer and to direct information between the computer and its peripheral devices. In most microcomputers, generally the size of an electric typewriter, the CPU is composed of a microprocessor, usually containing a single chip. The larger minicomputer, usually the size of an office desk, contains a miniprocessor that is composed of a collection of chips mounted on a single board approximately one-foot square by two-feet square. The even-larger mainframe computer, several of which can occupy the floor space of a good-sized room, is composed of a mainframe processor that contains many boards of chips. This central processing unit— regardless of whether it is configured to serve the needs of a microcomputer, minicomputer, or mainframe computer—in order to function needs to be connected by the wires emanating from its chips to sources of information via input devices and must also be able to transmit information to the user via output devices.

Input Devices

An *input device* is a piece of equipment that permits the user to transmit information or instructions to a computer CPU. Input devices are analogous to the "eyes" and "ears" of the computer. The most commonly recognized input device is the *keyboard*. Every letter on the keyboard has an assigned electronic code. Under each key there are seven different switches that open and close. Just as an automobile can pass over a drawbridge when it is closed, so electricity can pass through when switches are closed. When a key is pressed, a series of electronic signals pass on to the computer's CPU. The pattern of electric impulses "tells" the CPU which key was pressed, thereby permitting the CPU to display a familiar English character on the screen. This is akin to pressing a piano key that causes a hammer to strike a specific string producing the desired sound.

There are a number of less familiar input devices. Among these are the card reader, the paper-tape reader, microphones, modem with telephone, optical-scanning devices, light-sensing devices, pressure sensors, movement sensors, voltage sensors, and the unique palm-temperature sensors that read the hand temperature of each individual.

Output Devices

An *output device* is a piece of equipment that allows a computer to communicate with the user by permitting information to be retrieved or accessed from the computer. Output devices are analagous to the mouth of the computer. The most familiar output device is the *cathode-ray tube* (CRT), which is a televisionlike picture tube that allows a visual display of information. Such information may appear in black and white or in color. It may appear in the form of alphabet letters, words, numbers, or graphics patterns. Another familiar output device is a *printer,* which transmits information from the computer to the user on paper.

There are a number of less familiar output devices. Among these are modem with telephone, speakers, punch tape, muscle probes, voice simulators (used by the telephone company in lieu of a human voice), music simulators (used in computer-created musical compositions), and a variety of robotic devices used in industrial plants for welding units, for tightening bolts, for controlling wrenches, and for painting vehicles, to name just a few.

To manipulate and transmit information, the computer generally must possess the capacity to store that information in a kind of memory bank. Temporary memory is provided by integrated circuit chips that store information electronically. When the computer's power supply is turned off, whatever was stored in memory is eradicated. Permanent memory is available by the careful and proper storage of information on either magnetic tapes or disks. These were discussed in detail in chapters 1 and 4. It may be useful to review that material before proceeding.

The Impact of Computers on Society

Computers are continuing to have a powerful impact on society by affecting directly or indirectly virtually every conceivable occupational endeavor and by influencing significantly options in recreational activities of adults and children.

According to recent reports in numerous periodicals computers are being used to write and edit speeches, compose and play music, serve food, create hairdos, assist in coaching ball teams, and even analyze pitching in baseball.

It has long been common public knowledge that professional football organizations utilize computers and the specialized information they store for selection of optimum plays to be run in given situations. Computers are now to be utilized by the Golden Gloves, an amateur boxing organization. The 27 December 1982 issue of the *New York Daily News,* in Tommy Hanrahan's column, "The Golden Gloves," indicates that the Golden Gloves is beginning the computerization of records of all fighters "for safekeeping and easy retrieval." This will allow officials to monitor and track the health records of all fighters so that any previous injuries that may have been sustained earlier in the fighter's career will be instantly available. In this way instantaneous medical judgments can be made so that fighters who are not in proper physical condition can be prevented from entering the ring. Increasingly, organized sports, a major business entity in the United States, is availing itself of benefits that may result from high technology.

Computers are also challenging many of the fundamental precepts and values on which U.S. educational systems have been developed. In an official statement on 16 September 1982, Secretary Bell observed: "Of greater importance to the future of American education, we are rediscovering the need for going beyond the basics in reading and writing skills. If we talk about reading, we emphasize comprehension. If we talk about writing, we emphasize precision and clarity. . . . We hear a new kind of literacy—computer literacy—discussed with justifiable vigor. As a nation, we have moved full-force into the computer age. Today, more and more administrators and teachers are using new technology as a teaching tool. Our students will hereafter have a better introduction to the world of work when they emerge from school systems that have exposed them to the computer and its role in today's world." In an address on 27 September 1982, Secretary Bell admonished: "If American education does not prepare its students to live, work, and compete in this fast paced and interdependent world, all America will be the loser in the battle for international survival."

Leading educators have also noted the impact that computers are expected to have on all aspects of U.S. society. In an August 1981 article in *The New Liberal Arts,* Stephen White of the Alfred P. Sloan Foundation states that computers are having an impact on the way we think just as earlier developments in technology had an impact on the physical labor that human beings had to perform. Computers are assisting mankind in manipulating data rapidly just as the earlier machines assisted us in performing manual labor faster and more efficiently.

Other educators are now coming to grips with the reality of the computer's presence. In the 27 December 1982 *Newsweek*, the article, "The Great Computer Frenzy,"; by Dennis A. Williams and Dianne H. McDonald, makes the point that parents throughout the nation are pressuring school officials to introduce computer education at the earliest possible time. This has created controversy as to how and when to bring children into contact with this new technology.

Why is the computer phenomenon generating such intensive thinking, evaluation, activity, and controversy among so many individuals and organizations in our society? It is evident that the realization has set in that computers are here to stay. Because their value has been and continues to be demonstrated in so many sectors of life in the United States and their still-untapped potential is acknowledged, there seems to be relentless pressure on those in positions of leadership to confront the evidence, the realities, the implications, and the responsibility for ensuring that U.S. youth will be prepared adequately to cope with the future.

It is highly doubtful that the business community could function effectively without computers. Innumerable applications have been found for these machines. Among these are:(1) word processing that has revolutionized the methods used for the preparation of written communications, (2) payroll preparation that has mechanized the generation of paychecks and government reports, (3) inventory control that allows for the instantaneous accessing of many kinds of essential information, (4) accounts receivable, and (5) accounts payable. In the state of California, computerized bartering has a place in the economy.

The rapid rate of acceptance of computers by the public and by industry has generated much controversy as to the impact of high technology on society. The anxieties expressed by leaders in the international community merit consideration. Unless such reservations are evaluated objectively, we will be remiss in our responsibility to present both the positive and possibly negative impact that the use of computers may have on society.

The 18 October 1982 issue of *Newsweek* cites the warning by French President Valery Giscard d'Estaing that computerization could destroy 30 percent of the jobs in French banking and insurance industries. The same article examines the impact of computers in the United States. The article reports that computers have already replaced thousands of bank tellers and suggests that in the near future computers will be replacing many thousands of other clerks. Interviews with bank executives have been quite revealing. The reduction of tellers and staff may be attributed directly to the increasing rapidity with which computers are able to process information. As a result, commercial banks that formerly offered the public five basic types of accounts are now able to offer many new products by increasing the options available to approximately twenty new types of accounts. This reduction of staff has also afforded bank management tremendous annual savings in salaries. The flip side of the coin, however, is interesting as well. Bank executives are experiencing burnout at a more rapid rate and at earlier stages in their careers. Although computers have no difficulty in handling thousands of bits of information instantaneously, executives are experiencing trauma and exhaustion in trying to assimilate and internalize vast amounts of constantly changing information. On a given day, bank executives may be briefed with innumerable details and are expected to be able to explain each set of options to customers the following day. Not only are they expected to communicate the advantages offered by their own bank, but they must also be aware of the advantages and disadvantages of different types of accounts offered by competitive banks and firms specializing in money-market accounts. Executives are finding that their working day has been prolonged significantly, often extending into the late evening hours, for them to stay abreast of the volume of information generated by computers that fill their trays to overflowing. Such problems will have to be addressed and resolved.

Other aspects of industry cannot avoid being affected by computerization. *Newsweek* 18 (October 1982) cites the prediction by David Varway, professor of economics at Wayne State University that many thousands of workers in the automobile industry will never be able to return to their jobs because the work they used to perform has been made obsolete because of robotics and other computer activity. *Newsweek* also quotes Thomas G. Gunn, managing director of Arthur D. Little's Computer-Integrated Manufacturing Group. He suggests that a similar impact will be experienced as a result of the new technology in robots. Workers on assembly lines in many fields will be replaced because management will have to choose between making significant layoffs and going out of business. *Newsweek* also revealed in that article that General Motors Corporation plans to buy 14,000 industrial robots over the next ten years and cites the prediction of technology analyst Harley Shaiken of the Massachusetts Institute of Technology that computer robots may well replace tens of thousands of workers in these automobile plants.

The message is clear. Industry measures progress by profits and profits can be realized only from an ever-increasing productivity. Computers contribute to increasing that productivity. Not only do they perform assigned tasks tirelessly with an even consistency in the production of goods and services, but they also permit the reduction of human labor previously required for the achievement of such industrial objectives. Without training and the development of adequate skills necessary for making possible the transition to high-technology industries, displaced workers, who possess skills no longer in demand, will continue to flounder among the growing numbers of unemployed. Those who do find jobs will have to face the bleak prospects of earning considerably less. One of the costs of progress is bound to be human anguish. *Newsweek* (18 October 1982) cites S. Martin Taylor of the Employment Security Commission as saying that in Michigan unemployment has been a direct cause of alcoholism, family breakdown, and child abuse. It is essential that mechanisms be identified for coping with such trauma so that human beings and long-cherished values are not destroyed in the name of progress.

The professions have also found computers extremely helpful. In medicine, computers have been used to control large pieces of equipment so that cat-scan diagnoses can be made. They have been used to monitor the condition of patients in cardiac cases. In patients where damage to the spinal column has resulted in paralysis, computers are now being used to bypass messages sent from the brain so that mobility of limbs may be achieved. The benefits of such utilization cannot be measured. Physicians can now input to a computer highly specific information about individual patients (for example, age, gender, blood type, blood pressure, ethnicity, occupation, and other relevant factors), specific symptoms, and any other appropriate medical observations. The computer will then suggest a diagnosis of one or more possible diseases, advise of specific physicians who treat each such possible disease and the mode of treatment used by each, and recommend possible treatments. The implications are clear. The computer in assisting the physician with instantaenous diagnoses and suggestions of possible treatment may ultimately benefit the patient. Continued reliance on computers, however, may result in the eventual weakening of the physician's self-confidence; dependence on information resulting from generalization rather than from specificity; a diminished tendency to follow instincts developed in training and practice; and the loss of ability to diagnose under stress, in emergency situations, and in the event of power failure.

Some hospital peer-review committees rely on data provided by computers to evaluate the extent to which individual physicians are treating patients according to acceptable standards. By measuring the statistical performance of one physician compared to that of other colleagues and the deviation from a preestablished norm, the effect may be to pressure physicians to adopt uniform practices that inhibit creativity and the following of instincts—which, in the end, could result in disservice to patients. Caution and alertness are needed to guide the activities of such committees. Impressive statistics do not necessarily make good medicine.

In the legal profession, attorneys now have access to computerized services (one of which is called LEXUS) that permit the typing of a few key words requesting information on legal decisions involved in specific types of cases. LEXUS instantaneously scans every legal decision involving those typed-in words in specified communities within a given time period and provides a synopsis of those decisions. The implications are clear as to the future of law libraries and the methods of research to be employed.

Attorneys now also have access to computerized information about the profiles of prospective jurors. Such data is gleaned from a variety of sources, such as commercially available lists. Again, the implications are sobering. Can such information work for the administration of justice or can the employment of computerized information work to the detriment of the legal system? Will only the affluent be in a position to avail themselves of such services? Clearly the problem has to be addressed.

The field of engineering was the first to harness the computer to any great extent. Used initially to perform intricate numeric calculations, the computer made the public at large aware of its presence, quite dramatically, first as an instrument for predicting the outcome of national elections and then as a tool used in a variety of capacities for sending rockets and then human beings to the moon. Its future solidly assured, computers began to play an increasingly important role in virtually all phases of industry. Problems began to emerge, many of which remain unresolved to this day. One point is clear. The computer, as with all powerful tools and weapons, remains quite indifferent to the roles assigned to it by society. The atom cannot be blamed for the destructive role it has been harnessed to play. It may also not take credit for the potential good that its use may contribute. The same is true for computers. Unless human beings are determined to cope humanely and wisely with those problems generated by the continuing roles assigned to computers, such problems can only become more exacerbated and the eventual impact to be experienced by society is open to the widest speculation.

Government at the local, state, and federal levels is using computers in a wide variety of roles. In his remarks on 15 September 1982, U.S. Secretary of Education Bell observed: "Students of all ages are living in a world of dramatic change and fantastic knowledge explosion. . . . Today we have created a thing called artificial intelligence-capability not only to store, retrieve, and regurgitate information but also to manipulate it, analyze it, and print out various options, possibilities, and potentials." Government agencies, to ensure their ability to function effectively, are expanding their use of computers for precisely the purposes indicated by Secretary Bell.

Local police as well as federal investigative agencies are employing computers to accumulate and store information about motor-vehicle offenses, serious crimes, identification of criminals and their modus operandi, fingerprints, and outstanding warrants. The dispatch of police, fire, and sanitation vehicles, the control of banks of traffic lights, and communications systems depend increasingly on the use of computers. According to Secretary Bell, an electronic mail service may be introduced in the not-too-distant future. The agency responsible for overseeing the Social Security System now uses computers to determine the amount of each check due individuals depending on changes in status, to print the actual checks mailed to recipients, and to transfer electronically the amount of checks to individual banking accounts. The Internal Revenue Service stores all information obtained from tax forms in computers, which determine those individuals to be audited.

Access to and the use of information can be a two-edged sword. Individuals can be helped or hurt, even inadvertently, as a result of government agencies having control of so much information. In an open, democratic society where the right to privacy of each individual has been carefully cherished and guarded, there is fear that this right may be eroded as government agencies continue to accumulate information about citizens. No matter how seemingly proper the ultimate purpose, individuals in positions of bureaucratic authority have the power to misuse that information and to invade the privacy of U.S. citizens. Unless this problem is confronted and safeguards are established to protect the rights guaranteed to citizens in the Constitution, the use of computers for improper purposes may become a practice that can destroy the fabric of our democratic society.

Controlling the Computer

The last of the four principal elements in a comprehensive computer-literacy program is computer control. There are two kinds of people who are involved with computers—those who control them and those who are controlled by them. Those who control computers by communicating sets of precise technical instructions (programs) are known as *programmers*. Those who operate computers without necessarily understanding anything related to those sets of instructions responsible for the functioning of computers are referred to as *users*. Most individuals who interact with computers are users. They respond to questions put to them on a computer screen by typing responses on a keyboard. They are then asked to respond to a series of additional questions put to them one at a time. Each response generates either new questions or directions. At the conclusion of such interactive processes, specific tasks are accomplished. Youngsters playing electronic games; bank tellers making electronic entries; accountants inputing data into computers when grappling with the completion of tax forms; doctors typing symptoms of an illness into a computer with the expectation of assistance in arriving at accurate diagnoses; attorneys scanning a computer printout of informtion about the interests, likes, and dislikes of prospective jurors; supermarket checkout clerks passing cans and packaged goods over electronically lighted glass panels are all examples of computer users. None of these individuals need understand how a computer operates in order to accomplish assigned tasks.

A simple simulation of a "conversation" between a physician and a computer may illustrate the kind of interaction that takes place between a user and a set of specific intructions that have been input into a computer by a programmer:

> *Computer:* Please type your patient's name.
> *Physician:* John J. Jones
> *Computer:* Type the patient's age.
> *Physician:* 39
> *Computer:* Type the patient's gender.
> *Physician:* Male
> *Computer:* Type the patient's race.
> *Physician:* Caucasian
> *Computer:* Type the patient's ethnic affiliation.
> *Physician:* Polish-American
> *Computer:* Type the patient's occupation.
> *Physician:* Librarian
> *Computer:* What is the patient's oral temperature expressed in Fahrenheit?
> *Physician:* 99.3
> *Computer:* Describe the patient's skin-moisture level.
> *Physician:* Wet
> *Computer:* Type the patient's blood pressure.
> *Physician:* 140/80
> *Computer:* Is there any visible rash?
> *Physician:* Yes
> *Computer:* Type in the location of the rash.
> *Physician:* Lower abdomen . . .
>
> *Computer:* Your patient seems to be suffering from . . . . Three treatments have been used successfully with patients having this disease. Based upon your patient's age, gender, other physical characteristics, and information that you have supplied, the treatment most likely to succeed is . . .

Notice that the physician has responded in English to questions and directions that appeared on the computer's screen. At no time was the doctor called upon to understand how the program was configured, how computers work, or to help make adjustments in the technical set of instructions that were previously communicated to the computer. The physician's role was solely that of a user interested in achieving a particular objective, which in this instance was the diagnosis and treatment of an illness in which the physical symptom of a rash had appeared.

A programmer is a person who devises sets of technical instructions in a language the computer "understands" or "comprehends" and configures the computer so that it will perform a specific task or series of tasks for a user. The individual who configured the computer in the previous simulated interaction to ask questions and to analyze responses made by the user is a programmer. Programmers who are engaged in the process of creating complicated programs generally work closely with experts in the particular field of endeavor that the program is designed to serve. In the previous illustration, a programmer would have been assisted by a team of medical specialists if the computer was to have the capacity to truly diagnose a disease from given symptoms and then recommend an appropriate treatment pattern. Such a computer program, and the data it manipulates, would be regularly updated so that it would be able to accommodate the ever-changing field of medical diagnosis and treatment.

Computer Literacy in Schools

Many educators feel that computer-literacy training should begin in the earliest possible school grades. In Community School District 22 in Brooklyn, New York, a district with more than twenty-three thousand children in grades from prekindergarten through grade nine, children are exposed to all four components of computer literacy. The magnitude and intensity of such exposure varies from grade to grade and is adjusted to accommodate the academic, social, and emotional needs of the children in each class.

In the earliest grades, children are encouraged to talk with parents about computers that may be utilized in places of employment. Youngsters are also encouraged to inquire about how such computers are used. Teachers provide opportunities for children to share such information. Children are also taught how to type their names on a keyboard. Much excitement is engendered when simple programs have been configured to cause the computer to print each child's name on the screen a number of times.

A precise curriculum is established for the inclusion of all four components of computer literacy at each grade level. By the time the children reach the upper grades, classroom discussion provides for a consideration and evaluation of the many different social problems generated by society's increasing use of computers. Students are afforded opportunities to do research and write term papers about individuals who have contributed to the development of computers and the applications for which they may have been used. Sequential instruction is provided so that students learn how to write computer programs that may be used by the teacher with other youngsters who may require remedial assistance. The programs alluded to in chapter 9 are extremely useful, having been configured by teachers and students.

The key to a successful computer-literacy program in the schools is teacher training. This can best be provided by a central full-time coordinator who has demonstrated expertise in training teachers. Such a coordinator can set up teacher workshops during the school year and during summer vacations. More extensive inservice courses can be developed under the coordinator's supervision. Bulletins and notices can be issued periodically. Among the coordinator's most important role is that of resource for the purchase of equipment, the development and sharing of in-house software, and the writing of curriculum and syllabi appropriate to the needs of individual schools in the district.

To attempt to suggest a particular brand of machine or type of software without knowing the specific problems and limitations of a given school district is nonproductive and misleading. Some guidelines, however, are possible. For example, many school districts have found that in the lower elementary-school grades, one computer shared by every five teachers provides maximum utilization. In the middle school, ten machines concentrated in a single centralized laboratory environment will probably afford optimum utilization. In the senior-high school where concentration primarily has been on instructing students how to write programs in a computer-laboratory environment, more effective articulation is needed if the fuller definition of computer literacy is to be realized. It should also be noted that it is highly impractical for the authors to attempt instruction in writing programs because so many different models of computers are available. Experience has shown that the development of a quality, comprehensive computer-literacy program at each educational level may be achieved more smoothly if a central coordinator of computer education is selected. Fewer costly mistakes are likely to occur. Quality computer facilities and programs are likely to be developed that can best serve the needs of each school, student body, and community.

Administrators and supervisors can no longer delay coming to grips with the need to develop computer facilities in each school. A comprehensive computer-literacy program is essential for each school Procrastination cannot be afforded because each community expects and will demand that its schools and the educational programs offered by them reflect the reality of the times.

12 National Trends in the Computer Revolution

Overview

Computers have invaded our national consciousness. U.S. Secretary of Education T.H. Bell, in an address on 15 September 1982, pinpointed the directions in which computers are taking U.S. society: "Computers in the classroom, computers in industry, computers in our workplaces are just going to be commonplace." Leading national magazines and newspapers increasingly advertise the sale of personal computers and computer-related products. Television commercials incessantly bombard the viewer with the message of the blessing to be derived from owning a personal computer, a word processor, and a seemingly infinite variety of ever-new electronic games. A major trend toward an increasing use of computers by Americans is not difficult to discern. Any wonder then that *Time* selected the computer as Man of the Year for 1982. This controversial inanimate entity that has made its impact felt on such a wide spectrum of activity in the United States was singled out for recognition over many other well-known international personalities. It seems highly proper, therefore, to conclude this book with an examination of the major national trends in the use of computers.

In the same way that our society experienced an increase in productivity when it shifted gears from an agricultural to an industrial economy in the latter part of the nineteenth century, we can now anticipate a similar productivity increase as a result of the introduction of high-technology computers. In retrospect, the Industrial Revolution has represented an evolutionary process in which machines have helped human beings to do their work and to standardize the ways in which that work could be accomplished. The Computer Revolution is now enabling human beings to gain further control over those machines. Computers allow for increased speed and a tirelessness in the quest to produce a more uniform and satisfying finished product.

Secretary Bell in an address on 15 September 1982, alludes to the prediction made by Dr. Christopher Evans in his book, *The Micro-Millenium*, that by 1990 everything will be in electronic print and the silicon chip will replace the book. Secretary Bell then ventures the view: "I'm not sure this is coming that soon but I know it's coming. It's a great landmark development in the march of mankind. Whether you think it's progress or not, it's here. You can't hold it back. We're going to have paperless newspapers.

We're going to have bookless schools and libraries. It will soon be inefficient and costly to print on paper and bind it into books for storing and retrieving information.''

In an article, ''Computers And The Schools,'' by former California Governor Edmund G. Brown, Jr., in the September 1982 issue of *T.H.E. Journal*, the governor tells us that in the coming years we will all have a need to process increasing amounts of information and the new technology will permit us to have access to ''global networks of knowledge inconceivable even today to the average American.''

These are indeed highly sobering, thought-provoking comments from informed individuals who are able to discern and monitor trends in computer utilization that Americans may well expect to materialize in the not-too-distant future. Why then has there been resistance to the computer by many in U.S. society?

Resistance to Computers

Throughout history, there has always been apprehension about trading the familiar for the unknown. Though the desire for progress has been regularly used either as motivation or as the ultimate objective, many human beings have been reluctant to accept change. There always has been anxiety about possibilities of disruption, replacement, and displacement. There always has been resistance to having to make adjustments. There always has been concern about the rearrangement of priorities. There always has been mistrust of procedural changes for accomplishing desired tasks. There always has been a reluctance to yielding the uniquely creative skills of the craftsman enjoyed by the relatively few so that a higher standard of living might be enjoyed by the many.

The process of change, of forward motion, however, has never been halted for long. The art of hieroglyphics gave way to the alphabet. Hand lettering yielded to the printing press. The art of typesetting yielded to lithography and then to computerized printing. The art of letter writing was replaced by the art of the instantaneous telephone conversation, which in the near future will become visualized. The art of listening and imagining that was needed for the enjoyment of radio yielded to the multisensory appeal needed for the enjoyment of television. The art of reading and sober reflection about the specific meaning and intent of words yielded to the bombardment of the senses with instantaneous news and canned presentations by the mass media. The art of appreciating finely bound books yielded to the demands of a growing mass market for less expensive and more available and expendable paperback editions. The analogies are endless.

It is inconceivable that human beings will stand ready to abandon the lifestyles that such changes have brought regardless of the discomforts, adjustments, emotional depression, or loss of individual self-image that may have resulted. Many people, however, continue to resist the changes in lifestyle that informed individuals predict use of the computer will bring. Even though they may be well aware that change is inevitable, they continue to have deep-felt reservations about the quality of life that may eventually result. The reasons for their anxieties about the purported blessing computers will bring to society merit consideration.

Reservations and Fears

As was mentioned in chapter 3, the 7 September 1982 issue of the *New York Daily News* reports that many individuals, particularly office workers, are now afflicted with cyberphobia, an as yet unexplained fear of computers. They experience major distress when in the presence of these machines and may suffer from nausea, hysteria, stomachaches, or cold sweat. Such fears are real and although they have not yet been adequately explained, as with other phobias, the distress they cause cannot be disregarded. In large measure this condition can be attributed to the lack of previous experiences in the area of computer management. It is the fear of the unknown that is being expressed.

Other individuals feel that by accepting computers, by becoming accustomed to their presence, and perhaps by becoming increasingly dependent on these inanimate electronic devices, some degree of dehumanization may result. There is fear that there will occur an erosion of the unique attributes of human beings, namely the ability to reason, to feel, and to behave with compassion. There is fear that by accepting the passive role of sitting in front of computers for significant periods of time and interacting with these mechanical entities, human beings will further weaken their ability to relate to other human beings. They cite a loss in the art of conversation, a growing inability of people to communicate with each other, and a reinforcement of passivity brought on by extensive television viewing with exacerbation of the problem projected in the future by protracted interaction with computers. They also point to an alienation of children from relationships with members of the family. They cite an increase in loneliness, a disease now afflicting large segments of U.S. society despite the entertainment value offered by television, radio, stereo equipment, and computer games.

Many individuals are concerned that there may develop a willingness to trade the individual's love of the arts, aesthetics, and indefiniteness for the less desirable world of technology, plastics, and precision. There is genuine concern that human beings will forego long-cherished human traits. Many have reservations about accepting reassurance that the growing appreciation of the power of a silicon chip does not preclude the continued pleasure that comes from caring for and valuing a book or a phonograph record.

The reservations of still other individuals are rooted in fears of a more mundane nature. As was indicated in the last chapter, there is genuine concern that the very fabric of a democratic society may be threatened by the invasion of every individual's right to privacy. There is fear that those with access to the mass of information continually being stored in and generated by computers about each individual may misuse their position and authority to the detriment of civil liberties. For example, government agencies such as the Federal Bureau of Investigation and the Internal Revenue Service maintain files on U.S. citizens that contain not only information related to possible criminal offenses but information related to marriage, divorce, health, bank accounts, credit ratings, membership in organizations, and motor-vehicle records, to name only a few. Much of this information has been acquired legally from census reports, published lists, and other sources. That it is being stored systematically and electronically poses a potential threat to the right of privacy and may be used to infringe on constitutionally guaranteed civil liberties.

Other individuals feel that this electronic information explosion may assist banks and real-estate interests in successfully implementing "redlining" policies. Access to such vast amounts of computer-stored information may assist organizations to draw conclusions about specific regions and communities that may lead to possible inequities, such as the targeting of some areas for mailings and the exclusion of others. Access to computer codes may assist some individuals with the execution of white-collar crimes such as electronically stealing money and stock certificates. Access to information stored in computers can facilitate the illegal modification of a wide variety of records that can result in misrepresentation of credentials in many fields. Access to information stored in computers can facilitate tampering with credit records; violating the sanctity of legally protected information such as sealed bids; and selling for profit information contained in census reports, motor-vehicle registration forms, and voter registration forms.

Other individuals are gravely concerned about the psyche and self-image of the U.S. worker. The demands of the information revolution may require that workers who once took deep pride in the skills industry utilized may have to learn the new and possibly much less satisfying skills necessary for employment in high-technology industries. *Newsweek* (18 October 1982) quotes Columbia University professor, Martin K. Starr, who expresses concern that workers who once took pride in their skills will be required to make major adjustments in their attitudes toward their jobs. They will essentially become machine babysitters. Although the work they perform will be important it will not be very interesting or very demanding. They will be controlling machines that require little skill to manage. There is growing concern that many individuals may be denied even the illusion of making a meaningful contribution to their families and to the national community.

To date, opportunities for retraining have been limited and many workers remain idle. As a result, *Newsweek* observes that depression has so overtaken workers who have been unemployed for significant periods that many of them "refuse to leave their beds." The leadership of a society that has long taken pride in its humanitarianism will not be able to ignore the desperation of millions of workers whose skills no longer seem to have a place in the U.S. economy.

There is fear that Thoreau's observation that "men have become the tools of their tools" will become even more of a reality because of computers. Perhaps such deep-felt reservations and anxieties suggest the need to pause and reflect on the choices that will have to be made. Certainly it is important for society to retain its unique attributes even as it strives to learn how to control human excesses and weaknesses. Unless the computer is harnessed so that its role is severely limited, society will experience the blessings as well as the curses of high technology. At the same time that computers help us to have more free time to enjoy enlivening pursuits they can create great trouble for those who are not prepared to meet the future.

Educational Observers View the National Scene

In the September 1982 issue of *T.H.E. Journal*, Governor Brown expresses his conviction that just as Americans once made a commitment to providing a free public education for everyone, there will now have to be a commitment to introduce computers into the educational process.

On 15 September 1982, Secretary Bell commented: "As far as education is concerned, the next few years are going to be the most exciting years in the history of mankind." Many problems may result. On 27 September 1982, Secretary Bell continued his observations: "This country took upon itself the challenge of offering a free education to any citizen who desired it. To add to that challenge, we also offered the opportunity for higher education to anyone who sought it. . . . But simply offering an education is not enough. If that education is not relevant, if it is not an education of quality, if it does not challenge the learner to expand his intellectual capacities to their fullest, it is simply not good enough. . . . As educators, we owe students the opportunity to gain the knowledge and skills that will make them employable. The future is going to mean literally millions of new jobs in computers and related technological fields."

Secretary Bell went on to quote *Washington Post* columnist Dorothy Gilliam who urged parents of disadvantaged youngsters to recognize that "computer literacy is high priority."[a] She warned that their children "will remain at a disadvantage unless computer literacy becomes part of the public school systems."

---

[a] *Washington Post*, September 1982. Reprinted with permission.

Secretary Bell put the problem squarely before the U.S. people: "The information explosion is bringing a new trend to the job market of our country, a new trend to our entire culture. It will be national suicide if education continues to drag its feet in this area because if we do, the rest of the world will run right over us."

It is clear that those in a position to observe the Computer Revolution and its implications on a national scope are strong in the conviction that our nation can no longer afford to procrastinate in taking steps to making effective computer-literacy education a reality in our nation's schools.

Movement in the Nation's Colleges

Carnegie-Mellon's president, Richard M. Cyert, announced that computer literacy, the ability to use a computer in their studies, was nearly universal among students in the university's colleges of science, engineering, humanities, and social sciences and is increasing in the colleges of fine arts by students and faculty.

At Dartmouth College, with approximately three thousand students on campus, there are about eight hundred computer terminals of which one-hundred-fifty are specifically designated for student use. The college has begun to sell and rent computer terminals to students who will then have the option of selling their computers or terminals back to the college should they no longer be needed. A survey in 1981 showed that 93 percent of students while attending Dartmouth, without being required to do so, had used a computer; 83 percent of the student body had written a computer program; 53 percent of first-year students had used a computer prior to arrival at Dartmouth; and 86 percent of first-year students had used a computer during the year.

Allegheny College, in establishing a major in computer science, adopted a faculty proposal taking the position that a liberal-arts college has a responsibility to offer a quality program in computer science.

At Cornell University, in a freshman English seminar on "Mastering the Essay," students write essays on computers. Instructors have found that the quality of the essays is better because students are more willing to modify their papers when they can be changed electronically without their having to retype the entire paper. Electronic word processing may soon replace the electric typewriter for many students.

Stephen White (in *The New Liberal Arts*, an Alfred P. Sloan Foundation publication) suggests that it is necessary that the introduction of new curriculum be accompanied by the training of faculty. Recognizing that colleges must keep up with the demands of changing times, several institutions now require computer literacy for graduation. At many others, computers are being used regularly by students and faculty in every field of study.

The Rochester Institute of Technology has announced that it will invest $4.2 million in new computer equipment. In addition, this institution has announced a computer-literacy program for faculty and students. Of the four hundred faculty members on staff, three hundred applied for a two-week summer workshop in 1982 to better understand computers. Every student to be graduated with an undergraduate or graduate degree will be required to demonstrate a level of computer skill appropriate to the current state of computing in his or her field. Students will be required to provide evidence of having mastered fundamental computer literacy. The school is also requiring that a substantial majority of full-time faculty members in each program possess a basic level of computer literacy.

At Wells College, a two-week course was offered for faculty who had no previous computer experience. The program was well attended by faculty members including instructors in French and philosophy, who were able to write their own computer programs for use by students in their classes.

The New England Regional Computing Program announced a one-week summer workshop in 1982 at Bowdoin College that required a fee of $4,000, which provided for the purchase of a personal computer, instruction, food, and lodging. The program was so successful that the workshop was repeated at Connecticut's Trinity College. Once again the workshop was a tremendous success.

At the colleges of the City University of New York, courses in computer science are proliferating. The colleges are hard pressed to keep up with student demand. Washington Post columnist Dorothy Gilliam (quoted by Secretary Bell in his 27 September 1982 address) was evidently quite right when she observed that students "will play the rules of the game and master those subjects once they know that the bottom line will be the money to permit them to live in the manner in which they wish to live."

Movement in Primary and Secondary Schools

Throughout the United States, educators are grappling with many problems related to the introduction of comprehensive computer-literacy programs in the nation's elementary and secondary schools. There is tremendous controversy among educators as to how computers should be used in the schools. Some believe that the utilization of computers for drill and practice is wasteful because other less expensive media can be used to accomplish the same objectives. Others however, cannot ignore the demands of parents that the schools find a way to provide meaningful computer-oriented education for their children. Parents are often impatient with excuses and explanations and demand an end to procrastination.

As educators strive to provide meaningful courses in computer literacy, they must find a way to make a place for these new studies in an already-crowded curriculum. Providing for the inclusion of computer studies necessitates the selective exclusion of other courses that may be favored by one or another highly vocal group in the community. They must resolve the many problems related to teacher training for which money may not be available. On the elementary-school level, teachers need to learn about each of the four elements of computer literacy so that they can prepare meaningful lessons in each area. On the junior- and senior-high-school levels, decisions must be made as to whether to offer computer literacy as an elective or required course. The benefits of having computer-literacy courses given by one department must be weighed against spreading the responsibilities among a number of departments. School districts must decide whether to select a central coordinator. Supervisors and administators must undergo training. Books and materials have to be purchased and made available to students even though choices may be highly limited. Although these are not easy problems to resolve, pressure by parents for the introduction of computer-literacy courses continues to increase.

To understand the major trends involving the use of computers in schools, nationally, it is instructive to focus on developments in New York, Minnesota, and California. New York State will now require all individuals seeking state certification as teachers to be computer literate. This will require colleges to provide computer courses as part of their teacher-training programs. As was indicated in the last chapter, New York City local-community school districts have already introduced comprehensive computer-literacy programs. Brooklyn's Community School District #22, for example, has been instrumental in developing a sequential curriculum from kindergarten through grade nine, in establishing teacher, parent, and supervisor workshops during school hours, in after-school sessions, and during summers. The district has seen the need to involve both the parents and the community in its attempt to foster computer literacy. To this end they have sanctioned presentations before meetings of parent teachers associations and public meetings of the school board. These presentations have shared the board's plans and concerns with the entire community. Each presentation was well received and warmly applauded. The district has made the staff aware of college-level computer-science courses, has issued notices and bulletins, has encouraged the presentation of assembly programs related to computer education, and has recommended that students be taken on trips to computer facilities. It has made recommendations for the purchase and distribution of computers, peripheral hardware, and appropriate software. Other areas of activity include the development of a meaningful articulation program with senior-high schools. Central-board-of-education officials have supported the development of a computer-literacy program that will serve the needs of the city's youngsters. The adage seems to apply, "where there is a will there's a way!"

Dennis A. Williams and Tracey Robinson report in their article, "Minnesota Leads The Way," in the 22 November 1982 *Newsweek* that although a lack of funds required Minneapolis to close 30 percent of its high schools it nonetheless is continuing to spend many thousands of dollars to train teachers in the use of microcomputers. In Minnesota, children from preschool age through college are being afforded the opportunity to have a computer-oriented education.

In California, former Governor Edmund G. Brown, Jr., ("Computers and The Schools," *T.H.E. Journal*, September 1982) put a series of innovative proposals before the state legislature. He recommends: (1) the establishment of computer demonstration centers throughout the state with nineteen such centers to be modeled on those already in operation in Santa Clara, San Mateo, and Alameda; (2) that one of the nineteen computer demonstration centers to be established be designated as a coordinating center entitled to receive extra funds to coordinate the evaluation and dissemination of quality computer software; (3) that provision be made for teacher stipends and release-time expenses to assist teachers in the study of computer-aided instruction; (4) that funding be provided for the sponsorship of summer training programs for staff and for teacher inservice training programs during the school year; (5) the creation of a California Council on Technological Education that would assist in the development of in-depth training programs for teachers; and (6) that funds be provided to make innovative software programs more widely known throughout the state.

For many schools, the selection of hardware is generally easier than choosing software. Curriculum must be established before software can be purchased with which to implement that curriculum. As was indicated earlier in this book, the search for appropriate quality software often is frustrating. User groups, reviews in magazines, recommendations of other schools, and first-hand trial and evaluation are recommended approaches. While outside organizations such as Consumers Union and The Educational Products Information Exchange Institute offer to provide schools with an evaluation of available hardware and software we feel that such a service, no matter how well meaning, can never replace a knowledgeable staff making their own evaluations for their own students in their own schools.

The University of Minnesota, the State University of Minnesota, community-college systems, and the Minnesota Department of Education formed an agency, the Minnesota Educational Computing Consortium (MECC) in 1973, and has paired professional curriculum experts with skilled programmers to develop software for the state's schools. It has encouraged the widest cooperation among the state's educational organizations and has provided for a previously unavailable articulation among academic levels. MECC has arranged for equipment purchase discounts and has linked more than four hundred school districts in a computer timesharing network.

Other communities such as Lyons Township District in LaGrange, Illinois, are also developing their own software by teaming teachers and supervisors with expert programmers. Many school districts are determined to keep the federal government a healthy distance from curriculum development, which they insist belongs under the aegis of local communities. Each community must identify and define its own problems and needs so that the children attending individual schools may be most effectively served. In his address on 15 September 1982 Secretary Bell may have discerned a national trend: "In today's elementary school, many youngsters are not only using published courseware, but many of them are doing some of their own computer program development."

The National Science Foundation (NSF) predicts that by the end of the twentieth century the entire structure and organization of the nation's schools may be altered. The increasing numbers of children and adults actively involved with computers at home is likely to result in the breakdown of peer relationships. Schools may have to organize classes by grouping people according to common interests, skills, and perhaps specialized languages rather than grouping them by age. If the NSF proves to be correct, school administrators will have to cope with a whole new range of problems that at present have probably not even been considered.

Progress is also being made to assist some of our nation's handicapped. The Rochester Institute for Technology (RIT) has been engaged in a highly specialized research project to assist the deaf. Ross Stuckless, director of RIT's National Technical Institute for the Deaf, said in an interview with *Higher Education Daily* (17 May 1982) that research has shown that deaf adults (and presumably children as well) can learn to process information visually with the aid of a computer more effectively than by the use of interpreters or other technological devices.

The same article reports that at RIT, approximately fifty deaf students have taken classes using a new computer system and prefer it to interpreters. "The professor speaks, and three seconds later, the lecture appears word for word." The material is then available as a printout that is displayed on computer screens placed at various points in the classroom or can be projected on a large screen in front of the room. The computer is at present only about 92 percent accurate because some technical terms and proper names are not in its vocabulary and because certain homonyms cause confusion. Stuckless is confident that the problems will be resolved. The utilization of the computer makes it possible to educate both deaf and nondeaf students together.

The utilization of computers to assist the deaf and to provide paraplegics with the ability to walk will have an impact on the nation's primary and secondary schools. The harnessing of computers will provide large numbers of human beings with a new lease on life. Although an infinite variety of new problems will result from such developments, it is difficult to conceive that programs designed to assist the afflicted will face significant opposition.

The Role of the Federal Government

The U.S. Congress has been grappling with the question of how much responsibility is to be assumed by the federal government in assisting states and local communities with adequate funding to make possible the introduction of computers into elementary and secondary schools. John Gibbons, director of Congress's Office of Technology Assessment, summarized the problem (*Education Daily*, 15 September 1982) when he pinpointed the problems of initial high cost, the lack of quality software, and the inadequate training of personnel.

In his remarks on 27 September 1982, Secretary Bell outlined the reasons for concern. He indicated that some of the nation's schools were designed for chalkboard lectures and are not equipped to handle the introduction of computers, that decisions about classroom scheduling and organization have not yet been concretized, and that shortages of computer-literate teachers necessitate the development of teacher-training programs. The lack of quality software was singled out as another major problem. Lastly, even though the cost of computer hardware is dropping, many schools, particularly those in disadvantaged areas, continue to face budgetary limitations.

Recognizing that the problem of assisting the nation's schools will not disappear, the Office of Technology Assessment advised two House of Representatives educational panels that "the federal government must stand ready to dispense money, advice, and tax breaks if the nation's schools are to fulfill the promise inherent in the new educational technologies." The Office of Technology Assessment also advised Congress to provide tax incentives for donations of computers to schools, to subsidize the development of software, and to fund directly school technology purchases or fund demonstration projects and teacher training.

Many professional observers have suggested that the private sector will not by itself invest in the development of quality software and therefore it is necessary for the federal government to participate in the introduction of computer literacy in our nation's schools.

The House of Representatives responded with the passage of H.R. 5373 with 323 voting for enactment of the bill and only 62 voting against. This legislation, known as the Apple Bill, named for the Apple Computer Company, its architect and promoter, would have permitted computer manufacturers "to take a tax write-off of approximately twice the manufacturing cost of each machine donated to schools, colleges, museums, or libraries." According to Congressman Daniel Rostenkowski, chairman of the House

Ways and Mean Committee, the measure was designed to encourage computer manufacturing firms to donate computers for use in classrooms around the country so that students could become trained in this new technology. The bill his committee recommended for enactment stipulated that computers must have been manufactured no more than six months prior to their donation so that schools would not receive outdated equipment, that the computers be used for the purpose of educating students, and that the companies avoid concentrating their donations in one geographic area or at one socioeconomic level. The bill actually provided that companies making donations could deduct the cost of the equipment plus half the difference between the cost and the fair-market value of the equipment but that the deduction could not exceed twice the value of the property to the manufacturer.

In his address on 27 September 1982, Secretary Bell expressed the view that "business and private enterprise will be one of the greatest benefactors of a student populace educated in the new technologies." In the same address Secretary Bell expressed the view that private companies "should be encouraged to provide more support and interest in education programs that support the very skills they require of their employees." The Apple Company expressed its intention to donate a computer to every accredited school in the United States.

The House bill, however, never reached the Senate floor for a variety of reasons. There were pressures to consider the enactment of other measures to be sure but it seems that the principal obstacle was the opposition to the bill by a number of powerful education lobbies. There was fear of Congress gaining control over school curricula. At the time it had been found in many school districts that machines on hand were not being used because of inadequate teacher training. The view was expressed that if computer-literacy programs were to be effective each school would require large numbers of machines, the funding for which would prove excessive. Others in opposition pointed to the lack of appropriate quality software. Others indicated concern that the computers to be donated might be incompatible with other peripheral equipment, such as printers and software, that might also be donated.

There is much concern that unless adequate funding is provided by Congress only students in wealthy communities will become computer literate and the education of youngsters in disadvantaged areas will suffer. Although the Apple Bill was not enacted last year, as problems and reservations held by education groups are resolved, new measures will be put before the Congress that may gain the necessary support for enactment. To delay may permit other nations such as Japan to gain the upper hand in computer literacy, a reality from which the United States may never recover. A national commitment is in order to ensure that the creativity of the U.S. people is not destroyed because of a lack of such national will.

Occupational Projections

It is extremely difficult to attempt to identify precisely those occupations for which the youth of the United States should prepare. For many years the automobile industry served as the hub of the U.S. economy employing one in every five workers. Should that industry recover from the continuing slump it has been experiencing, prospects for future employment are highly limited because of increased automation. Experts in government and the private sector identify two general areas that should serve as the hub of future opportunities for employment. The umbrella term, *conservation*, may offer job prospects in health care, solar energy, raw-material utilization, solar energy, occupational and physical therapy, speech pathology, technician-administered medical and dental care, geriatric social work, genetic engineering, and bionic medicine. A second umbrella term, *information*, should be the satellite around which other types of job opportunities develop. The Bureau of Labor Statistics and other forecasting agencies estimate that opportunities will open in the fields of computer technology, industrial-robot production, industrial-laser processing, optical-fiber maintenance, and genetic engineering.

Until the middle 1980s, many traditional categories of employment such as medicine, law, banking, engineering, and teaching should continue to offer limited opportunities. By the end of the decade, however, a whole new spectrum of occupations may appear. The problem will be to match employable skills to available jobs. In his address of September 27 Secretary Bell forecasts: "Our schools are unprepared for one of the decade's major challenges, retraining millions of workers whose jobs will be wiped out by the world's technological revolution. . . . The nation has about a decade to retool the work force for the kinds of jobs that already are emerging." In the same address Secretary Bell predicts that "90 percent of the American work force in 1990 will be adults already working, many of them in jobs that will be made obsolete by high technology."

According to the *New York Daily News* (24 October 1982), there are now 1.25 million computers in use in the United States and by 1990 the number may jump to 100 million. Although computers have been identified as one of the major areas of future employment, the true picture has not yet come into focus. For example, the Bureau of Labor Statistics indicates that occupations such as data-processing machine mechanics have grown by 157.1 percent, that occupations as computer-systems analysts have grown by 112.4 percent, and that the occupation of computer programmer has grown by 77.2 percent. Also projected by 1990 is a shortage of 577,000 computer operators, systems analysts, and maintenance technicians. In his address of 15 September 1982, Secretary Bell quotes Peter Drucker of the *Wall Street Journal* as having projected that "the fastest growing industry today may be the continuing education of highly schooled mid-career adults.'' Secretary Bell went on to predict that the adult learner may become the focus of educational technology in the next few years. He estimates that currently ''three out of every ten people in the United States are involved in education as their full-time endeavor,'' spending over two-hundred-billion dollars a year for education.

Former Governor Brown focuses on the impact that high technology has had in California (*T.H.E. Journal*, September 1982). He reports that the high-technology industries will be responsible for creating 40 percent of all of the new jobs in California during the 1980s. This trend is expected to have national implications. Without computer-literacy education students throughout the nation will be at a disadvantage when seeking employment. Many respected organizations estimate that more than 80 million Americans will be using computers in their workplaces by the year 1990.

It is important that some of the implications of these projections be considered. Unless the federal government modifies its recent position on aid to education, many adults, particularly those who are unemployed, may experience real difficulty in finding the money to support their own educational retraining while trying to finance the educations of their children. It is important also to recognize the need to separate opportunities for employment in the next few years from the realities of the next decade. Presently there is a need for computer programmers, computer-systems analysts, and computer operators. At the rate at which high technology is making current models of computers obsolete, by the 1990s these currently viable occupatons may also be obsolete. If yet-to-be-developed computers will permit users to communicate directly by sound in some yet-to-be-developed language, then there is every probability that the need for programmers that exists presently will disappear.

The last element that merits consideration when attempting to make occupational projections is the threat to our industrial sector posed by Japan. *Washington Post* columnist Stuart Auerbach quotes U.S. Commerce Undersecretary Lionel H. Olmer (*Washington Post*, 25 November 1982) who advises us that we are threatened by ''Japan's targeted industry practice.'' This informal partnership between the Japanese government and the industrial sector has operated successfully by allowing the government to select specific targets for Japanese business to attempt world market domination. Undersecretary Olmer projects that U.S. industry will experience a competitive decline because the financial support of the Japanese government for selected target industries provides a significant advantage. One of Japan's major target industries is in the development and production of microelectronic chips on which the future of computers depends. Although the 64K RAM silicon chip was initially developed in the United States, Japan has managed to gain control of more than half the world's market for this chip, which expects to exceed one-billion dollars in sales in the near future. Such intense, effective competition by the Japanese must be a matter of real concern in the United States when attempting to project future employment opportunities. Unless the federal government comes to terms with the realities and develops an updated viable national plan to permit the U.S. people to compete, attempts to provide accurate projections of future employment opportunities will be replete with unreliable statistical information and misdirection.

The trends described to this point affect U.S. society and the schools that society supports. Although future projections seem clouded at present, no viable alternative exists to provide meaningful educational programs in computer literacy for the youngsters who attend those schools. Although educators have experienced many frustrations over the years, the effective application of computers in the future may help to resolve many of the problems that currently exist. Administrators will find that computers will offer real solutions to the complex process of school record keeping. Many large metropolitan school districts are already maintaining data banks of student and staff information that enable them to better analyze and meet administrative responsibilities. Individual schools are beginning to adopt this pattern of administration and supervision. The classroom teacher's drill-and-practice approach of the past with its inherent nightmare of record keeping is being replaced in some schools by electronic computer-aided instruction. Within the next ten years it is very likely that the use of computers for administrative and instructional purposes will become commonplace in most school systems throughout the United States. The rapid increase in computer utilization by almost every field of employment will by necessity pressure forward-looking school systems throughout the nation to provide meaningful educational programs in computer literacy so that an entry-level work force may be adequately prepared for absorption into projected high-technology industries in the United States. U.S. schools are the key to the development of a trained work force that will allow U.S. industry to compete successfully with the challenges of other nations. If the schools are to succeed there must be a collective will to face the future unafraid. The computer must be harnessed and made to serve U.S. society beneficially and the most important place to begin this activity is in the nation's schools.

Appendix A:
Commercial Software
Vendors

The following is a selective listing of qualified vendors of educational software. The credentials of these firms have been established and assure that the software they offer has been of consistently good quality. Although it is hardly possible to evaluate each piece of software produced by each vendor, a sampling of each firm's software production has been highly satisfactory. Because there has been a continuous, significant proliferation of educational software, it is strongly recommended that whenever possible, before making purchase, there be onsite testing and evaluation of each piece of software under consideration to ensure that the product will meet the expectations of teachers and the needs of students in each school. Programs that are effective in one educational environment are not necessarily appropriate for or effective in others.

3R Software
P.O. Box 3115
Jamaica, New York   11431

Academic Computing Association
P.O. Box 27561
Phoenix, Arizona   85061

Academic Software
C/O Software City
22 East Quackenbush Avenue
Dumont, New Jersey   07628

Acorn Software Products, Inc.
634 N. Caroline Avenue, S.E.
Washington, D.C.   20003

Activity Resources Company, Inc.
P.O. Box 4875
Hayward, California   94540

Addison-Wesley Publishing Company
2725 Sand Hill Road
Menlo Park, California   94025

Stephen Radin and Fayvian Lee, *Computers in the Classroom: A Survival Guide for Teachers* (Chicago: Science Research Associates, Inc., 1983). Printed with permission.

Advanced Computer Products, Inc.
P.O. Box 17329
Irvine, California   92713

Adventure International, Inc.
P.O. Box 729
Casselberry, Florida   32707

Alternate Source
704 Pennsylvania Street
Lansing, Michigan   48906

American Micro Media
P.O. Box 306
Red Hook, New York   12571

Analysts International Corporation
295 Madison Avenue
Suite 930
New York, New York   10017

Aquarius Publishers, Inc.
P.O. Box 128
Indian Rocks Beach, Florida   33535

Aries Information Systems, Inc.
Suite 370
7400 Metro Boulevard
Minneapolis, Minnesota   55435

Avant-Garde Creations
P.O. Box 30160
Eugene, Oregon   97403

Avas Corporation
196 Holt Street
Hackensack, New Jersey   07602

Basics and Beyond, Inc.
P.O. Box 10
Amawalk, New York   10501

Bertamax Inc.
101 Nickerson
Suite 550
Seattle, Washington   98109

Bluebird's Computer Software
2267 23rd Street
Wyandotte, Michigan   48192

Borg-Warner Educational System
600 West University Drive
Arlington, Illinois   60004-1889

Brain Box
601 W. 26th Street
New York, New York   10001

Camelot Publishing Company
P.O. Box 1357
Ormond Beach, Florida   32074

Carolina Biological Supply Company
Burlington, North Carolina   27215

Chang Laboratories
10228 North Stelling Road
Cupertino, California   95014

Charles Clark Company, Inc.
168 Express Drive South
Brentwood, New York   11717

Charles Mann and Associates
55722 Santa Fe Trail
Yucca Valley, California   92284

The Classroom Answer
Houghton Mifflin
One Beacon Street
Boston, Massachusetts   02107

Classroom Consortia Media
28 Bay Street
Staten Island, New York   10301

Cognitive Research Group
Education Development Center, Inc.
55 Chapel Street
Newton, Massachusetts   02160

Coin
1546 Dartford Road
Maumee, Ohio   43537

Comm Data Systems Inc.
P.O. Box 325
Milford, Michigan   48042

Compak, Inc.
10309 Talleyran Drive
Austin, Texas   78750

Compress
A Division of Science Books International, Inc.
P.O. Box 102
Wentworth, New Hampshire   03282

Compu-Tations, Inc.
P.O. Box 502
Troy, Michigan   48099

Computer Cat
3005 West 74th Avenue
Westminister, Colorado   80030

Computer Concepts
509 Chestnut Street
Cedarhurst, New York   11516

Computer Courseware Services
Changing Times Education Service
300 York
St. Paul, Minnesota   55101

Computer Discount of America, Inc.
West Milford Mall
West Milford, New Jersey   07480

Computer Motivated Learning Lab
Random House School Division
201 East 50th Street
New York, New York   10022

Computer Systems International, Inc.
539 Durie Avenue
Closter, New Jersey   07624

Conduit
100 Lindquist Center
P.O. Box 338
University of Iowa
Iowa City, Iowa   52244

Courseware Magazine
4919 W. Millbrook, #222
Fresno, California 93726

Creative Computing
39 East Hanover Avenue
Morris Plains, New Jersey   07950

Creative Publications
Computer Products
3977 East Bayshore Road
P.O. Box 10328
Palo Alto, California   94303

Cross Educational Software
P.O. Box 1536
Ruston, Louisiana   71270

Cuisenaire Company of America, Inc.
12 Church Street
P.O. Box D
New Rochelle, New York   10805

Curriculum Applications
P.O. Box 264
Arlington, Massachusetts   02174

Data Command
P.O. Box 548
Kankakee, Illinois   60901

Developmental Learning Materials
One DLM Park
P.O. Box 4000
Allen, Texas   75002

Dilithium Software
P.O. Box 606
Beaverton, Oregon   97075

Disney Electronics
6153 Fairmount Avenue
San Diego, California   92120

Dolphin Computer-Based Instruction
TSC, A Houghton Mifflin Company
Box 683
Hanover, New Hampshire   03755

Dorsett Educational Systems, Inc.
P.O. Box 1226
Norman, Oklahoma   73070

Dynacomp, Inc.
1427 Monroe Avenue
Rochester, New York   14618

George Earl
1302 South General McMullen
San Antonio, Texas   78237

Earthware Computer Services
P.O. Box 30039
Eugene, Oregon   97403

EDCO
P.O. Box 30846
Orlando, Florida   32862

Edu-Soft
4639-G Spruce Street
Philadelphia, Pennsylvania   19139

Educational Activities, Inc.
P.O. Box 392
Freeport, New York   11520

Educational Audio Visual, Inc.
Pleasantville, New York   10570

Educational Computing Systems, Inc.
106 Fairbanks
Oak Ridge, Tennessee   37830

Educational Connection
1508 Coffee Road
Suite J
Modesto, California   95355

Educational Courseware
3 Nappa Lane
Westport, Connecticut   06880

Educational Development Corporation
P.O. Box 45663
Tulsa, Oklahoma   74145

Educational Dimensions Group
P.O. Box 126
Stamford, Connecticut   06904

Educational Materials and Equipment Company
P.O. Box 17
Pelham, New York   10803

Educational Micro Systems, Inc.
P.O. Box 471
Chester, New Jersey   07930

Educational Services Management Corporation
Software Support Division
P.O. Box 12599
Research Triangle Park, North Carolina   27709

Educational Software, Inc.
Soquel, California   95073

Educational Software Midwest
414 Rosemere Lane
Maquoketa, Iowa   52060

Educational Systems Software
23720 El Toro Road, Suite C
P.O. Box E
El Toro, California   92630

Educational Teaching Aids
159 W. Kinzie Street
Chicago, Illinois   60610

Edu-Soft
4639 Spruce Street
Philadelphia, Pennsylvania   19139

Edutech, Inc.
634 Commonwealth Avenue
Newton Centre, Massachusetts   02159

Eduware Services Inc.
28035 Dorothy Drive
Agoura, California   91301

Electronic Courseware Systems, Inc.
P.O. Box 2374, Station A
Champaign, Illinois   61820

Encyclopedia Britannica Educational Company
425 North Michigan Avenue
Chicago, Illinois   60611

Entelek
P.O. Box 1303
Portsmouth, New Hampshire   03801

Evans Newton, Inc.
7745 E. Redfield Road
Scottsdale, Arizona   85260

Eye Gate Media, Inc.
146-01 Archer Avenue
Jamaica, New York   11435

Fisher Scientific Company
Educational Materials Division
4901 W. Lemoyne Street
Chicago, Illinois   60651

Follett Library Book Company
4506 Northwest Highway
Crystal Lake, Illinois   60014

Foreign Language CAI Software
Gessler Publishing Company
900 Broadway
Suite 10A
New York, New York   10003

Fullmer Associates
1132 Via Jose
San Jose, California   95120

Gamco Industries Inc.
P.O. Box 310 P
Big Spring, Texas   79720-0120

George Madden and Associates
3101 Fourth Avenue
San Diego, California   92103

Gladstone Electronics
901 Fuhrmann Boulevard
Buffalo, New York   14203

Greg Campbell
Borg Warner Educational Systems
600 West University Drive
Arlington Heights, Illinois   60004

H & E Computronics, Inc.
50 N. Pascack Road
Spring Valley, New York   10977

J.L. Hammett Company
P.O. Box 545
Braintree, Massachusetts   02184

Harcourt Brace Jovanovich
School Department
757 Third Avenue
New York, New York   10017

Harper and Row/Conduit
110 East 53rd Street
College Division
Suite 3D/Conduit
New York, New York   10022

Hartley Courseware, Inc.
Department CND
P.O. Box 431
Dimondale, Michigan   48821

Hayden Educational Software
50 Essex Street
Rochelle Park, New Jersey   07662

Holt, Rinehart and Winston
383 Madison Avenue
New York, New York   10017

Houghton Mifflin Microcourse
Language Arts
Houghton Mifflin
One Beacon Street
Boston, Massachusetts   02107

Houghton Mifflin Microcourse
Reading
Houghton Mifflin
One Beacon Street
Boston, Massachusetts   02107

I.S.A., Inc.
P.O. Box 7186
Wilmington, Delaware   19803

Ideatech Company
P.O. Box 62451
Department 88
Sunnyvale, California   94088

Information Unlimited Software, Inc.
281 Arlington Avenue
Berkeley, California   94707

Instant Software
Peterborough, New Hampshire   03458

ICT—Instructional/Communications Technology Inc.
10 Stepar Place
Huntington Station, New York   11746

Instructional Development Systems
1927 Virginia Beach Boulevard
Virginia Beach, Virginia   23452

Interpretive Education, Inc.
157 South Kalamazoo Mall
P.O. Box 3126
Kalamazoo, Michigan   49003-3126

J & S Software
140 Reid Avenue
Port Washington, New York   11050

Jadee Enterprises
1799 Meadowlake
Charleston, Illinois   61920

Jinsam Micro-Systems Inc.
P.O. Box 274E
Kingsbridge Station
Riverdale, New York   10463

John Wiley and Sons, Inc.
Attention Clayton Gordon
605 Third Avenue
New York, New York   10158

Kensington Microware
300 E. 54th Street
New York, New York   10022

K8 Software
P.O. Box 248
Canton, Connecticut   06019

K-12 Micromedia, Inc.
P.O. Box 17
Valley Cottage, New York, 10989

Krell Software
1320 Stony Brook Road
Suite 219
Stony Brook, New York   11790

Lanier Learning Center
1700 Chantilly Drive N.E.
Atlanta, Georgia   30324

The Learning Company
4370 Alpine Road
Portola Valley, California   94025

Learning Systems, Ltd.
P.O. Box 9046
Fort Collins, Colorado   80525

Learning Tools, Inc.
686 Massachusetts Avenue
Cambridge, Massachusetts   02139

Level IV Products, Inc.
32461 Schoolcraft Street
Livonia, Michigan   48150

Magic Lanterns Computers
406 South Park Street
Madison, Wisconsin   53715

Marck
280 Linden Avenue
Branford, Connecticut   06405

Math Software
1233 Blackhorn Place
Deerfield, Illinois   60015

Mathware/Math City
4040 Palos Verdes Drive North
Rolling Hills Estates, California   90274

MCE Educational Programs
Interpretive Education, Inc.
157 South Kalamazoo Mall
Kalamazoo, Michigan   49007

McGraw Hill Technology Marketing Manager
School Division
McGraw Hill Book Company
1221 Avenue of the Americas
New York, New York   10020

Med Systems Software
P.O. Box 2674
Chapel Hill, North Carolina   27514

Media Materials, Inc.
2936 Remington Avenue
Baltimore, Maryland   21211

Meka Publishing Company
9120 Galaxie Drive
Indianapolis, Indiana   46227

Mercer Systems, Inc.
87 Scooter Lane
Hicksville, New York   11801

The Micro Center
P.O. Box 6
Pleasantville, New York   10570

Microcomputer Education Applications Network (Mean)
256 N. Washingotn Street
Falls, Church, Virginia   22046

Microcomputer Workshops
103 Puritan Drive
Port Chester, New York   10573

Microcomputers Corporation
P.O. Box 8
Armonk, New York   10504

Micro-Ed, Inc.
P.O. Box 24156
Minneapolis, Minnesota   55424

Micrograms, Inc.
P.O. Box 2146
Loves Park, Illinois   61130

Micro Lab, Inc.
2310 Skokie Valley Road
Highland Park, Illinois   60035

Micro Learningware
P.O. Box 2134
North Mankato, Minnesota   56001

Microphys Programs
2048 Ford Street
Brooklyn, New York   11229

Micro Power and Light Company
12820 Hillcrest Road, #224
Dallas, Texas   75230

Microsoftware Services
P.O. Box 776
Harrisonburg, Virginia   22801

Midwest Visual Equipment Company
6500 North Hamlin Avenue
Chicago, Illinois   60645

Milliken Publishing Company
1100 Research Boulevard
St. Louis, Missouri   63132

Milton Bradley Educational Division
443 Shaker Road
East Longmeadow, Massachusetts   01028

Minnesota Educational Computing Consortium (MECC)
2520 Broadway Drive
Saint Paul, Minnesota   55113

Monument Computer Service
Village Data Center
P.O. Box 603
Joshua Tree, California   92252

MSSS D, Inc.
3412 Binkley
Dallas, Texas   75205

Muse Software
330 N. Charles Street
Baltimore, Maryland   21201

Opportunities for Learning, Inc.
8950 Lurline Avenue
Department 2
Chatsworth, California   91311

Opportunities for Learning, Inc.
8950 Lurline Avenue
Department A7401
Chatsworth, California   91311

Orange Cherry Media
7 Delano Drive
Bedford Hills, New York   10507

Oryx Press
2214 North Central at Encanto
Phoenix, Arizona   85004

Powersoft
P.O. Box 157
Pitman, New Jersey   08071

Prescription Learning
5240 S. Sixth Street Road
Springfield, Illinois   62707

Prismatron Productions, Inc.
155 Buena Vista Avenue
Mill Valley, California   94941

Program Design, Inc.
11 Idar Court
Greenwich, Connecticut   06830

The Programmers, Inc.
P.O. Box 1207
211 Cruz Alta
Taos, New Mexico   87571

Programs Unlimited
P.O. Box 265
Jerico, New York   11753

Programs Unlimited
131 Mamaroneck Avenue
White Plains, New York   10606

Quality Educational Designs
P.O. Box 12486
Portland, Oregon   97212

Queue, Inc.
5 Chapel Hill Drive
Fairfield, Connecticut   06432

Radio Shack Education Division
Department 82-A-324
1300 One Tandy Center
Fort Worth, Texas   76102

Random House School Division
201 East 50th Street
New York, New York   10022

Random House School Division
400 Hahn Road
Westminster, Maryland   21157

Reader's Digest Services, Inc.
Educational Division
Pleasantville, New York   10570

Reston Publishing Company
11480 Sunset Hills Road
Reston, Virginia   22090

Right on Programs
Divison Computeam, Inc.
P.O. Box 977
Huntington, New York   11743

RMI Media Productions, Inc.
120 West 72nd Street
Kansas City, Missouri   64114

Sandura Training Systems, Inc.
1249 Greentree Lanes
Narberth, Pennsylvania   19072

S.V.E., Inc.
1345 Diversey Parkway
Chicago, Illinois   60614

Scholastic Microcomputer Materials
Scholastic, Inc.
904 Sylvan Avenue
Englewood Cliffs, New Jersey   07632

Science Research Associates, Inc.
155 North Wacker Drive
Chicago, Illinois   60606

Scott Foresman and Company
1900 E. Lake Avenue
Glenview, Illinois   60025

SEI (SLINA Enterprises, Inc.)
P.O. Box 7266-CD
Hampton, Virginia   23666

Sled Software
P.O. Box 16322
Minneapolis, Minnesota   55416

The Software House, Inc.
695 E. Tenth North
Logan, Utah   84321

Spinnaker Software Corporation
215 First Street
Cambridge, Massachusetts   02142

Sterling Swift Publishing Company
1600 Fortview Road
Austin, Texas   78704

Storybooks of the Future
527-41st Avenue
San Francisco, California   94121

Sunburst Communications
Room VF #4
39 Washington Avenue
Pleasantville, New York   10570

Synergistic Software
5221 120th Avenue S.E.
Bellevue, Washington   98006

Tara, Ltd.
P.O. Box 118
Seiden, New York   11784

Teach Yourself by Computer Software (TYC)
40 Stuyvesant Manor
Genesco, New York   14454

Teacher's Pet
1517 Holly Street
Berkeley, California   94703

Teaching Tools: Microcomputer Services
P.O. Box 50065
Palo Alto, California   94303

Teck Associates
P.O. Box 8732
White Bear Lake, Minnesota   55110

Telephone Software Connection, Inc.
P.O. Box 6548
Torrance, California   90504

Terrapin, Inc.
380 Green Street
Cambridge, Massachusetts   02139

Texas Instruments
P.O. Box 10508
Mail Station 5849
Lubbock, Texas   79408

T.H.E.S.I.S.
P.O. Box 147
Garden City, Michigan   48135

The Center for Humanities
Communications Park
P.O. Box 1000
Mount Kisco, New York   10549

The Code Works
P.O. Box 550
Goleta, California   93116

The Micro Center
P.O. Box 6
Pleasantville, New York   10570

T.I.E.S.
1925 West County Road, BZ
Saint Paul, Minnesota   55113
Attention: Distribution

The Software Exchange
6 South Street
Milford, New Hampshire   03055

Triangle Audio Visual Media, Inc.
141 N. Main Street
P.O. Box 2248
Branford, Connecticut   06405

TSE Hardside
6 South Street
Milford, New Hampshire   03055

TYC Software
40 Stuyvesant Manor
Geneseo, New York   14454

Tycom Associates
68 Velma Avenue
Pittsfield, Massachusetts   01201

UNICOM
297 Elmwood Avenue
Providence, Rhode Island   02907

Versa Computing, Inc.
3541 Old Condjo Road
Suite 104
Newbury Park, California   91320

Visual Materials, Inc.
4170 Grove Avenue
Gurnee, Illinois   60031

Wise Owl Workshop
1168 Avenida de Las Palmas
Livermore, California   94550

Xtrasoft
P.O. Box 91063
Louisville, Kentucky   40291

Zweig Associates
1711 McGraw Avenue
Irvine, California   92714

Appendix B:
Computer Magazines

The following is a list of magazines that focus on computers, peripheral equipment, hardware, and software. Each magazine is a good source of informative articles that can contribute significantly to strengthening computer literacy. Each magazine is also a major source for securing a variety of professional evaluations of the latest products, announcements of current and projected computer shows, and the most recent comparative costs of equipment. After an evaluation of trial copies of a sampling of the magazines listed, administrators and supervisors are strongly urged to have their schools subscribe to several of the publications that seem most appropriate. Remaining current is essential to effective decision making.

General Educational Computing Magazines

Classroom Computing News
Intentional Educations, Inc.
341 Mount Auburn St.
Watertown, Massachusetts   02172

Educational Technology
140 Sylvan Avenue
Englewood Cliffs, New Jersey   07632

Electronic Learning
Scholastic, Inc.
902 Sylvan Avenue
Box 2001
Englewood Cliffs, New Jersey   07632

Instructional Innovator
AECT
1126 Sixteenth Street, NW
Washington, D.C.   20036

Interface: The Computer Education Quarterly
915 River Street
Santa Cruz, California   95060

Stephen Radin and Fayvian Lee, *Computers in the Classroom: A Survival Guide for Teachers* (Chicago: Science Research Associates, Inc., 1983). Printed with permission.

Journal of Computer Based Instruction
ADCIS
409 Miller Hall
Western Washington University
Bellingham, West Virginia   98225

School Microcomputer Bulletin
Learning Publications, Inc.
Box 1326
Holmes Beach, Florida   33509

The Computing Teacher
Department of Computer Education and Information Science
University of Oregon
Eugene, Oregon   97403

T.H.E. Magazine
Information Synergy, Inc.
P.O. Box 992
Acton, Massachusetts   01720

General Computer-Information Publications

Byte Magazine
70 Main Street
Peterboro, New Hampshire   03458

Kilobaud Microcomputing
1001001 Incorporated
Peterboro, New Hampshire   03458

Personal Computing
Hayden Publishing Company, Inc.
50 Essex Street
Rochelle Park, New Jersey   07662

**Magazines Designed to Serve the Owners of
Specific Brands of Machines**

80 U.S. Journal
80 Northeast Publishing, Inc.
3838 South Warner Street
Tacoma, Washington   98409-4698
(TRS80)

80 Microcomputing
1001001 Incorporated
80 Pine Street
Peterboro, New Hampshire   03458
(TRS80)

Compute
Small Systems Services, Inc.
P.O. Box 5406
Greensboro, North Carolina   27403
(Pet, Atari)

Creative Computing Magazine
P.O. Box 789M
Morristown, New Jersey   07960
(TRS80, Apple, Pet, Atari, Sol)

Dr. Dobbs Journal
People's Computing Company
P.O. Box E
1263 El Camino Real
Menlo Park, California   94025
(Small computer-systems users)

H & E Computronics
50 North Pascack Road
Spring Valley, New York   10977
(TRS80)

Personal Computer
Software Communications, Inc.
1239 21st Avenue
San Francisco, California   94122
(IBM Personal Computer)

Recreational Computing
People's Computing Company
P.O. Box E
1263 El Camino Real
Menlo Park, California   94025
(Small computer-systems users)

Softside Magazine
Softside Publications, Inc.
6 South Street
Milford, New Hampshire   03055
(Apple, Atari, TRS80)

Softalk
11021 Magnolia Blvd.
North Hollywood, California   91601
(Apple)

General Industry and Business Information

Interface Age
McPheters, Wolfe and Jones
16704 Marquardt Avenue
Cerritos, California   90701

Mini Microsystems
Cahners Publishing Company
Division of Reed Holdings, Inc.
221 Columbus Avenue
Boston, Massachusetts   02116

Appendix C:
Computer-Hardware
Vendors

The computer market is constantly undergoing rapid change. The line of microcomputers offered by manufacturers reflects an overall ongoing improvement in technology. In addition, new firms enter the field with an attractive array of products and high-powered advertising campaigns. Such factors make it difficult to compile a current listing of vendors that may be considered reliable. As a result, only those firms whose products have had a positive impact and whose reputations and longevity reasonably assure their continued future involvement with computer education in the schools have been included in this listing.

Microcomputer Manufacturers

Apple Computer, Inc.
10260 Bandley Drive
Cupertino, California   95014

Commodore, Inc.
487 Devon Park Drive
Wayne, Pennsylvania   19087

Digital Equipment Corporation
129 Parker Street
Maynard, Massachusetts   01754

IBM Corporation
Old Orchard Road
Armonk, New York   10504

Monroe Systems for Business
The American Road
Morris Plains, New Jersey   07950

Radio Shack
1300 One Tandy Center
Forth Worth, Texas   76102

Stephen Radin and Fayvian Lee, *Computers in the Classroom: A Survival Guide for Teachers* (Chicago: Science Research Associates, Inc., 1983). Printed with permission.

Texas Instruments, Inc.
P.O. Box 2909
Austin, Texas   78769

Timex Computer Corporation
Waterbury, Connecticut   06725

Integrated-Circuit-Chip Manufacturers

Intel Corporation
3065 Bowers Avenue
Santa Clara, California   95051

Motorola, Inc.
3501 Ed Bluestein Boulevard
Austin, Texas   78721

Zilog, Inc.
1315 Dell Avenue
Campbell, California   95008

Appendix D:
Program-Utilization
Information

General Information

The following information should be of assistance when utilizing the series of programs that have been discussed in chapters 7 and 9 (and that are provided in appendixes E and F). If the suggestions made are followed precisely, errors that are usually made and much unneeded frustration will be avoided.

The programs that have been recommended for use are written in the computer language, BASIC, and when copied, may be used with the Radio Shack TRS80 or IBM Personal Computer without change. These programs may be modified with ease for use with other computers. Any individual who has had formal training in computer-programming techniques and has attained a level of expertise can make them compatible with other microcomputers such as the Apple and the Commodore Pet. Complex programming statements have been deliberately omitted so that modifications of these programs may be accomplished without difficulty.

The programs provide for the inclusion of a number of REM statements so that as administrators, supervisors, and teachers continue to gain expertise, they may enjoy the option of further modifying each program to accommodate the changing needs of students. Such REM statements are not executed when the programs are run but allow for personal notations to be made about specific lines and objectives.

Typing Instructions

Each program often contains individually numbered lines that are longer than those that actually appear on a screen line. Each such program line must be typed with consecutive numbers. Therefore, the ENTER or RETURN key must not be pressed until each numbered line has been completed. The typing of each line should continue unbroken until it has been completed. When a numbered line has been completed and the programmer is ready to type a new line number, *only then* should the ENTER or RETURN key be pressed.

The screen line for which the included programs have been configured is approximately sixty-four characters in length. Should your computer ac-

Stephen Radin and Fayvian Lee, *Computers in the Classroom: A Survival Guide for Teachers* (Chicago: Science Research Associates, Inc., 1983). Printed with permission.

commodate either a longer or shorter line capacity, you may logically expect that either more or less information will fit on one of your computer's screen lines. This variation will not present a problem. Avoid inserting extra carriage returns anywhere other than at the end of a numbered line so that problems may be avoided.

As was indicated above, the programs included in this book were configured for use on the TRS80 or IBM Personal Computer and were written in MICROSOFT BASIC (c). This assures that the programs will run without modification on any TRS80 microcomputer (that is, Model I, Model II, and Model III). These programs will also run, with modification, on such microcomputers as the Apple II (+ or E), the Sinclair, the Commodore Pet, and many others. Specific instructions as to how to modify these programs are provided later in Appendix D. Follow instructions for such modification of programs carefully and precisely.

User Suggestions

Avoid typing commas when entering any kind of data as a user. Most computers use the comma as a delimiter. Confusion occurs when commas appear in the body of user entries.

The programs that have been included, from time to time, offer the user various selections. For example, one choice given the user is (S)creen or (P)rinter. It is intended that the user select the letter contained within the parentheses that identifies the option preferred. If the user presses the S key, the computer will treat the selection as though the word *screen* had been typed and the information to be accessed will appear only on the screen. On the other hand, the selection of P will cause the computer to have the information to be accessed printed only on paper.

Unless otherwise indicated, all responses made by the user should be consistently uniform. For example, a date may be entered as March 7 1931 or 3/7/31 or 03/07/31. The microcomputer will accept any of these variations. It is important, however, to be uniformly consistent, to select one specific form, and to use it throughout. Should the user type a date as March 7 1931 and then at some later time expect the machine to find 3/7/31 or 03/7/31, the computer will be unable to access the information. The computer is only able to understand codes in the form of electronic symbols. Uniformity and consistency are necessary if user frustration is to be avoided.

Running the Programs

Only a computer for which the program has either been configured or modified may be used to run a program. The computer must also be equipped with the peripheral equipment specified in the program.

Media-Handling Suggestions

Whereas cassettes and diskettes are usually reliable for permanent data storage, they are not infallible. If the data contained on cassettes and diskettes are to be safeguarded from erasure, care must be exercised to avoid placing these storage devices in the proximity of magnets or equipment that contains magnets or electrical impulses. Three specific practices are strongly recommended when storing data:

1. Before typing any data be certain that each computer program does exactly what is intended, that it fulfills your specific needs and objectives, and that you understand completely how the program has been configured to work. Do not commit valuable data to a computer unless you are convinced that it will perform as you would like. No computer program can ever be truly perfect.

2. Maintain a back-up system. For example, in a program such as that used in the treasurer's office (described in chapter 7), maintain a separate set of written transactions that are noted as checks arrive and are processed. For the program on student profiles also described in chapter 7), admit forms for each student should be saved. Such written records ensure the rebuilding of a file should the diskette or cassette either not function or be inadvertently erased.

3. Maintain at least one copy of each diskette or cassette on which data has been stored. Such back-up copies should be stored in locations other than where the original is kept. The procedure for saving data should be in the form of a habit of stopping entry and saving after each fifteen-minute interval. Another recommended programming practice is to back-up the data being accumulated on diskette or cassette at the end of each day.

Program-Modification Instructions

To successfully modify the programs that have been included for use on microcomputers other than those for which the programs have been configured, administrators are strongly advised to secure the assistance of individuals with expertise in programming. The programs were written in the computer language, Microsoft BASIC (c). The TRS80 and the IBM Personal Computer permit the programs included to be run without modification. With modification, these programs can also be run on a large variety of other microcomputers.

Those program lines that contain statements that are machine dependent have been marked with an asterisk. *Machine dependent* refers to the compatibility of a program with a particular microcomputer; the program will run on one microcomputer but not on others unless modifications are made within the program. Should your microcomputer be a brand other than the TRS80 or the IBM Personal Computer, it is important for the individual making the necessary modifications to consult the Language Reference Manual that comes supplied with the machine. This manual will identify the equivalent of each statement marked with an asterisk so that necessary adjustments can be made.

The list of Microsoft BASIC (c) words that follows contains instructions that apply to all the programs included in chapters 7 and 9. The instructions are provided so that you may determine the appropriate equivalents that will operate on your machine.

A hyphen is included at the beginning and end of each defined term so that its precise length and character can be ascertained by the reader.

-ASC(B$)-   This statement causes the machine to return the ASCII value of the first character of the string variable, B$. Should your microcomputer not allow this function, it must be omitted and the programmed section must be rewritten so that ASC is not needed.

-CLEAR-   This statement is required by some microcomputers in that an adequate amount of memory be set aside when using string variables. If your machine does not require a CLEAR statement, then omit the line from the program.

-CLS-   This statement causes the computer's screen to be cleared of all data. On some machines, the BASIC word, HOME, serves this function.

-DEFINT A-Z-   This statement causes all variables automatically to be declared as integers unless otherwise specified by affixing a symbol such as a dollar sign ($), exclamation point (!), or other such keyboard character to the letters in the variable. On machines that do not allow the DEFINT function, omit it from the program.

-DIM A$(3)-   This statement appears in either of two forms, (1) DIM A$(5) and (2) DIM A$(6,7). Some machines will not allow a two-dimensional array. Should your machine be one that does not allow for this function, the program will not RUN because there is no way to provide for an equivalent function. Some machines will run out of memory if the DIM constants are too large. Should your microcomputer not have enough memory to handle the demands of the program, replace the DIM A$(250) with DIM A$(200). This modification will reduce the number files the microcomputer can store and will permit the program to RUN on your machine.

-IF-THEN-ELSE-   This statement causes the machine to perform the first command if the condition is met, or the second command if the condition is not met. For example, in the statement, IF A = 2 THEN PRINT "HELLO" ELSE PRINT "GOODBYE," the machine will PRINT the word, HELLO, if the variable, A, is 2 or it will PRINT the word, GOODBYE, if the variable, A, is 1. This statement can be replaced with two separate statements:

IF A = 2 THEN PRINT "HELLO"

IF A < > 2 THEN PRINT "GOODBYE"

-INPUT A$-   If an input statement appears in a program, some machines, such as the Commodore Pet, will not permit the pressing of the RETURN key without the user having previously entered other data. Should your microcomputer have such a limitation this section of the program will have to be rewritten to include a PRINT statement that advises the user to enter data before pressing the carriage-return key.

-LINE INPUT A$-   This is a programming statement that causes the computer to input information even if delimiters such as the comma, semicolon, or colon are present in the string. These LINE INPUT statements can be replaced by the simpler term, INPUT. If such replacement is effected, then delimiters may not be included in the data.

-LPRINT-   This is a Microsoft BASIC (c) word that instructs the computer to PRINT the information on paper via a printer rather than on the microcomputer's screen. Some microcomputers such as the Apple II require a command statement to print via a specific output port and then the standard word, PRINT, is used.

-ON A GOTO 1000, 2000, 3000-   This statement causes the machine to transfer the program flow, (GOTO), either line number 1000, line number 2000, or line number 3000, depending on the value of the variable, A. If A = 1, the machine will transfer control of the program to line 1000. If A = 2, the program will GOTO line 2000. If A = 3, the next line to be executed will be 3000. On some machines the statement would read: GOTO ON A 1000, 2000, 3000. If this or any other form of the statement is used on your microcompuer, then modify this line. If no such statement is available in the version of BASIC compatible with your microcomputer, replace the one statement with the following three statements.

If A = 1 THEN GOTO 1000

If A = 2 THEN GOTO 2000

If A = 3 THEN GOTO 3000

-PRINT "PRESS THE ENTER KEY WITHOUT DATA TO . . ."- or
-PRINT "TYPE ENTER TO CONTINUE"- These are command statements that are not allowed on some machines. If your microcomputer will not allow a nul-input command (INPUT without data),
change this statement to advise the user to type a single blank space
or some other identifiable message, followed by pressing the car-
riage-return key. (See INPUT A$ above).

-VAL (B$)- This statement causes the machine automatically to calcu-
late the value of the string, B$. Usually, the function appears in the
form, -C = VAL(B$)-. If B$ does not consist of digits (that is, 0, 1,
2, 3, 4, . . . 9), the value of C is zero. If your microcomputer does
not allow this function, then the program must be modified to accommodate the INPUT of a number rather than a string.

The following seven words are used to open, to use, and to close sequential access-disk files. If your microcomputer is not equipped with disk
drives, replace each of these words with the equivalent sequential access-
cassette term found in your computer manual.

-CLOSE- This term instructs the computer to CLOSE all files that are
OPEN. Some computers require that files must be closed one at a
time. On such machines, the words CLOSE#1, CLOSE#2, and so
on, may have to be typed one at a time to accomplish this objective.

-INPUT#1,A$- This term requires a computer to retrieve a single string
from a file that is already OPEN. Because it is a sequential-access
term, it will always retrieve the next string in the file.

-LINE INPUT #1,A$- This is a statement that causes the computer to
input information from a file (see INPUT #1 above) even if a
comma, semicolon, or other delimiter is present in the string. These
statements can be replaced with the simpler command, INPUT#1,A$.
Should this be the case, no INPUT data may include delimiters.

-OPEN"E",1,C$- This statement requires the computer to OPEN a
sequential file that is named by the variable, C$, for the purpose of
ADDING new information to the end of that file. On some machines
a file may not be identified by a variable. If your microcomputer is

such a machine, then C$ must be replaced with a file identification such as GRADES. On some machines this function is accomplished with an OPEN APPEND command. The manual that comes with your machine should be checked to identify the proper term or format for this command.

-OPEN"I",1,C$-   This statement instructs the computer to OPEN a sequential file that is named by the variable, C$, for the purpose of RETRIEVING information from that file. On some machines a file may not be identified by a variable. If your computer is such a machine, then C$ must be replaced with a file specification such as NAMES.

-OPEN"O",1,C$-   This statement requires the computer to OPEN a sequential file that is named by the variable, C$, for the purpose of ADDING new information to that file. On some machines a file may not be identified by a variable. If your computer is such a machine, then C$ must be replaced with a file identification such as NAMES. This command causes information to be added from the beginning of the file and as a consequence it will destroy any file with the name C$ that may already exist on the disk.

-PRINT#1,A$-   This is a term that commands the computer to add the string held in the variable, A$, to the OPEN file (#1).

Appendix E: Program Listings: Administrative and Supervisory

The following programs are described in chapter 7. They are examples of in-house administrative software. For further information about their recommended use please refer to chapter 7 and appendix D. It is especially important to remember that administrative software must be tested over and over again until users are assured that it will operate without error. This point cannot be stressed enough.

I N V E N T O R

```
       1000 REM ***     INVENTORY MANAGEMENT PROGRAM            ***
   *   1010 CLEAR 15000
       1020 X=1000
   *   1030 DIM A1$(X),A2$(X),A3$(X),A4$(X)
   *   1040 CLS
   *   1050 CLS:X=0
   *   1060 CLS
       1070 PRINT
       1080 PRINT"WOULD YOU LIKE TO "
       1082 PRINT" 1 ADD A NEW INVENTORY RECORD"
       1084 PRINT" 2 DELETE AN INVENTORY RECORD"
       1086 PRINT" 3 MODIFY AN INVENTORY RECORD"
       1090 PRINT" 4 SEARCH THROUGH RECORDS"
       1095 PRINT" 5 PRINT OUT INVENTORY RECORDS"
       1100 INPUT A$
   *   1110 CLS
   *   1120 A=VAL(A$)
   *   1130 CLS:IF A<1OR A>6THEN PRINT"SORRY BUT CHOICE ";A$;" IS
            NOT AN ACCEPTABLE CHOICE":GOTO 1070
   *   1140 A6$="INVEN:1"
       1150 IF A>1 THEN GOSUB 2350
   *   1160 CLS:ON A GOTO 1170,1320,1490,1690,2070
       1170 PRINT"WE ARE GOING TO ADD RECORDS TO A FILE NOW."
       1180 PRINT"IF THIS IS THE FUNCTION YOU DESIRE, PRESS THE"
       1190 PRINT"WHITE ENTER KEY.  IF IT IS NOT THEN TYPE THE
            WORD"
       1200 PRINT"NO FOLLOWED BY THE ENTER KEY"
       1210 B$="":INPUT B$
       1220 IF LEFT$(B$,1)="N" THEN GOTO 1070
   *   1230 PRINT"PRESS THE ENTER KEY TO TERMINATE THIS
            OPERATION":A1$=""
       1240 INPUT"PLEASE TYPE IN THE ITEM NAME NOW";A1$
   *   1250 IF A1$="" THEN CLOSE:GOTO 1080
       1260 X=X+1:INPUT"PLEASE TYPE IN THE ITEM NUMBER NOW";A2$
       1270 INPUT"PLEASE TYPE IN THE RESPONSIBLE PERSON'S NAME
            NOW";A3$
       1280 INPUT"I NEED THE ITEM LOCATION NOW";A4$
   *   1290 CLS:CLOSE
       1300 GOSUB 2280
       1310 GOTO 1230
       1320 PRINT"WE ARE GOING TO DELETE RECORDS NOW. IF THAT"
       1330 PRINT"IS CORRECT THEN PRESS THE ENTER KEY. IF IT IS"
       1340 PRINT"NOT THEN TYPE NO FOLLOWED BY THE ENTER KEY"
       1350 N$="":INPUT N$
       1360 IF LEFT$(N$,1)="N" THEN GOTO 1080
       1370 PRINT"TELL ME THE ITEM'S NAME"
       1380 INPUT Z1$:L1=LEN(Z1$)
```

```
1390 INPUT"TELL ME THE SERIAL NUMBER OF THE
     ITEM";Z2$:L2=LEN(Z2$)
1400 FOR Z=1TOX
1410 SW=0
1420 IF Z1$=LEFT$(A1$(Z),L1) AND Z2$=LEFT$(A2$(Z),L2) THEN
     SW=1:GOTO 1440
1430 NEXT
1440 IF SW=0 THEN PRINT"SORRY BUT THERE IS NO ITEM IN MY
     FILE WITH":PRINT"AN ITEM NAME OF ";Z1$;" AND AN ITEM
     SERIAL NUMBER OF ";Z2$:PRINT"TRY AGAIN":GOTO 1320
1450 FOR V=Z TO X-1
1460 A1$(V)=A1$(V+1): A2$(V)=A2$(V+1): A3$(V)=A3$(V+1):
     A4$(V)=A4$(V+1)
1470 NEXT V:X=X-1
1480 CLS:GOSUB 2450:GOTO 1070
1490 PRINT"WE ARE GOING TO MODIFY RECORDS NOW. IF THAT"
1500 PRINT"IS CORRECT THEN PRESS THE ENTER KEY. IF IT IS"
1510 PRINT"NOT THEN TYPE NO FOLLOWED BY THE ENTER KEY"
1520 N$="":INPUT N$
1530 IF LEFT$(N$,1)="N" THEN GOTO 1080
1540 PRINT"TELL ME THE ITEM NAME "
1550 INPUT Z1$:L1=LEN(Z1$)
1560 INPUT"TELL ME THE ITEM'S SERIAL NUMBER"; Z2$:
     L2=LEN(Z2$)
1570 FOR Z=1TOX
1580 SW=0
1590 IF Z1$=LEFT$(A1$(Z),L1) AND Z2$=LEFT$(A2$(Z),L2) THEN
     SW=1:GOTO 1610
1600 NEXT
1610 IF SW=0 THEN PRINT"SORRY BUT THERE IS NO ITEM IN MY
     FILE WITH":PRINT"AN ITEM NAME OF ";Z1$;" AND AN ITEM
     NUMBER OF ";Z2$:PRINT"TRY AGAIN":GOTO 1490
1620 PRINT"I FOUND IT !"
1625 PRINT"PLEASE TYPE IN THE CORRECT INFORMATION NOW."
1630 INPUT"PLEASE TYPE IN THE ITEM NAME NOW";A1$(Z)
1640 INPUT"PLEASE TYPE IN THE ITEM NUMBER NOW";A2$(Z)
1650 INPUT"PLEASE TYPE IN THE RESPONSIBLE PARTY NOW";
     A3$(Z)
1660 INPUT"I NEED THE ITEM LOCATION NOW";A4$(Z)
1670 GOSUB 2450
1680 CLS:GOTO 1070
1690 PRINT"WE ARE GOING TO SEARCH FOR RECORDS NOW. IF
     THAT"
1700 PRINT"IS CORRECT THEN PRESS THE ENTER KEY. IF IT IS"
1710 PRINT"NOT THEN TYPE  NO  FOLLOWED BY THE ENTER KEY."
1720 S6=0:N$="":INPUT N$
1730 IF LEFT$(N$,1)="N" THEN GOTO 1080
1740 PRINT"YOU CAN SEARCH ACCORDING TO ANY OF THE
     FOLLOWING CRITERIA"
1750 PRINT"SELECT ONE NOW"
1752 PRINT" 1 - ITEM NAME"
1754 PRINT" 2 - SERIAL NUMBER"
1756 PRINT" 3 - RESPONSIBLE PARTY"
1758 PRINT" 4 - LOCATION"
1760 INPUT SR$
1770 SR=VAL(SR$):IF SR<1 OR SR>4 THEN CLS:PRINTSR$;" IS
     NOT ALLOWED AS A CHOICE":GOTO 1750
1780 IF SR=1 THEN PRINT"TELL ME THE ITEM NAME NOW ":
     INPUT Q$
```

```
        1790 IF SR=2 THEN PRINT"TELL ME THE ITEM SERIAL NUMBER
             NOW ":INPUT Q$
        1800 IF SR=3 THEN PRINT"TELL ME THE RESPONSIBLE PERSON'S
             NAME NOW":INPUT Q$
        1810 IF SR=4 THEN PRINT"ITEM LOCATION NOW ":INPUT Q$
        1820 L1=LEN(Q$)
        1830 FOR Z=1TOX
        1840 SW=0
        1850 IF SR=1 AND Q$=LEFT$(A1$(Z),L1) THEN SW=1:GOTO 1900
        1860 IF SR=2 AND Q$=LEFT$(A2$(Z),L1) THEN SW=1:GOTO 1900
        1870 IF SR=3 AND Q$=LEFT$(A3$(Z),L1) THEN SW=1:GOTO 1900
        1880 IF SR=4 AND Q$=LEFT$(A4$(Z),L1) THEN SW=1:GOTO 1900
        1890 NEXT
        1900 IF SW=0 THEN PRINT"BASED ON THE PARAMETERS YOU
             INDICATED ": PRINT "THERE IS NO ADDITIONAL
             INFORMATION THAT CAN BE PROVIDED.": PRINT:GOTO 1690
        1910 IFS6=0 THEN PRINT"WOULD YOU LIKE TO PRINT ON THE
             (S)CREEN OR (P)APER"
        1920 IF S6=0 THEN INPUTM$:M$=LEFT$(M$,1):IF M$<>"S" AND
             M$<>"P" THEN GOTO 1910
        1930 IF M$="S" THEN GOTO 1990
        1940 S6=1:LPRINT"ITEM'S NAME - ";A1$(Z)
        1950 LPRINT"ITEM SERIAL NUMBER - ";A2$(Z)
        1960 LPRINT"RESPONSIBLE PARTY - ";A3$(Z)
        1970 LPRINT"ITEM LOCATION - ";A4$(Z)
   *    1980 LPRINT:IF Z<X THEN GOTO 1890 ELSE CLS:GOTO 1070
        1990 S6=1:PRINT"ITEM'S NAME - ";A1$(Z)
        2000 PRINT"ITEM'S SERIAL NUMBER - ";A2$(Z)
        2010 PRINT"RESPONSIBLE PARTY - ";A3$(Z)
        2020 PRINT"ITEM LOCATION - ";A4$(Z)
   *    2030 PRINT"PRESS ANY KEY TO SEE MORE"
        2040 INPUT AV$
   *    2050 CLS
   *    2060 PRINT:IF Z<X THEN GOTO 1890 ELSE CLS:GOTO 1070
        2070 PRINT"WE ARE GOING TO PRINT OUT RECORDS NOW. IF THAT
             IS "
   *    2080 M$="":PRINT"O.K. PRESS THE ENTER KEY. IF NOT THEN
             TYPE NO AND PRESS ENTER": INPUTM$: IF LEFT$(M$,1)="N"
             THEN CLS: GOTO 1070
        2090 PRINT"WOULD YOU LIKE TO PRINT ON THE (S)CREEN OR
             (P)APER "
        2100 INPUTM$:M$=LEFT$(M$,1):IF M$<>"S" AND M$<>"P" THEN
             GOTO 2090
        2110 IF M$="S" THEN GOTO 2190
        2120 FOR Z=1 TO X
        2130 LPRINT"ITEM'S NAME - ";A1$(Z)
        2140 LPRINT"ITEM'S SERIAL NUMBER - ";A2$(Z)
        2150 LPRINT"RESPONSIBLE PARTY - ";A3$(Z)
        2160 LPRINT"ITEM LOCATION - ";A4$(Z)
        2170 LPRINT" "
   *    2180 NEXT Z:CLS:CLOSE:GOTO 1070
        2190 FOR Z=1 TO X
        2200 PRINT"ITEM'S NAME - ";A1$(Z)
        2210 PRINT"ITEM NUMBER - ";A2$(Z)
        2220 PRINT"RESPONSIBLE PARTY - ";A3$(Z)
        2230 PRINT"ITEM LOCATION - ";A4$(Z)
   *    2240 PRINT"PRESS ANY KEY AND ENTER TO SEE MORE"
   *    2250 INPUT AV$
   *    2260 CLS
```

```
*       2270 NEXT Z:CLS:CLOSE:GOTO 1070
        2280 REM*** THIS SECTION OPENS A FILE AND ADDS DATA ***
*       2290 OPEN"E",1,A6$
*       2300 PRINT#1,A1$
*       2310 PRINT#1,A2$
*       2320 PRINT#1,A3$
*       2330 PRINT#1,A4$
*       2340 RETURN
        2350 REM *** THIS SECTION READS IN A FILE ***
*       2360 OPEN"I",1,A6$
        2370 X=0
*       2380 IF EOF(1) THEN CLOSE:RETURN
        2390 X=X+1
*       2400 LINE INPUT#1,A1$(X)
*       2410 LINE INPUT#1,A2$(X)
*       2420 LINE INPUT#1,A3$(X)
*       2430 LINE INPUT#1,A4$(X)
        2440 GOTO 2380
        2450 REM *** THIS SECTION WRITES OUT A FILE ***
*       2460 OPEN"O",1,A6$
        2470 FOR Z=1 TO X
*       2480 PRINT#1,A1$(Z)
*       2490 PRINT#1,A2$(Z)
*       2500 PRINT#1,A3$(Z)
*       2510 PRINT#1,A4$(Z)
        2520 NEXT Z
*       2530 CLOSE:RETURN


                       T R E A S U R Y


        1000 REM ***    SCHOOL TREASURY MAINTENANCE PROGRAM     ***
*       1010 CLEAR 1000
        1020 X=200
        1030 DIM A1$(X),A2$(X),A3$(X),A4$(X),A5$(X),A6(X),A7$(X)
*       1040 CLS
        1050 PRINT
*       1060 CLS:X=0
*       1070 CLS
        1080 PRINT"WHAT WOULD YOU LIKE TO CALL THIS FILE ?"
        1090 PRINT"SELECT A NAME THAT INCLUDES DESCRIPTIVE
             INFORMATION"
        1100 PRINT"ABOUT THE FILE.  IT MUST BEGIN WITH A LETTER
             AND MUST"
        1110 PRINT"CONTAIN ONLY LETTERS AND NUMBERS.  IT MUST NOT
             INCLUDE"
        1120 PRINT"SPACES AND MUST BE 8 OR LESS KEYBOARD
             CHARACTERS IN
        1130 PRINT"LENGTH.  EXAMPLE: A PAYROLL FILE MAY BE CALLED"
        1140 PRINT"PAYSEP81 OR PAY8182.  TYPE IN THE NAME OF THIS
             FILE."
        1150 INPUT AA$
*       1160 CLS
*       1170 CLOSE:PRINT
        1180 PRINT"WOULD YOU LIKE TO
             1 ADD A NEW TRANSACTION RECORD
             2 DELETE A TRANSACTION RECORD
             3 MODIFY A TRANSACTION RECORD"
        1190 PRINT"        4 SEARCH THROUGH RECORDS
```

```
                  5 PRINT OUT TRANSACTION RECORDS"
      1200 INPUT A$
*     1210 CLS
      1220 A=VAL(A$)
*     1230 CLS:IF A<1OR A>5THEN PRINT"SORRY BUT CHOICE ";A$;" IS
                  NOT AN ACCEPTABLE CHOICE":GOTO 1170
      1240 AB$=AA$+":1"
      1250 IF ASC(LEFT$(AA$,1))<65 OR ASC(LEFT$(AA$,1))>90 THEN
                  PRINT"SORRY BUT ";AA$;" IS NOT AN ACCEPTABLE NAME"
                  :GOTO 1080
      1260 IF A>1 THEN GOSUB 2910
      1270 ON A GOTO 1280,1480,1750,2100,2540
*     1280 CLS:PRINT"RECORDS MAY NOW BE ADDED TO YOUR FILE " ;
                  AA$; "."
      1290 GOSUB 3140
      1300 IF SW=1 THEN SW=0ELSE GOTO 1170
      1310 PRINT"EACH TIME THAT YOU ARE ASKED TO SUPPLY A
                  NAME,":A1$=""
*     1320 PRINT"YOU MAY TERMINATE THIS FUNCTION BY PRESSING THE
                  ENTER KEY."
      1330 PRINT
      1340 PRINT"TYPE THE NAME OF THE PERSON RESPONSIBLE FOR
                  THIS"
      1350 INPUT"TRANSACTION. ";A1$
*     1360 IF A1$="" THEN CLOSE:GOTO 1170
      1370 PRINT"TYPE THE NAME OF THE SCHOOL ACCOUNT
                  RESPONSIBLE"
      1380 INPUT"FOR THIS TRANSACTION";A2$
      1390 PRINT"TYPE THE TRANSACTION DATE IN THE FORM 01/02/81"
      1400 INPUT A3$
      1410 PRINT"TYPE IN THE VENDOR'S NAME."
      1420 INPUT A4$
      1430 INPUT"TYPE IN THE CHECK NUMBER ";A5$
      1440 PRINT"TYPE IN THE  AMOUNT OF THE TRANSACTION IN THE
                  FORM 42.21"
      1450 INPUT"OMIT THE DOLLAR SIGN ";A6
      1460 GOSUB 2830
      1470 GOTO 1280
*     1480 CLS:SW=0:PRINT"I AM READY TO DELETE RECORDS FROM YOUR
                  FILE ";AA$
      1490 GOSUB 3140
      1500 IF SW=1 THEN SW=0 ELSE GOTO 1170
      1510 PRINT"I NEED INFORMATION ABOUT THE FILE WHICH YOU
                  WANT ME TO DELETE."
      1520 PRINT"TELL ME THE NAME OF THE PERSON REQUESTING THE
                  TRANSACTION."
      1530 INPUT Q1$
      1540 PRINT"TELL ME THE AMOUNT OF MONEY WHICH WAS
                  INVOLVED."
      1550 INPUT Q2
      1560 FOR Y=1TO X
      1570 IF Q1$<>LEFT$(A1$(Y),LEN(A1$(Y))) OR Q2<>A6(Y) THEN
                  GOTO 1720
      1580 PRINT"I HAVE FOUND A RECORD WITH THE FOLLOWING
                  INFORMATION:"
      1590 PRINT"NAME OF PERSON REQUESTING TRANSACTION - ";
                  A1$(Y)
      1600 PRINT"ACCT NAME - ";A2$(Y)
      1610 PRINT"DATE OF TRANSACTION - ";A3$(Y)
```

```
1620 PRINT"OUTSIDE PARTY - ";A4$(Y)
1630 PRINT"CHECK NUMBER - ";A5$(Y)
1640 PRINT"AMOUNT OF TRANSACTION - ";A6(Y)
1650 PRINT"IS THAT THE TRANSACTION YOU WANT ME TO DELETE "
1660 PRINT"TYPE YES OR NO. THEN PRESS THE ENTER KEY."
1670 INPUT VV$:IF LEFT$(VV$,1)<>"Y" THEN GOTO 1720
1680 FOR Z=YTOX-1
1690 A1$(Z)=A1$(Z+1): A2$(Z)=A2$(Z+1): A3$(Z)=A3$(Z+1):
     A4$(Z)=A4$(Z+1): A5$(Z)=A5$(Z+1): A6(Z)=A6(Z+1):X=X-1
1700 NEXT Z:GOSUB 3030
1710 SW=1
1720 NEXT Y
1730 IF SW=0 THEN SW=1: PRINT"I HAVE NOT FOUND ANY RECORDS
     WITH THOSE PARAMETERS.":INPUT"TYPE ENTER TO CONTINUE"
     ;ZZ$:GOTO 1480
1740 GOTO 1170
*    1750 CLS:PRINT"THE RECORDS OF FILE ";AA$;" MAY NOW BE
          MODIFIED."
1760 GOSUB 3140
1770 IF SW=1 THEN SW=0 ELSE GOTO 1170
1780 PRINT"I NEED INFORMATION ABOUT THE FILE WHICH YOU
     WANT ME TO MODIFY."
1790 PRINT"TYPE THE NAME OF THE PERSON REQUESTING THE
     TRANSACTION."
1800 INPUT Q1$
1810 PRINT"TYPE THE AMOUNT OF THE ORIGINAL TRANSACTION IN
     THE FORM 22.33"
1820 PRINT"OMIT THE DOLLAR SIGN."
1830 INPUT Q2
1840 FOR Y=1TO X
1850 IF Q1$<>A1$(Y) OR Q2<>A6(Y) THEN GOTO 2070
1860 PRINT"THE FOLLOWING RECORD IS ON FILE :"
1870 PRINT"NAME OF PERSON REQUESTING TRANSACTION - "
     ;A1$(Y)
1880 PRINT"ACCT NAME - ";A2$(Y)
1890 PRINT"DATE OF TRANSACTION - ";A3$(Y)
1900 PRINT"VENDOR OR OUTSIDE OR PARTY - ";A4$(Y)
1910 PRINT"CHECK NUMBER - ";A5$(Y)
1920 PRINT"AMOUNT OF TRANSACTION - ";A6(Y)
1930 PRINT"IS THAT THE TRANSACTION YOU WANT ME TO MODIFY "
1940 PRINT"TYPE YES OR NO THEN PRESS THE ENTER KEY."
1950 INPUT VV$:IF LEFT$(VV$,1)<>"Y" THEN GOTO 2070
1960 PRINT:PRINT"PLEASE TYPE IN THE NEW INFORMATION AS
     REQUESTED BELOW."
1970 INPUT"TYPE THE NAME OF THE INDIVIDUAL REQUESTING THE
     TRANSACTION ";A1$(Y)
1980 INPUT"NOW TYPE THE NAME OF THE SCHOOL ACCOUNT "
     ;A2$(Y)
1990 PRINT"NOW I NEED THE TRANSACTION DATE IN THE FORM
     01/02/81 "
2000 INPUT A3$(Y)
2010 PRINT"TYPE THE NAME OF THE OUTSIDE AGENT INVOLVED IN
     THIS":INPUT"TRANSACTION ";A4$(Y)
2020 INPUT"NOW I NEED THE CHECK NUMBER ";A5$(Y)
2030 PRINT"NOW TYPE THE AMOUNT OF THE TRANSACTION IN THE
     FORM 22.99  ."
2040 INPUT"OMIT  THE DOLLAR SIGN.";A6(Y)
2050 GOSUB 3030
2060 SW=1
```

```
      2070 NEXT Y
      2080 IF SW=0 THEN PRINT"I HAVE NOT FOUND ANY RECORDS WITH
           THOSE PARAMETERS.":INPUT"TYPE ENTER TO CONTINUE"
           ;ZZ$:GOTO 1750
      2090 GOTO 1170
*     2100 CLS:PRINT"THE SEARCH OF YOUR FILE ";AA$;" WILL NOW
           BEGIN."
      2110 GOSUB 3140
      2120 IF SW=1 THEN SW=0 ELSE GOTO 1170
      2130 PRINT"SELECT ONE OF THE FOLLOWING CATEGORIES AND TYPE
           THE NUMBER"
      2140 PRINT"OF THE CATEGORY THAT YOU WISH TO EXAMINE."
      2150 PRINT"1 - AMOUNT OF TRANSACTION
           2 - DATE OF TRANSACTION
           3 - PERSON RESPONSIBLE"
      2160 PRINT"4 - VENDOR
           5 - CHECK NUMBER
           6 - ACCOUNT NAME"
      2170 INPUT C$
      2180 C=VAL(C$):IFC<1ORC>6 THEN GOTO 2150
      2190 IF C=1 THEN INPUT"TYPE IN THE AMOUNT YOU ARE LOOKING
           FOR ";Q$:Q=VAL(Q$)
      2200 IF C=2 THEN INPUT"TYPE IN THE DATE YOU ARE SEARCHING
           FOR ";Q$
      2210 IF C=3 THEN INPUT"TYPE IN THE NAME OF THE RESPONSIBLE
           FOR THE TRANSACTION ";Q$
      2220 IF C=4 THEN INPUT"TYPE IN THE NAME OF VENDOR ";Q$
      2230 IF C=5 THEN INPUT"TYPE IN THE CHECK NUMBER ";Q$
      2240 IF C=6 THEN INPUT"TYPE IN THE ACCOUNT ";Q$
      2250 FOR Y=1TOX
      2260 IF C=1 AND Q<>A6(Y) THEN GOTO 2510
      2270 IF C=2 AND Q$<>LEFT$(A3$(Y),LEN(Q$)) THEN GOTO 2510
      2280 IF C=4 AND Q$<>LEFT$(A4$(Y),LEN(Q$)) THEN GOTO 2510
      2290 IF C=5 AND Q$<>LEFT$(A5$(Y),LEN(Q$)) THEN GOTO 2510
      2300 IF C=3 AND Q$<>LEFT$(A1$(Y),LEN(Q$)) THEN GOTO 2510
      2310 IF C=6 AND Q$<>LEFT$(A2$(Y),LEN(Q$)) THEN GOTO 2510
      2320 PRINT"TYPE S FOR THE SCREEN AND P FOR PAPER"
*     2330 INPUT V1$:IF V1$="" THEN GOTO 2330
      2340 V1$=LEFT$(V1$,1)
      2350 IF V1$="S" THEN GOTO 2430
      2360 LPRINT A1$(Y);"    ";
      2370 LPRINT A2$(Y)
      2380 LPRINT A3$(Y);"    ";
      2390 LPRINT A4$(Y)
      2400 LPRINT A5$(Y);"    ";
      2410 LPRINT A6(Y)
      2420 LPRINT"  "  ,
      2430 PRINT A1$(Y)
      2440 PRINT A2$(Y)
      2450 PRINT A3$(Y)
      2460 PRINT A4$(Y)
      2470 PRINT A5$(Y)
      2480 PRINT A6(Y)
      2490 PRINT
      2500 INPUT"PRESS THE ENTER KEY TO CONTINUE ";AV$
      2510 NEXT
      2520 PRINT"YOU HAVE SEEN ALL OF THE FILES WHICH MEET YOUR
           CRITERIA ":PRINT"PRESS ENTER TO CONTINUE ":INPUT ZZ$
      2530 GOTO 1170
```

```
*       2540 CLS:PRINT"I AM READY TO PRINT OUT RECORDS FROM YOUR
             FILE ";AA$
        2550 GOSUB 3140
        2560 IF SW=1 THEN SW=0 ELSE GOTO 1170
        2570 PRINT"YOU MAY CHOOSE EITHER S FOR SCREEN OR P FOR
             PAPER. "
        2580 INPUTM$:M$=LEFT$(M$,1):IF M$<>"S" AND M$<>"P"  THEN
             GOTO 2570
        2590 IF M$="S" THEN GOTO 2690
        2600 FOR Z=1 TO X
        2610 LPRINT"TEACHER'S NAME - ";A1$(Z)
        2620 LPRINT"ACCOUNT NAME - ";A2$(Z)
        2630 LPRINT"TRANSACTION DATE - ";A3$(Z)
        2640 LPRINT"OUTSIDE PARTY - ";A4$(Z)
        2650 LPRINT"CHECK NUMBER - ";A5$(Z)
        2660 LPRINT"AMOUNT OF TRANSACTION - ";A6(Z)
        2670 LPRINT" "
*       2680 NEXT Z:CLS:CLOSE:GOTO 1170
        2690 FOR Z=1 TO X
        2700 PRINT"TEACHER'S NAME - ";A1$(Z)
        2710 PRINT"ACCOUNT NAME - ";A2$(Z)
        2720 PRINT"TRANSACTION DATE - ";A3$(Z)
        2730 PRINT"OUTSIDE PARTY - ";A4$(Z)
        2740 PRINT"CHECK NUMBER - ";A5$(Z)
        2750 PRINT"TRANSACTION AMOUNT - ";A6(Z)
*       2760 PRINT"PRESS THE ENTER KEY SEE ADDITIONAL FILES "
*       2770 INPUT AV$
*       2780 CLS
*       2790 NEXT Z:CLS:CLOSE:GOTO 1170
        2800 GOTO 1170
        2810 GOTO 1170
        2820 REM*** THIS SECTION OPENS A FILE AND ADDS DATA ***
*       2830 CLOSE:OPEN"E",1,AB$
*       2840 PRINT#1,A1$
*       2850 PRINT#1,A2$
*       2860 PRINT#1,A3$
*       2870 PRINT#1,A4$
*       2880 PRINT#1,A5$
*       2890 PRINT#1,A6
        2900 RETURN
        2910 REM *** THIS SECTION READS IN A FILE ***
*       2920 OPEN"I",1,AB$
        2930 X=0
*       2940 IF EOF(1) THEN CLOSE:RETURN
        2950 X=X+1
*       2960 LINE INPUT#1,A1$(X)
*       2970 LINE INPUT#1,A2$(X)
*       2980 LINE INPUT#1,A3$(X)
*       2990 LINE INPUT#1,A4$(X)
*       3000 LINE INPUT#1,A5$(X)
*       3010 INPUT#1,A6(X)
        3020 GOTO 2940
        3030 REM *** THIS SECTION WRITES OUT A FILE ***
*       3040 OPEN"O",1,AB$
        3050 FOR Z=1 TO X
*       3060 PRINT#1,A1$(Z)
*       3070 PRINT#1,A2$(Z)
*       3080 PRINT#1,A3$(Z)
*       3090 PRINT#1,A4$(Z)
```

```
*      3100 PRINT#1,A5$(Z)
*      3110 PRINT#1,A6(Z)
       3120 NEXT Z
*      3130 CLOSE:RETURN
       3140 PRINT"IF THIS IS THE FUNCTION THAT YOU WANT, PRESS
            THE"
       3150 PRINT"ENTER KEY.  IF NOT, TYPE THE WORD    NO    AND
            PRESS THE ENTER"
       3160 PRINT"KEY."
       3170 B$="":INPUT B$
       3180 IF B$="" THEN B$="YES"
       3190 IF LEFT$(B$,1)<>"N" THEN SW=1 ELSE SW=0
       3200 RETURN
```

TEACHER FILE MANAGEMENT PROGRAMS

The next five programs allow a user to create, modify, print, search through, and delete records from a teacher file. For additional information refer to appendix D as well as to the description of these programs that appears in chapter 7. The next two sets of programs allow supplementary categories of information to be stored and manipulated through the use of codes. A qualified programmer can assist with any modifications that may be necessary.

```
       1000 REM ***** ADDS TEACHER RECORDS TO A FILE  *****
*      1010 CLEAR 18000:X=0:CLS
       1020 PRINT"THIS PROGRAM WILL ALLOW YOU TO ADD RECORDS TO
            YOUR TEACHER DATA"
       1030 PRINT"FILE.  IF THIS IS WHAT YOU WANT THEN TYPE THE
            WORD   YES   AND"
       1040 PRINT"PRESS THE <ENTER> KEY.  IF NOT THEN TYPE   NO
            AND PRESS <ENTER>"
       1050 INPUT A$
       1060 IF A$="NO" THEN END
       1070 A3$="SCHOOL"
       1080 AA$="SCHOOL:1"
*      1090 CLS
       1100 PRINT"PRESS THE ENTER KEY TO TERMINATE THIS
            OPERATION" :A1$=""
       1110 INPUT"PLEASE TYPE IN THE LAST NAME ";A1$
*      1120 IF A1$="" THEN CLOSE:GOTO 1030
       1130 X=X+1:INPUT"PLEASE TYPE IN THE FIRST NAME ";A2$
       1140 INPUT"PLEASE TYPE IN THE STREET ADDRESS ";A4$
       1150 LINE INPUT"PLEASE TYPE THE CITY AND STATE ";A5$
       1160 INPUT"PLEASE TYPE IN TEACHER'S ZIP CODE ";A6$
       1170 INPUT"PLEASE TYPE THE TEACHER'S PHONE NUMBER ";A7$
       1180 INPUT"PLEASE TYPE THE FILE NUMBER ";B3$
       1190 INPUT"NOW I NEED THE SOC. SEC. NUMBER ";B4$
       1200 PRINT"PLEASE TYPE IN THE LICENSE LEVEL "
       1210 INPUT"(CB, JHS, HS, OR OTHER) ";A8$
       1220 INPUT"NOW I NEED THE SUBJECT OF LICENSE ";A9$
       1230 INPUT"SUBJECT TAUGHT ";B1$
       1240 INPUT"IS THE TEACHER (T)ENURED OR (P)ROBATIONARY ";
            B2$
       1250 INPUT"I NEED THE DATE OF APPOINTMENT NEXT ";B5$
       1260 INPUT"NOW I NEED THE SENIORITY DATE ";B6$
       1270 INPUT"WHAT IS THE PRESENT LEAVE STATUS ";B7$
       1280 PRINT"SEX, RACE, OTHER CODE NOW (EACH IS 1 CHARACTER)
            IE. MO OR FB"
       1290 INPUT"PLEASE TYPE IN THE CODE ";B8$
*      1300 CLS:CLOSE
```

```
      1310 GOSUB 1330
      1320 GOTO 1100
      1330 REM*** THIS SECTION OPENS A FILE AND ADDS DATA ***
*     1340 OPEN"E",1,AA$
*     1350 PRINT#1,A1$
*     1360 PRINT#1,A2$
*     1370 PRINT#1,A3$
*     1380 PRINT#1,A4$
*     1390 PRINT#1,A5$
*     1400 PRINT#1,A6$
*     1410 PRINT#1,A7$
*     1420 PRINT#1,A8$
*     1430 PRINT#1,A9$
*     1440 PRINT#1,B1$
*     1450 PRINT#1,B2$
*     1460 PRINT#1,B3$
*     1470 PRINT#1,B4$
*     1480 PRINT#1,B5$
*     1490 PRINT#1,B6$
*     1500 PRINT#1,B7$
*     1510 PRINT#1,B8$
      1520 RETURN


      1000 REM *** THIS PROGRAM ALLOWS MODIFICATION OF TEACHER
           RECORDS ***
*     1010 CLEAR 18000:X=150:CLS
      1020 DIM A1$(X), A2$(X), A4$(X), A5$(X), A6$(X), A7$(X),
           A8$(X), A9$(X), B1$(X), B2$(X), B3$(X), B4$(X),
           B5$(X), B6$(X), B7$(X), B8$(X)
*     1030 CLS:X=0
      1040 A=VAL(A$)
      1050 A3$="SCHOOL"
      1060 AA$="SCHOOL:1"
      1070 PRINT"WE ARE GOING TO MODIFY RECORDS NOW. IF THAT"
      1080 PRINT"IS CORRECT THEN PRESS THE ENTER KEY. IF IT IS"
      1090 PRINT"NOT THEN TYPE  NO  FOLLOWED BY THE ENTER KEY."
      1100 N$="":INPUT N$
      1110 GOSUB 1420
      1120 IF LEFT$(N$,1)="N" THEN END
      1130 PRINT"TELL ME THE LAST NAME OF THE TEACHER"
      1140 INPUT Z1$:L1=LEN(Z1$)
      1150 INPUT"TELL ME THE TEACHER'S FILE NUMBER"; Z2$:
           L2=LEN(Z2$)
      1160 FOR Z=1TOX
      1170 SW=0
      1180 IF Z1$=LEFT$(A1$(Z),L1) AND Z2$=LEFT$(B3$(Z),L2) THEN
           SW=1:GOTO 1200
      1190 NEXT
      1200 IF SW=0 THEN PRINT"SORRY BUT THERE IS NO TEACHER IN
           MY FILE WITH":PRINT"A LAST NAME OF ";Z1$;" AND A FILE
           NUMBER OF ";Z2$:PRINT"TRY AGAIN":GOTO 1070
      1210 PRINT"TYPE IN THE NEW INFORMATION AS REQUESTED
           BELOW."
      1220 INPUT"PLEASE TYPE IN THE LAST NAME ";A1$(Z)
      1230 INPUT"PLEASE TYPE IN THE FIRST NAME ";A2$(Z)
      1240 INPUT"PLEASE TYPE IN THE STREET ADDRESS ";A4$(Z)
      1250 LINE INPUT"I NEED THE CITY AND STATE ";A5$(Z)
      1260 INPUT"PLEASE TYPE IN TEACHER'S ZIP CODE ";A6$(Z)
```

```
      1270 INPUT"I NEED THE TEACHER'S PHONE NUMBER ";A7$(Z)
      1280 INPUT"NOW I NEED THE FILE NUMBER ";B3$(Z)
      1290 INPUT"NOW I NEED THE SOC. SEC. NUMBER ";B4$(Z)
      1300 PRINT"PLEASE TYPE IN THE LICENSE LEVEL "
      1310 INPUT"(CB, JHS, HS, OR OTHER) ";A8$(Z)
      1320 INPUT"NOW I NEED THE SUBJECT OF LICENSE ";A9$(Z)
      1330 INPUT"SUBJECT TAUGHT ";B1$(Z)
      1340 INPUT"IS THE TEACHER (T)ENURED OR (P)ROBATIONARY ";
           B2$(Z)
      1350 INPUT"TYPE THE DATE OF APPOINTMENT ";B5$(Z)
      1360 INPUT"TYPE THE SENIORITY DATE ";B6$(Z)
      1370 INPUT"WHAT IS THE PRESENT LEAVE STATUS ";B7$(Z)
      1380 PRINT"SEX, RACE, OTHER CODE NOW (EACH IS 1 CHARACTER)
           IE. MO OR FB"
      1390 INPUT"PLEASE TYPE IN THE CODE ";B8$(Z)
      1400 GOSUB 1650
*     1410 CLS:GOTO 1030
      1420 REM *** THIS SECTION READS IN A FILE ***
*     1430 OPEN"I",1,AA$
      1440 X=0
*     1450 IF EOF(1) THEN CLOSE:RETURN
      1460 X=X+1
*     1470 LINE INPUT#1,A1$(X)
*     1480 LINE INPUT#1,A2$(X)
*     1490 LINE INPUT#1,A3$
*     1500 LINE INPUT#1,A4$(X)
*     1510 LINE INPUT#1,A5$(X)
*     1520 LINE INPUT#1,A6$(X)
*     1530 LINE INPUT#1,A7$(X)
*     1540 LINE INPUT#1,A8$(X)
*     1550 LINE INPUT#1,A9$(X)
*     1560 LINE INPUT#1,B1$(X)
*     1570 LINE INPUT#1,B2$(X)
*     1580 LINE INPUT#1,B3$(X)
*     1590 LINE INPUT#1,B4$(X)
*     1600 LINE INPUT#1,B5$(X)
*     1610 LINE INPUT#1,B6$(X)
*     1620 LINE INPUT#1,B7$(X)
*     1630 LINE INPUT#1,B8$(X)
      1640 GOTO 1450
      1650 REM *** THIS SECTION WRITES OUT A FILE ***
*     1660 OPEN"O",1,AA$
      1670 FOR Z=1 TO X
*     1680 PRINT#1,A1$(Z)
*     1690 PRINT#1,A2$(Z)
*     1700 PRINT#1,A3$
*     1710 PRINT#1,A4$(Z)
*     1720 PRINT#1,A5$(Z)
*     1730 PRINT#1,A6$(Z)
*     1740 PRINT#1,A7$(Z)
*     1750 PRINT#1,A8$(Z)
*     1760 PRINT#1,A9$(Z)
*     1770 PRINT#1,B1$(Z)
*     1780 PRINT#1,B2$(Z)
*     1790 PRINT#1,B3$(Z)
*     1800 PRINT#1,B4$(Z)
*     1810 PRINT#1,B5$(Z)
*     1820 PRINT#1,B6$(Z)
*     1830 PRINT#1,B7$(Z)
```

```
*     1840 PRINT#1,B8$(Z)
      1850 NEXT Z
*     1860 CLOSE:RETURN


      1000 REM *** THIS PROGRAM PRINTS OUT TEACHER RECORDS ***
*     1010 CLEAR 18000:X=150:CLS
      1020 DIM A1$(X), A2$(X), A4$(X), A5$(X), A6$(X), A7$(X),
           A8$(X), A9$(X), B1$(X), B2$(X), B3$(X) ,B4$(X),
           B5$(X), B6$(X), B7$(X), B8$(X)
      1030 A3$="SCHOOL":X=0
      1040 AA$="SCHOOL:1"
      1050 GOSUB 1520
*     1060 CLS
      1070 PRINT"WE ARE GOING TO PRINT OUT RECORDS NOW. IF THAT
           IS "
      1080 M$="":PRINT"O.K. PRESS THE ENTER KEY.  IF NOT THEN
           TYPE NO AND PRESS ENTER":INPUTM$:IF LEFT$(M$,1)="N"
           THEN END
      1090 PRINT"WOULD YOU LIKE TO PRINT ON THE (S)CREEN OR
           (P)APER OR (L)ABELS"
      1100 INPUTM$:M$=LEFT$(M$,1):IF M$<>"S" AND M$<>"P" AND
           M$<>"L" THEN GOTO 1090
      1110 IF M$="S" THEN GOTO 1320
      1120 IF M$="L" THEN INPUT"WHAT NUMBER SHOULD I BEGIN
           WITH "; AX
      1130 FOR Z=1 TO X
*     1140 IF M$="L" THEN LPRINTAX;" ";A1$(Z);", "; A2$(Z):
           LPRINT" ": LPRINT" ": LPRINT" ": LPRINT" ":
           AX=AX+1:GOTO 1300
*     1150 LPRINT"TEACHER'S NAME - ";A1$(Z);"    ";A2$(Z)
*     1160 LPRINT"STREET ADDRESS - ";A4$(Z)
*     1170 LPRINT"CITY, STATE AND ZIP - ";A5$(Z);" ";A6$(Z)
*     1180 LPRINT"HOME PHONE NUMBER - ";A7$(Z)
*     1190 LPRINT"FILE NUMBER - ";B3$(Z);" ";
*     1200 LPRINT"SOC. SEC. NUMBER - ";B4$(Z)
*     1210 LPRINT"SCHOOL - ";A3$
*     1220 LPRINT"LICENSE LEVEL - ";A8$(Z);" ";
*     1230 LPRINT"SUBJECT OF LICENSE - ";A9$(Z)
*     1240 LPRINT"SUBJECT TAUGHT - ";B1$(Z);" ";
*     1250 LPRINT"(T)ENURED OR (P)ROBATIONARY - ";B2$(Z)
*     1260 LPRINT"DATE OF APPOINTMENT - ";B5$(Z)
*     1270 LPRINT"SENIORITY DATE - ";B6$(Z)
*     1280 LPRINT"PRESENT LEAVE STATUS - ";B7$(Z)
*     1290 LPRINT"SPECIAL CODE NOW - ";B8$(Z)
*     1300 LPRINT" "
*     1310 NEXT Z:CLS:CLOSE:GOTO 1030
      1320 FOR Z=1 TO X
      1330 PRINT"TEACHER'S NAME - ";A1$(Z);"    ";A2$(Z)
      1340 PRINT"STREET ADDRESS - ";A4$(Z)
      1350 PRINT"CITY, STATE AND ZIP - ";A5$(Z);" ";A6$(Z)
      1360 PRINT"HOME PHONE NUMBER - ";A7$(Z)
      1370 PRINT"FILE NUMBER - ";B3$(Z);" ";
      1380 PRINT"SOCIAL SECURITY NUMBER - ";B4$(Z)
      1390 PRINT"SCHOOL - ";A3$
      1400 PRINT"LICENSE LEVEL - ";A8$(Z);" ";
      1410 PRINT"SUBJECT OF LICENSE - ";A9$(Z)
      1420 PRINT"SUBJECT TAUGHT - ";B1$(Z);" ";
      1430 PRINT"(T)ENURED OR (P)ROBATIONARY - ";B2$(Z)
```

```
     1440 PRINT"DATE OF APPOINTMENT - ";B5$(Z)
     1450 PRINT"SENIORITY DATE - ";B6$(Z)
     1460 PRINT"PRESENT LEAVE STATUS - ";B7$(Z)
     1470 PRINT"SPECIAL CODE NOW - ";B8$(Z)
*    1480 PRINT"PRESS ANY KEY AND ENTER TO SEE MORE"
     1490 INPUT AV$
*    1500 CLS
*    1510 NEXT Z:CLS:CLOSE:GOTO 1030
     1520 REM *** THIS SECTION READS IN A FILE ***
*    1530 OPEN"I",1,AA$
     1540 X=0
*    1550 IF EOF(1) THEN CLOSE:RETURN
     1560 X=X+1
*    1570 LINE INPUT#1,A1$(X)
*    1580 LINE INPUT#1,A2$(X)
*    1590 LINE INPUT#1,A3$
*    1600 LINE INPUT#1,A4$(X)
*    1610 LINE INPUT#1,A5$(X)
*    1620 LINE INPUT#1,A6$(X)
*    1630 LINE INPUT#1,A7$(X)
*    1640 LINE INPUT#1,A8$(X)
*    1650 LINE INPUT#1,A9$(X)
*    1660 LINE INPUT#1,B1$(X)
*    1670 LINE INPUT#1,B2$(X)
*    1680 LINE INPUT#1,B3$(X)
*    1690 LINE INPUT#1,B4$(X)
*    1700 LINE INPUT#1,B5$(X)
*    1710 LINE INPUT#1,B6$(X)
*    1720 LINE INPUT#1,B7$(X)
*    1730 LINE INPUT#1,B8$(X)
     1740 GOTO 1550


     1000 REM *** SEARCH THROUGH TEACHER RECORDS ***
*    1010 CLEAR 18000:X=150
     1020 DIM A1$(X), A2$(X), A4$(X), A5$(X), A6$(X), A7$(X),
          A8$(X), A9$(X) ,B1$(X), B2$(X), B3$(X), B4$(X),
          B5$(X), B6$(X) ,B7$(X), B8$(X)
*    1030 CLS:X=0
     1040 A3$="SCHOOL"
     1050 AA$="SCHOOL:1"
     1060 GOSUB 1680
     1070 PRINT"WE ARE GOING TO SEARCH FOR RECORDS NOW. IF
          THAT"
     1080 PRINT"IS CORRECT THEN PRESS THE ENTER KEY. IF IT IS"
     1090 PRINT"NOT THEN TYPE NO FOLLOWED BY THE ENTER KEY"
     1100 S6=0:N$="":INPUT N$
     1110 IF LEFT$(N$,1)="N" THEN END
     1120 PRINT"YOU CAN SEARCH ACCORDING TO ANY OF THE
          FOLLOWING CRITERIA"
     1130 PRINT"SELECT ONE NOW"
     1140 PRINT"   1 - SEX"
     1150 PRINT"   2 - ETHNICITY"
     1160 PRINT"   3 - LEAVE STATUS"
     1170 PRINT"   4 - SUBJECT TAUGHT"
     1180 PRINT"   5 - PROBATIONARY STATUS"
     1190 PRINT"   6 - TEACHER'S NAME"
     1200 PRINT"   7 - ZIP CODE"
     1210 PRINT"   8 - SPECIAL CODE"
```

```
1220 INPUT SR$
1230 Q4$="3"
* 1240 SR=VAL(SR$):IF SR<1 OR SR>8 THEN CLS:PRINTSR$;" IS
     NOT ALLOWED AS A CHOICE":GOTO 1130
1250 IF SR=1 THEN PRINT"TELL ME THE SEX NOW (1
     LETTER)":INPUT Q$
1260 IF SR=2 THEN PRINT"TELL ME THE ETHNICITY NOW (1
     LETTER)":INPUT Q$
1270 IF SR=3 THEN PRINT"TELL ME THE LEAVE STATUS
     NOW":INPUT Q$
1280 IF SR=4 THEN PRINT"SUBJECT TAUGHT NOW ":INPUT Q$
1290 IF SR=5 THEN PRINT"TELL ME THE PROBATIONARY STATUS
     NOW (P OR T)":INPUT Q$
1300 Q1$="":Q2$="":IF SR=6 THEN INPUT"TELL ME THE LAST
     NAME NOW";Q1$:INPUT"TELL ME THE FIRST NAME NOW";Q2$
1310 IF SR=7 THEN INPUT"TELL ME THE ZIP CODE NOW ";Q$
1320 L1=LEN(Q$):L2=LEN(Q1$):L3=LEN(Q2$)
1330 IF SR=8 THEN PRINT"TELL ME THE CHARACTER I'M TO
     SEARCH FOR NOW":INPUTQ$:PRINT"NOW THE POSITION (3, 4,
     OR 5)":INPUT Q4$
1340 IF SR=8 AND Q4$<>"3"ANDQ4$<>"4"ANDQ4$<>"5" THEN
     PRINT"SORRY ";Q4$;" IS NOT ACCEPTABLE ":GOTO 1120
1350 FOR Z=1TOX
1360 SW=0
1370 IF SR=1 AND Q$=LEFT$(B8$(Z),1) THEN SW=1:GOTO 1460
1380 IF SR=2 AND Q$=MID$(B8$(Z),2,1) THEN SW=1:GOTO 1460
1390 IF SR=3 AND Q$=LEFT$(B7$(Z),L1) THEN SW=1:GOTO 1460
1400 IF SR=4 AND Q$=LEFT$(B1$(Z),L1) THEN SW=1:GOTO 1460
1410 IF SR=5 AND Q$=LEFT$(B2$(Z),L1) THEN SW=1:GOTO 1460
1420 IF SR=6 AND Q1$=LEFT$(A1$(Z),L2) AND Q2$=
     LEFT$(A2$(Z),L3) THEN SW=1:GOTO 1460
1430 IF SR=7 AND Q$=A6$(Z) THEN SW=1:GOTO 1460
1440 IF SR=8 AND Q$=MID$(B8$(Z),VAL(Q4$),1) THEN SW=1:
     GOTO 1460
1450 NEXT
1460 IF SW=0 THEN PRINT "YOU HAVE SEEN ALL THAT MEET YOUR
     STATED CRITERIA. ":PRINT:GOTO 1070
1470 IFS6=0 THEN PRINT"WOULD YOU LIKE TO PRINT ON THE
     (S)CREEN OR (P)APER   OR (L)ABELS"
1480 IF S6=0 THEN INPUTM$:M$=LEFT$(M$,1):IF M$<>"S" AND
     M$<>"P" AND M$<>"L" THEN GOTO 1470
1490 IF M$="S" THEN GOTO 1580
* 1500 IF M$="L" THEN LPRINTA1$(Z);" ";A2$(Z): LPRINTA4$(Z):
     A5$(Z);" ";A6$(Z): LPRINT: LPRINT: GOTO 1570
* 1510 S6=1:LPRINT"TEACHER'S NAME - ";A1$(Z);"   ";A2$(Z)
* 1520 LPRINT"STREET ADDRESS - ";A4$(Z)
* 1530 LPRINT"CITY, STATE AND ZIP - ";A5$(Z);" ";A6$(Z)
* 1540 LPRINT"HOME PHONE NUMBER - ";A7$(Z)
* 1550 LPRINT"FILE NUMBER - ";B3$(Z);" ";
* 1560 LPRINT"SOC. SEC. NUMBER - ";B4$(Z)
* 1570 LPRINT:IF Z<X THEN GOTO 1450 ELSE CLS:GOTO 1030
1580 S6=1:PRINT"TEACHER'S NAME - ";A1$(Z);"   ";A2$(Z)
1590 PRINT"STREET ADDRESS - ";A4$(Z)
1600 PRINT"CITY, STATE AND ZIP - ";A5$(Z);" ";A6$(Z)
1610 PRINT"HOME PHONE NUMBER - ";A7$(Z)
1620 PRINT"FILE NUMBER - ";B3$(Z);" ";
1630 PRINT"SOCIAL SECURITY NUMBER - ";B4$(Z)
* 1640 PRINT"PRESS ANY KEY AND ENTER TO SEE MORE"
1650 INPUT AV$
```

```
*      1660 CLS
*      1670 PRINT:IF Z<X THEN GOTO 1450 ELSE CLS:GOTO 1030
       1680 REM *** THIS SECTION READS IN A FILE ***
*      1690 OPEN"I",1,AA$
       1700 X=0
*      1710 IF EOF(1) THEN CLOSE:RETURN
       1720 X=X+1
*      1730 LINE INPUT#1,A1$(X)
*      1740 LINE INPUT#1,A2$(X)
*      1750 LINE INPUT#1,A3$
*      1760 LINE INPUT#1,A4$(X)
*      1770 LINE INPUT#1,A5$(X)
*      1780 LINE INPUT#1,A6$(X)
*      1790 LINE INPUT#1,A7$(X)
*      1800 LINE INPUT#1,A8$(X)
*      1810 LINE INPUT#1,A9$(X)
*      1820 LINE INPUT#1,B1$(X)
*      1830 LINE INPUT#1,B2$(X)
*      1840 LINE INPUT#1,B3$(X)
*      1850 LINE INPUT#1,B4$(X)
*      1860 LINE INPUT#1,B5$(X)
*      1870 LINE INPUT#1,B6$(X)
*      1880 LINE INPUT#1,B7$(X)
*      1890 LINE INPUT#1,B8$(X)
       1900 GOTO 1710


       1000 REM ***** DELETES RECORDS FROM A TEACHER FILE   *****
*      1010 CLEAR 18000:X=150:CLS
       1020 DIM A1$(X), A2$(X), A4$(X), A5$(X), A6$(X), A7$(X),
            A8$(X), A9$(X), B1$(X), B2$(X), B3$(X), B4$(X),
            B5$(X), B6$(X), B7$(X), B8$(X)
       1030 PRINT:X=0
       1040 A3$="SCHOOL"
       1050 AA$="SCHOOL:1"
*      1060 CLS:GOSUB 1250
       1070 PRINT"WE ARE GOING TO DELETE RECORDS NOW. IF THAT"
       1080 PRINT"IS CORRECT THEN PRESS THE ENTER KEY. IF IT IS"
       1090 PRINT"NOT THEN TYPE NO FOLLOWED BY THE ENTER KEY"
       1100 N$="":INPUT N$
       1110 IF LEFT$(N$,1)="N" THEN END
       1120 PRINT"TELL ME THE LAST NAME OF THE TEACHER"
       1130 INPUT Z1$:L1=LEN(Z1$)
       1140 INPUT"TELL ME THE TEACHER'S FIRST NAME"; Z2$:
            L2=LEN(Z2$)
       1150 FOR Z=1TOX
       1160 SW=0
       1170 IF Z1$=LEFT$(A1$(Z),L1) AND Z2$=LEFT$(A2$(Z),L2) THEN
            SW=1:GOTO 1190
       1180 NEXT
       1190 IF SW=0 THEN PRINT"SORRY BUT THERE IS NO TEACHER IN
            MY FILE WITH":PRINT"A LAST NAME OF ";Z1$;" AND A
            FIRST NAME OF ";Z2$:PRINT"TRY AGAIN":GOTO 1070
       1200 FOR V=Z TO X-1
       1210 A1$(V)=A1$(V+1): A2$(V)=A2$(V+1): A4$(V)=A4$(V+1):
            A5$(V)=A5$(V+1): A6$(V)=A6$(V+1): A7$(V)=A7$(V+1):
            A8$(V)=A8$(V+1): A9$(V)=A9$(V+1)
       1220 B1$(V)=B1$(V+1): B2$(V)=B2$(V+1): B3$(V)=B3$(V+1):
            B4$(V)=B4$(V+1): B5$(V)=B5$(V+1): B6$(V)=B6$(V+1):
```

```
          B7$(V)=B7$(V+1): B8$(V)=B8$(V+1)
  1230 NEXT V:X=X-1
* 1240 CLS:GOSUB 1480:GOTO 1030
  1250 REM *** THIS SECTION READS IN A FILE ***
* 1260 OPEN"I",1,AA$
  1270 X=0
* 1280 IF EOF(1) THEN CLOSE:RETURN
  1290 X=X+1
* 1300 LINE INPUT#1,A1$(X)
* 1310 LINE INPUT#1,A2$(X)
* 1320 LINE INPUT#1,A3$
* 1330 LINE INPUT#1,A4$(X)
* 1340 LINE INPUT#1,A5$(X)
* 1350 LINE INPUT#1,A6$(X)
* 1360 LINE INPUT#1,A7$(X)
* 1370 LINE INPUT#1,A8$(X)
* 1380 LINE INPUT#1,A9$(X)
* 1390 LINE INPUT#1,B1$(X)
* 1400 LINE INPUT#1,B2$(X)
* 1410 LINE INPUT#1,B3$(X)
* 1420 LINE INPUT#1,B4$(X)
* 1430 LINE INPUT#1,B5$(X)
* 1440 LINE INPUT#1,B6$(X)
* 1450 LINE INPUT#1,B7$(X)
* 1460 LINE INPUT#1,B8$(X)
  1470 GOTO 1280
  1480 REM *** THIS SECTION WRITES OUT A FILE ***
* 1490 OPEN"O",1,AA$
  1500 PRINT"D O N E   "
  1510 FOR Z=1 TO X
* 1520 PRINT#1,A1$(Z)
* 1530 PRINT#1,A2$(Z)
* 1540 PRINT#1,A3$
* 1550 PRINT#1,A4$(Z)
* 1560 PRINT#1,A5$(Z)
* 1570 PRINT#1,A6$(Z)
* 1580 PRINT#1,A7$(Z)
* 1590 PRINT#1,A8$(Z)
* 1600 PRINT#1,A9$(Z)
* 1610 PRINT#1,B1$(Z)
* 1620 PRINT#1,B2$(Z)
* 1630 PRINT#1,B3$(Z)
* 1640 PRINT#1,B4$(Z)
* 1650 PRINT#1,B5$(Z)
* 1660 PRINT#1,B6$(Z)
* 1670 PRINT#1,B7$(Z)
* 1680 PRINT#1,B8$(Z)
  1690 NEXT Z
* 1700 CLOSE:RETURN
```

STUDENT FILE MANAGEMENT PROGRAMS

The next eight programs allow a user to create, modify, print, search through, and delete records from a student file. They also permit staff members to perform attendance functions and to create mass student changes (for example, reading-test data and end-term class changes). For additional information refer to appendix D as well as to the description of these programs that appears in chapter 7.

```
        1000 REM ***            STUDENT ADD PROGRAM                    ***
   *    1010 CLEAR 8000
   *    1020 X=150:DEFINT C,V
   *    1030 CLS:X=0
        1040 PRINT"WE ARE GOING TO ADD RECORDS TO A FILE NOW."
        1050 PRINT"IF THIS IS THE FUNCTION YOU DESIRE, PRESS THE"
        1060 PRINT"WHITE ENTER KEY.  IF IT IS NOT THEN TYPE THE
             WORD"
        1070 PRINT"NO  AND PRESS THE ENTER KEY"
        1080 B$="":INPUT B$
        1090 IF LEFT$(B$,1)="N" THEN END
        1100 PRINT"NOW I NEED THE STUDENT'S CLASS ROOM NUMBER.
             PLEASE CALL IT"
        1110 LINE INPUT"240 OR 452 OR 134 OR 022 ETC; ONLY NUMBERS
             MAY BE USED. ";A3$
        1120 M$=LEFT$(A3$,1):IF ASC(M$)<48 OR ASC(M$)>57 THEN
             PRINT"SORRY BUT ";A3$;" IS NOT ACCEPTABLE":GOTO 1100
        1130 AA$="C"+A3$+":1"
        1140 PRINT"PRESS THE ENTER KEY WITHOUT DATA TO TERMINATE
             THIS OPERATION":A1$=""
        1150 LINE INPUT"PLEASE TYPE IN THE LAST NAME  ";A1$
   *    1160 IF A1$="" THEN CLOSE:END
        1170 X=X+1:LINE INPUT"PLEASE TYPE IN THE FIRST NAME  ";A2$
        1180 LINE INPUT"PLEASE TYPE IN THE STREET ADDRESS   ";A4$
        1190 LINE INPUT"I NEED THE CITY AND STATE   ";A5$
        1200 INPUT"PLEASE TYPE IN STUDENT'S ZIP CODE   ";A6
        1210 LINE INPUT"I NEED THE STUDENT'S PHONE NUMBER   ";A7$
        1220 LINE INPUT"NOW I NEED THE PARENT'S NAME ";B3$
        1230 LINE INPUT"NOW I NEED THE HOME CONTACT NUMBER ";B4$
        1240 LINE INPUT"OSIS NUMBER ";A8$
        1250 LINE INPUT"NEWEST READING TEST DATE ";B1$
        1260 INPUT"NEWEST READING TEST SCORE ";B2
        1270 LINE INPUT"MOST RECENT MATH TEST DATE ";B5$
        1280 INPUT"MOST RECENT MATH TEST SCORE ";B6
        1290 LINE INPUT"PREVIOUS SCHOOL IS NEXT ";B7$
        1300 PRINT"SEX, RACE, OTHER CODE NOW (EACH IS 1 CHARACTER)
             IE. MO OR FB":PRINT"FIVE CHARACTERS MAXIMUM FOR FIVE
             CATEGORIES WILL BE STORED"
        1310 LINE INPUT"PLEASE TYPE IN THE CODE ";B8$
        1320 IF LEN(B8$)<5 THEN B8$=B8$+".":GOTO 1320
        1330 INPUT"NUMBER OF DAYS LATE ";A9
        1340 INPUT"CONSECUTIVE ABSENCES ";B9
        1350 INPUT"NUMBER OF TOTAL ABSENCES THIS YEAR ";V
        1360 INPUT"NUMBER OF TIMES HELD OVER ";C1
   *    1370 CLS:CLOSE
        1380 GOSUB 1400
        1390 GOTO 1140
        1400 REM*** THIS SECTION OPENS A FILE AND ADDS DATA ***
   *    1410 OPEN"E",1,AA$
   *    1420 PRINT#1,A1$
   *    1430 PRINT#1,A2$
   *    1440 PRINT#1,A3$
   *    1450 PRINT#1,A4$
   *    1460 PRINT#1,A5$
   *    1470 PRINT#1,A6
   *    1480 PRINT#1,A7$
```

```
*      1490 PRINT#1,A8$
*      1500 PRINT#1,A9
*      1510 PRINT#1,B1$
*      1520 PRINT#1,B2
*      1530 PRINT#1,B3$
*      1540 PRINT#1,B4$
*      1550 PRINT#1,B5$
*      1560 PRINT#1,B6
*      1570 PRINT#1,B7$
*      1580 PRINT#1,B8$
*      1590 PRINT#1,B9
*      1600 PRINT#1,V
*      1610 PRINT#1,C1
       1620 RETURN



       1000 REM ***          STUDENT RECORD MODIFICATION     ***
*      1010 CLEAR 8000
*      1020 X=150:DEFINT C,V
       1030 DIM A1$(X), A2$(X), A4$(X), A5$(X), A6(X), A7$(X),
            A8$(X) ,A9(X), B1$(X), B2(X), B3$(X), B4$(X) ,B5$(X),
            B6(X) ,B7$(X), B8$(X), B9(X), C1(X), V(X)
*      1040 CLS:X=0
       1050 PRINT"WE ARE GOING TO MODIFY RECORDS NOW. IF THAT"
       1060 PRINT"IS CORRECT THEN PRESS THE ENTER KEY. IF IT IS"
       1070 PRINT"NOT THEN TYPE NO FOLLOWED BY THE ENTER KEY"
       1080 N$="":LINE INPUT N$
       1090 IF LEFT$(N$,1)="N" THEN END
       1100 PRINT"NOW I NEED THE STUDENT'S CLASS ROOM NUMBER.
            PLEASE CALL IT"
       1110 LINE INPUT"240 OR 452 OR 134 OR 022 ETC; ONLY
            NUMBERS !!!" ;A3$
       1120 M$=LEFT$(A3$,1):IF ASC(M$)<48 OR ASC(M$)>57 THEN
            PRINT"SORRY BUT ";A3$;" IS NOT ACCEPTABLE":GOTO 1100
       1130 AA$="C"+A3$+":1"
       1140 GOSUB 1500
       1150 PRINT"TELL ME THE LAST NAME OF THE STUDENT"
       1160 LINE INPUT Z1$:L1=LEN(Z1$)
       1170 LINE INPUT"TELL ME THE STUDENT'S FIRST
            NAME";Z2$:L2=LEN(Z2$)
       1180 FOR Z=1TOX
       1190 SW=0
       1200 IF Z1$=LEFT$(A1$(Z),L1) AND Z2$=LEFT$(A2$(Z),L2) THEN
            SW=1:GOTO 1220
       1210 NEXT
       1220 IF SW=0 THEN PRINT"SORRY BUT THERE IS NO STUDENT IN
            MY FILE WITH":PRINT"A LAST NAME OF ";Z1$;" AND A
            FIRST NAME OF ";Z2$:PRINT"TRY AGAIN":GOTO 1150
       1230 PRINT"WE'RE READY FOR THE CHANGE.  TYPE CAREFULLY!"
       1240 INPUT"PLEASE TYPE IN THE LAST NAME NOW ";A1$(Z)
       1250 INPUT"PLEASE TYPE IN THE FIRST NAME NOW ";A2$(Z)
       1260 INPUT"PLEASE TYPE IN THE STREET ADDRESS NOW ";A4$(Z)
       1270 LINE INPUT"I NEED THE CITY AND STATE NOW";A5$(Z)
       1280 INPUT"PLEASE TYPE IN STUDENT'S ZIP CODE NOW";A6(Z)
       1290 INPUT"I NEED THE STUDENT'S PHONE NUMBER NOW ";A7$(Z)
       1300 INPUT"NOW I NEED THE PARENT'S NAME ";B3$(Z)
       1310 INPUT"NOW I NEED THE HOME CONTACT PHONE NUMBER ";
            B4$(Z)
       1320 PRINT"NOW I NEED THE STUDENT'S CLASS. PLEASE CALL IT"
```

```
     1330 INPUT"240 OR 352 OR 423 OR 022 ETC; ONLY NUMBERS "
          ;A3$
     1340 M$=LEFT$(A3$,1):IF M$="" OR LEFT$(M$,1)<"0" OR
          LEFT$(M$,1)>"9" THEN PRINT"SORRY BUT ";A3$;" IS NOT
          ACCEPTABLE":GOTO 1320
     1350 INPUT"OSIS NUMBER ";A8$(Z)
     1360 INPUT"NOW I NEED THE MOST RECENT READING TEST DATE ";
          B1$(Z)
     1370 INPUT"NOW I NEED THE MOST RECENT READING TEST SCORE";
          B2(Z)
     1380 INPUT"NOW THE MOST RECENT MATH TEST DATE ";B5$(Z)
     1390 INPUT"NOW THE MOST RECENT MATH SCORE ";B6(Z)
     1400 INPUT"WHAT IS THE PREVIOUS SCHOOL ATTENDED ";B7$(Z)
     1410 PRINT"SEX, RACE, OTHER CODE NOW (EACH IS 1 CHARACTER)
          IE. MO OR FB":PRINT"FIVE CHARACTERS MAXIMUM FOR FIVE
          CATEGORIES WILL BE STORED"
     1420 INPUT"PLEASE TYPE IN THE CODE NOW ";B8$(Z)
     1430 IF LEN(B8$(Z))<5 THEN B8$(Z)=B8$(Z)+".":GOTO 1430
     1440 INPUT"NUMBER OF TIMES LATE ";A9(Z)
     1450 INPUT"CONSECUTIVE ABSENCES ";B9(Z)
     1460 INPUT"TOTAL NUMBER OF ABSENCES THIS YEAR ";V(Z)
     1470 INPUT"NUMBER OF TIMES HELD OVER ";C1(Z)
     1480 GOSUB 1760
*    1490 CLS:GOTO 1050
     1500 REM *** THIS SECTION READS IN A FILE ***
*    1510 OPEN"I",1,AA$
     1520 X=0
*    1530 IF EOF(1) THEN CLOSE:RETURN
     1540 X=X+1
*    1550 LINE INPUT#1,A1$(X)
*    1560 LINE INPUT#1,A2$(X)
*    1570 LINE INPUT#1,A3$
*    1580 LINE INPUT#1,A4$(X)
*    1590 LINE INPUT#1,A5$(X)
*    1600 INPUT#1,A6(X)
*    1610 LINE INPUT#1,A7$(X)
*    1620 LINE INPUT#1,A8$(X)
*    1630 INPUT#1,A9(X)
*    1640 LINE INPUT#1,B1$(X)
*    1650 INPUT#1,B2(X)
*    1660 LINE INPUT#1,B3$(X)
*    1670 LINE INPUT#1,B4$(X)
*    1680 LINE INPUT#1,B5$(X)
*    1690 INPUT#1,B6(X)
*    1700 LINE INPUT#1,B7$(X)
*    1710 LINE INPUT#1,B8$(X)
*    1720 INPUT#1,B9(X)
*    1730 INPUT#1,V(X)
*    1740 INPUT#1,C1(X)
     1750 GOTO 1530
     1760 REM *** THIS SECTION WRITES OUT A FILE ***
*    1770 OPEN"O",1,AA$
     1780 FOR Z=1 TO X
*    1790 PRINT#1,A1$(Z)
*    1800 PRINT#1,A2$(Z)
*    1810 PRINT#1,A3$
*    1820 PRINT#1,A4$(Z)
*    1830 PRINT#1,A5$(Z)
*    1840 PRINT#1,A6(Z)
```

```
*      1850 PRINT#1,A7$(Z)
*      1860 PRINT#1,A8$(Z)
*      1870 PRINT#1,A9(Z)
*      1880 PRINT#1,B1$(Z)
*      1890 PRINT#1,B2(Z)
*      1900 PRINT#1,B3$(Z)
*      1910 PRINT#1,B4$(Z)
.      1920 PRINT#1,B5$(Z)
*      1930 PRINT#1,B6(Z)
*      1940 PRINT#1,B7$(Z)
*      1950 PRINT#1,B8$(Z)
*      1960 PRINT#1,B9(Z)
*      1970 PRINT#1,V(Z)
*      1980 PRINT#1,C1(Z)
       1990 NEXT Z
*      2000 CLOSE:RETURN


       1000 REM ***    STUDENT RECORD PRINTING PROGRAM      ***
*      1010 CLEAR 8000
*      1020 X=150:DEFINT C,V
       1030 DIM A1$(X), A2$(X), A4$(X), A5$(X), A6(X), A7$(X),
            A8$(X) ,A9(X), B1$(X), B2(X) ,B3$(X), B4$(X), B5$(X),
            B6(X), B7$(X), B8$(X), B9(X), C1(X), V(X)
*      1040 CLS:X=0
       1050 PRINT"WE ARE GOING TO PRINT OUT RECORDS NOW. IF THAT
            IS "
       1060 M$="":PRINT"O.K. PRESS THE ENTER KEY.  IF NOT THEN
            TYPE NO AND PRESS ENTER":LINE INPUTM$:IF LEFT$(M$,1)
            = "N" THEN END
       1070 PRINT"NOW I NEED THE STUDENT'S CLASS ROOM NUMBER.
            PLEASE CALL IT"
       1080 LINE INPUT"240 OR 452 OR 134 OR 022 ETC; ONLY
            NUMBERS !!!";A3$
       1090 M$=LEFT$(A3$,1):IF ASC(M$)<48 OR ASC(M$)>57 THEN
            PRINT"SORRY BUT ";A3$;" IS NOT ACCEPTABLE":GOTO 1070
       1100 AA$="C"+A3$+":1"
       1110 GOSUB 1150
       1120 PRINT"WOULD YOU LIKE TO PRINT ON THE (S)CREEN OR
            (P)APER OR (L)ABELS"
       1130 LINE INPUTM$:M$=LEFT$(M$,1):IF M$<>"S" AND M$<>"P"
            AND M$<>"L" THEN GOTO 1120
       1140 GOTO 1410
       1150 REM *** THIS SECTION READS IN A FILE ***
       1160 OPEN"I",1,AA$
       1170 X=0
*      1180 IF EOF(1) THEN CLOSE:RETURN
       1190 X=X+1
*      1200 LINE INPUT#1,A1$(X)
*      1210 LINE INPUT#1,A2$(X)
*      1220 LINE INPUT#1,A3$
*      1230 LINE INPUT#1,A4$(X)
*      1240 LINE INPUT#1,A5$(X)
*      1250 INPUT#1,A6(X)
*      1260 LINE INPUT#1,A7$(X)
*      1270 LINE INPUT#1,A8$(X)
*      1280 INPUT#1,A9(X)
*      1290 LINE INPUT#1,B1$(X)
*      1300 INPUT#1,B2(X)
```

```
*       1310 LINE INPUT#1,B3$(X)
*       1320 LINE INPUT#1,B4$(X)
*       1330 LINE INPUT#1,B5$(X)
*       1340 INPUT#1,B6(X)
*       1350 LINE INPUT#1,B7$(X)
*       1360 LINE INPUT#1,B8$(X)
*       1370 INPUT#1,B9(X)
*       1380 INPUT#1,V(X)
*       1390 INPUT#1,C1(X)
        1400 GOTO 1180
        1410 IF M$="S" THEN GOTO 1640
        1420 FOR Z=1 TO X
*       1430 IF M$="L" THEN LPRINTA2$(Z);" ";A1$(Z): LPRINTA4$(Z):
             LPRINTA5$(Z);" ";A6(Z): LPRINT: LPRINT: LPRINT:
             GOTO 1630
*       1440 LPRINT"STUDENT'S NAME - ";A1$(Z);"     ";A2$(Z)
*       1450 LPRINT"STREET ADDRESS - ";A4$(Z)
*       1460 LPRINT"CITY, STATE AND ZIP - ";A5$(Z);" ";A6(Z)
*       1470 LPRINT"HOME PHONE NUMBER - ";A7$(Z);"   ";
*       1480 LPRINT"PARENT'S NAME - ";B3$(Z);" "
*       1490 LPRINT"HOME CONTACT NUMBER - ";B4$(Z);"   ";
*       1500 LPRINT"CLASS - ";A3$
*       1510 LPRINT"OSIS NUMBER - ";A8$(Z);" ";
*       1520 LPRINT"NUMBER OF TIMES LATE - ";A9(Z)
*       1530 LPRINT"RECENT READING TEST DATE - ";B1$(Z);" ";
*       1540 LPRINT"RECENT READING TEST SCORE - ";B2(Z)
*       1550 LPRINT"RECENT MATH TEST DATE - ";B5$(Z)
*       1560 LPRINT"RECENT MATH TEST SCORE - ";B6(Z)
*       1570 LPRINT"PREVIOUS SCHOOL - ";B7$(Z)
*       1580 LPRINT"SPECIAL CODE NOW - ";B8$(Z)
*       1590 IF A<>6 THEN LPRINT"CONSECUTIVE ABSENCES - ";B9(Z)
*       1600 LPRINT"TOTAL ABSENCES TO DATE - ";V(Z)
*       1610 IF A<>6 THEN LPRINT"NUMBER OF TIMES HELD OVER - "
             ;C1(Z)
*       1620 LPRINT
*       1630 NEXT Z:CLS:CLOSE:GOTO 1050
        1640 FOR Z=1 TO X
        1650 PRINT"STUDENT'S NAME - ";A1$(Z);"     ";A2$(Z)
        1660 PRINT"STREET ADDRESS - ";A4$(Z)
        1670 PRINT"CITY, STATE AND ZIP - ";A5$(Z);" ";A6(Z)
        1680 PRINT"HOME PHONE NUMBER - ";A7$(Z);"   "
        1690 PRINT"PARENT'S NAME - ";B3$(Z);" "
        1700 PRINT"HOME CONTACT NUMBER - ";B4$(Z);"   ";
        1710 PRINT"CLASS - ";A3$
        1720 PRINT"OSIS NUMBER - ";A8$(Z);" ";
        1730 PRINT"NUMBER OF TIMES LATE - ";A9(Z)
        1740 PRINT"RECENT READING TEST DATE.- ";B1$(Z);" ";
        1750 PRINT"READING SCORE - ";B2(Z)
        1760 PRINT"RECENT MATH TEST DATE - ";B5$(Z);
        1770 PRINT" RECENT MATH SCORE - ";B6(Z)
        1780 PRINT"PREVIOUS SCHOOL - ";B7$(Z);
        1790 PRINT" SPECIAL CODE NOW - ";B8$(Z)
        1800 IF A<>6 THEN PRINT"CONSECUTIVE ABSENCES - ";B9(Z);
        1810 PRINT"TOTAL ABSENCES TO DATE - ";V(Z)
        1820 IF A<>6 THEN PRINT" NUMBER OF TIMES HELD OVER - "
             ;C1(Z)
*       1830 PRINT"PRESS ANY KEY AND ENTER TO SEE MORE"
        1840 INPUT AV$
*       1850 CLS
```

```
*    1860 NEXT Z:CLS:CLOSE:GOTO 1050


     1000 REM ***          STUDENT CLASS LIST PRINTING          ***
*    1010 CLEAR 8000
*    1020 X=150:DEFINT C,V
     1030 DIM A1$(X), A2$(X), A4$(X), A5$(X), A6(X), A7$(X),
          A8$(X), A9(X), B1$(X), B2(X), B3$(X), B4$(X), B5$(X),
          B6(X), B7$(X), B8$(X), B9(X), C1(X), V(X)
*    1040 CLS:X=0
     1050 PRINT"WE ARE GOING TO PRINT OUT A CLASS LIST NOW."
     1060 PRINT"IF THIS IS THE FUNCTION YOU DESIRE, PRESS THE"
     1070 PRINT"WHITE ENTER KEY.  IF IT IS NOT THEN TYPE THE
          WORD"
     1080 PRINT"NO FOLLOWED BY THE ENTER KEY"
     1090 B$="":INPUT B$
     1100 IF LEFT$(B$,1)="N" THEN END
     1110 PRINT"NOW I NEED THE STUDENT'S CLASS ROOM NUMBER.
          PLEASE CALL IT"
     1120 LINE INPUT"240 OR 452 OR 134 OR 022 ETC; ONLY
          NUMBERS !!!";A3$
     1130 M$=LEFT$(A3$,1):IF ASC(M$)<48 OR ASC(M$)>57 THEN
          PRINT"SORRY BUT ";A3$;" IS NOT ACCEPTABLE":GOTO 1110
     1140 AA$="C"+A3$+":1"
     1150 GOSUB 1320
     1160 PRINT"PRESS THE ENTER KEY WITHOUT DATA TO TERMINATE
          THIS OPERATION":A1$=""
     1170 PRINT"WOULD YOU LIKE A (1) READING LIST (2) MATH LIST
          OR "
     1180 INPUT"(3) ONLY A LIST OF NAMES";VV
     1190 IF VV<>1 AND VV<>2 AND VV<>3 THEN GOTO 1170
     1200 GOSUB 1320
*    1210 LPRINT"CLASS ";A3$
*    1220 LPRINT
     1230 FOR Y=1TOX
*    1240 IF PD=0 THEN LPRINT A1$(Y);" ";A2$(Y); ELSE LPRINT
          TAB(32)A1$(Y);" ";A2$(Y);
*    1250 IF VV=1 AND PD=0 THEN LPRINT TAB(25) B2(Y);
*    1260 IF VV=1 AND PD=1 THEN LPRINT TAB(57) B2(Y);
*    1270 IF VV=2 AND PD=0 THEN LPRINT TAB(25) B6(Y);
*    1280 IF VV=2 AND PD=1 THEN LPRINT TAB(57) B6(Y);
*    1290 PD=PD+1:IF PD=2 THEN PD=0:LPRINT
     1300 NEXT Y
*    1310 CLOSE:GOTO 1050
     1320 REM *** THIS SECTION READS IN A FILE ***
*    1330 OPEN"I",1,AA$
     1340 X=0
*    1350 IF EOF(1) THEN CLOSE:RETURN
     1360 X=X+1
*    1370 LINE INPUT#1,A1$(X)
*    1380 LINE INPUT#1,A2$(X)
*    1390 LINE INPUT#1,A3$
*    1400 LINE INPUT#1,A4$(X)
*    1410 LINE INPUT#1,A5$(X)
*    1420   INPUT#1,A6(X)
*    1430 LINE INPUT#1,A7$(X)
*    1440 LINE INPUT#1,A8$(X)
*    1450 INPUT#1,A9(X)
*    1460 LINE INPUT#1,B1$(X)
```

```
*       1470 INPUT#1,B2(X)
*       1480 LINE INPUT#1,B3$(X)
*       1490 LINE INPUT#1,B4$(X)
*       1500 LINE INPUT#1,B5$(X)
*       1510 INPUT#1,B6(X)
*       1520 LINE INPUT#1,B7$(X)
*       1530 LINE INPUT#1,B8$(X)
*       1540 INPUT#1,B9(X)
*       1550 INPUT#1,V(X)
*       1560 INPUT#1,C1(X)
        1570 GOTO 1350


        1000 REM ***       STUDENT FILE SEARCH PROGRAM       ***
*       1010 CLEAR 8000
*       1020 X=150:DEFINT C,V
        1030 DIM A1$(X), A2$(X), A4$(X), A5$(X), A6(X) ,A7$(X),
             A8$(X), A9(X), B1$(X), B2(X), B3$(X), B4$(X),
             B5$(X), B6(X), B7$(X), B8$(X), B9(X), C1(X), V(X),
             B9$(X)
*       1040 CLS:X=0
        1050 PRINT"WE ARE GOING TO SEARCH FOR RECORDS NOW. IF
             THAT"
        1060 PRINT"IS CORRECT THEN PRESS THE ENTER KEY. IF IT IS"
        1070 PRINT"NOT THEN TYPE NO FOLLOWED BY THE ENTER KEY"
        1080 S6=0:N$="":INPUT N$
        1090 IF LEFT:(N$,1)="N" THEN END
        1100 PRINT"NOW I NEED THE STUDENT'S CLASS ROOM NUMBER.
             PLEASE CALL IT"
        1110 LINE INPUT"240 OR 452 OR 134 OR 022 ETC; ONLY
             NUMBERS !!!";A3$
        1120 M$=LEFT$(A3$,1):IF ASC(M$)<48 OR ASC(M$)>57 THEN
             PRINT"SORRY BUT ";A3$;" IS NOT ACCEPTABLE":GOTO 1100
        1130 AA$="C"+A3$+":1"
        1140 GOSUB 1720
        1150 PRINT"YOU CAN SEARCH ACCORDING TO ANY OF THE
             FOLLOWING CRITERIA"
        1160 PRINT"SELECT ONE NOW"
        1170 PRINT"    1 - SEX"
        1180 PRINT"    2 - ETHNICITY"
        1190 PRINT"    3 - RECENT READING SCORE"
        1200 PRINT"    4 - RECENT MATH SCORE"
        1210 PRINT"    5 - OTHER CODE"
        1220 LINE INPUT SR$
*       1230 SR=VAL(SR$):IF SR<1 OR SR>6 THEN CLS:PRINTSR$;" IS
             NOT ALLOWED AS A CHOICE":GOTO 1160
        1240 IF SR=1 THEN PRINT"TELL ME THE SEX NOW (1
             LETTER)":INPUT Q$
        1250 IF SR=2 THEN PRINT"TELL ME THE ETHNICITY NOW (1
             LETTER)":INPUT Q$
        1260 IF SR=3 THEN PRINT"TELL ME THE READING SCORE YOU ARE
             LOOKING FOR":LINE INPUTQ$:PRINT"WOULD YOU LIKE THOSE
             (1) EQUAL TO (2) GREATER THAN OR (3) LESS":
             PRINT"THAN";Q$:LINE INPUT Q4$
        1270 IF SR=4 THEN PRINT"TELL ME THE MATH SCORE YOU ARE
             LOOKING FOR":LINE INPUTQ$:PRINT"WOULD YOU LIKE THOSE
             (1) EQUAL TO (2) CREATER THAN OR (3) LESS":
             PRINT"THAN " ;Q$:LINE INPUT Q4$
        1280 IF SR=5 THEN PRINT"TELL ME THE CODE YOU ARE LOOKING
```

```
          FOR ":LINE INPUT Q$:LINE INPUT"WHICH CHARACTER NUMBER
          IS IT (3, 4 OR 5)";Q4$
    1290  IF (SR=3 OR SR=4) AND Q4$<>"1" AND Q4$<>"2" AND
          Q4$<>"3" THEN PRINT"SORRY BUT THAT IS NOT AN
          ACCEPTABLE ANSWER":GOTO 1150
    1300  IF SR=5 AND Q4$<>"3"ANDQ4$<>"4"ANDQ4$<>"5" THEN PRINT
          "SORRY BUT ";Q4$;" IS NOT AN ACCEPTABLE CHOICE ":
          GOTO 1150
    1310  IF SR=6 THEN LINE INPUT"TELL ME THE LAST NAME NOW";
          Q1$:LINE INPUT"TELL ME THE FIRST NAME NOW";Q2$
    1320  L1=LEN(Q$):L2=LEN(Q1$):L3=LEN(Q2$)
    1330  FOR Z=1TOX
    1340  SW=0
    1350  IF SR=1 THEN IF Q$=LEFT$(B8$(Z),1) THEN SW=1:
          GOTO 1460
    1360  IF SR=2 THEN IF Q$=MID$(B8$(Z),2,1) THEN SW=1:
          GOTO 1460
    1370  IF SR=3 THEN IF Q4$="1" AND VAL(Q$)=B2(Z) THEN
          SW=1:GOTO 1460
    1380  IF SR=3 THEN IF Q4$="2" AND VAL(Q$)<B2(Z) THEN
          SW=1:GOTO 1460
    1390  IF SR=3 THEN IF Q4$="3" AND VAL(Q$)>B2(Z) THEN
          SW=1:GOTO 1460
    1400  IF SR=4 THEN IF Q4$="1" AND VAL(Q$)=B6(Z) THEN
          SW=1:GOTO 1460
    1410  IF SR=4 THEN IF Q4$="2" AND VAL(Q$)<B6(Z) THEN
          SW=1:GOTO 1460
    1420  IF SR=4 THEN IF Q4$="3" AND VAL(Q$)>B6(Z) THEN
          SW=1:GOTO 1460
    1430  IF SR=5 THEN IF Q$=MID$(B8$(Z),VAL(Q4$),1) THEN
          SW=1:GOTO 1460
    1440  IF SR=6 THEN IF Q1$=LEFT$(A1$(Z),L2) AND
          Q2$=LEFT$(A2$(Z),L3) THEN SW=1:GOTO 1460
    1450  NEXT
    1460  IF SW=0 THEN PRINT "YOU HAVE SEEN ALL THAT MEET YOUR
          STATED CRITERIA. ":PRINT:GOTO 1150
    1470  IFS6=0 THEN PRINT"WOULD YOU LIKE TO PRINT ON THE
          (S)CREEN OR (P)APER OR (L)ABELS"
    1480  IF S6=0 THEN LINE INPUTM$:M$=LEFT$(M$,1):IF M$<>"S"
          AND M$<>"P" AND M$<>"L" THEN GOTO 1470
    1490  IF M$="S" THEN GOTO 1600
*   1500  S6=1:IF M$="L" THEN LPRINTA1$(Z);" ";A2$(Z):
          LPRINTA4$(Z): LPRINTA5$(Z);" "; A6(Z): LPRINT:
          LPRINT: GOTO 1590
*   1510  S6=1:LPRINT"STUDENT'S NAME - ";A1$(Z);"      ";A2$(Z)
*   1520  LPRINT"STREET ADDRESS - ";A4$(Z)
*   1530  LPRINT"CITY, STATE AND ZIP - ";A5$(Z);" ";A6(Z)
*   1540  LPRINT"HOME PHONE NUMBER - ";A7$(Z)
*   1550  LPRINT"PARENT'S NAME - ";B3$(Z);" ";
*   1560  LPRINT"HOME CONTACT NUMBER - ";B4$(Z)
*   1570  LPRINT"CLASS NUMBER -    ";A3$
*   1580  LPRINT"OSIS NUMBER - ";A8$(Z);" ";
*   1590  LPRINT" ":IF Z<X THEN GOTO 1450 ELSE CLS:GOTO 1150
    1600  S6=1:PRINT"STUDENT'S NAME - ";A1$(Z);"      ";A2$(Z)
    1610  PRINT"STREET ADDRESS - ";A4$(Z)
    1620  PRINT"CITY, STATE AND ZIP - ";A5$(Z);" ";A6(Z)
    1630  PRINT"HOME PHONE NUMBER - ";A7$(Z)
    1640  PRINT"PARENT'S NAME - ";B3$(Z);" ";
    1650  PRINT"HOME CONTACT NUMBER - ";B4$(Z)
```

```
      1660 PRINT"CLASS - ";A3$
      1670 PRINT"OSIS NUMBER - ";A8$(Z);" ";
*     1680 PRINT"PRESS ANY KEY AND ENTER TO SEE MORE"
      1690 INPUT AV$
*     1700 CLS
*     1710 PRINT:IF Z<X THEN GOTO 1450 ELSE CLS:GOTO 1150
      1720 REM *** THIS SECTION READS IN A FILE ***
*     1730 OPEN"I",1,AA$
      1740 X=0
*     1750 IF EOF(1) THEN CLOSE:RETURN
      1760 X=X+1
*     1770 LINE INPUT#1,A1$(X)
*     1780 LINE INPUT#1,A2$(X)
*     1790 LINE INPUT#1,A3$
*     1800 LINE INPUT#1,A4$(X)
*     1810 LINE INPUT#1,A5$(X)
*     1820 INPUT#1,A6(X)
*     1830 LINE INPUT#1,A7$(X)
*     1840 LINE INPUT#1,A8$(X)
*     1850 INPUT#1,A9(X)
*     1860 LINE INPUT#1,B1$(X)
*     1870 INPUT#1,B2(X)
*     1880 LINE INPUT#1,B3$(X)
*     1890 LINE INPUT#1,B4$(X)
*     1900 LINE INPUT#1,B5$(X)
*     1910 INPUT#1,B6(X)
*     1920 LINE INPUT#1,B7$(X)
*     1930 LINE INPUT#1,B8$(X)
*     1940 INPUT#1,B9(X)
*     1950 INPUT#1,V(X)
*     1960 INPUT#1,C1(X)
      1970 GOTO 1750


      1000 REM ***          STUDENT DELETION PROGRAM              ***
*     1010 CLEAR 8000
*     1020 X=150:DEFINT C,V
      1030 DIM A1$(X), A2$(X), A4$(X), A5$(X), A6(X), A7$(X),
           A8$(X), A9(X), B1$(X), B2(X), B3$(X), B4$(X), B5$(X),
           B6(X), B7$(X), B8$(X), B9(X), C1(X), V(X)
*     1040 CLS:X=0
      1050 PRINT"WE ARE GOING TO DELETE RECORDS NOW. IF THAT"
      1060 PRINT"IS CORRECT THEN PRESS THE ENTER KEY. IF IT IS"
      1070 PRINT"NOT THEN TYPE NO FOLLOWED BY THE ENTER KEY"
      1080 N$="":LINE INPUT N$
      1090 IF LEFT$(N$,1)="N" THEN END
      1100 PRINT"NOW I NEED THE STUDENT'S CLASS ROOM NUMBER.
           PLEASE CALL IT"
      1110 LINE INPUT"240 OR 452 OR 134 OR 022 ETC; ONLY
           NUMBERS !!!";A3$
      1120 M$=LEFT$(A3$,1):IF ASC(M$)<48 OR ASC(M$)>57 THEN
           PRINT"SORRY BUT ";A3$;" IS NOT ACCEPTABLE":GOTO 1100
      1130 AA$="C"+A3$+":1"
      1140 GOSUB 1280
      1150 PRINT"TELL ME THE LAST NAME OF THE STUDENT"
      1160 LINE INPUT Z1$:L1=LEN(Z1$)
      1170 LINE INPUT"TELL ME THE STUDENT'S FIRST NAME"; Z2$:
           L2=LEN(Z2$)
      1180 FOR Z=1TOX
```

```
      1190 SW=0
      1200 IF Z1$=LEFT$(A1$(Z),L1) AND Z2$=LEFT$(A2$(Z),L2) THEN
           SW=1:GOTO 1220
      1210 NEXT
      1220 IF SW=0 THEN PRINT"SORRY BUT THERE IS NO STUDENT IN
           MY FILE WITH":PRINT"A LAST NAME OF ";Z1$;" AND A
           FIRST NAME OF ";Z2$:PRINT"TRY AGAIN":GOTO 1150
      1230 FOR V=Z TO X-1
      1240 A1$(V)=A1$(V+1): A2$(V)=A2$(V+1): A4$(V)=A4$(V+1):
           A5$(V)=A5$(V+1): A6(V)=A6(V+1): A7$(V)=A7$(V+1):
           A8$(V)=A8$(V+1): A9(V)=A9(V+1)
      1250 B1$(V)=B1$(V+1): B2(V)=B2(V+1): B3$(V)=B3$(V+1):
           B4$(V)=B4$(V+1): B5$(V)=B5$(V+1): B6(V)=B6(V+1):
           B7$(V)=B7$(V+1): B8$(V)=B8$(V+1): B9(V)=B9(V+1):
           C1(V)=C1(V+1): V(V)=V(V+1)
      1260 NEXT V:X=X-1
*     1270 CLS:GOSUB 1540:GOTO 1040
      1280 REM *** THIS SECTION READS IN A FILE ***
*     1290 OPEN"I",1,AA$
      1300 X=0
*     1310 IF EOF(1) THEN CLOSE:RETURN
      1320 X=X+1
*     1330 LINE INPUT#1,A1$(X)
*     1340 LINE INPUT#1,A2$(X)
*     1350 LINE INPUT#1,A3$
*     1360 LINE INPUT#1,A4$(X)
*     1370 LINE INPUT#1,A5$(X)
*     1380 INPUT#1,A6(X)
*     1390 LINE INPUT#1,A7$(X)
*     1400 LINE INPUT#1,A8$(X)
*     1410 INPUT#1,A9(X)
*     1420 LINE INPUT#1,B1$(X)
*     1430 INPUT#1,B2(X)
*     1440 LINE INPUT#1,B3$(X)
*     1450 LINE INPUT#1,B4$(X)
*     1460 LINE INPUT#1,B5$(X)
*     1470 INPUT#1,B6(X)
*     1480 LINE INPUT#1,B7$(X)
*     1490 LINE INPUT#1,B8$(X)
*     1500 INPUT#1,B9(X)
*     1510 INPUT#1,V(X)
*     1520 INPUT#1,C1(X)
      1530 GOTO 1310
      1540 REM *** THIS SECTION WRITES OUT A FILE ***
*     1550 OPEN"O",1,AA$
      1560 FOR Z=1 TO X
*     1570 PRINT#1,A1$(Z)
*     1580 PRINT#1,A2$(Z)
*     1590 PRINT#1,A3$
*     1600 PRINT#1,A4$(Z)
*     1610 PRINT#1,A5$(Z)
*     1620 PRINT#1,A6(Z)
*     1630 PRINT#1,A7$(Z)
*     1640 PRINT#1,A8$(Z)
*     1650 PRINT#1,A9(Z)
*     1660 PRINT#1,B1$(Z)
*     1670 PRINT#1,B2(Z)
*     1680 PRINT#1,B3$(Z)
*     1690 PRINT#1,B4$(Z)
```

```
*    1700 PRINT#1,B5$(Z)
*    1710 PRINT#1,B6(Z)
*    1720 PRINT#1,B7$(Z)
*    1730 PRINT#1,B8$(Z)
*    1740 PRINT#1,B9(Z)
*    1750 PRINT#1,V(Z)
*    1760 PRINT#1,C1(Z)
     1770 NEXT Z
*    1780 CLOSE:RETURN


     1000 REM *** STUDENT RECORDS - ATTENDANCE FUNCTIONS ***
*    1010 CLEAR 8000
*    1020 X=150:DEFINT C,V
     1030 DIM A1$(X), A2$(X), A4$(X), A5$(X), A6(X), A7$(X),
          A8$(X), A9(X), B1$(X), B2(X), B3$(X), B4$(X), B5$(X),
          B6(X), B7$(X), B8$(X), B9(X), C1(X), V(X)
*    1040 CLS:X=0
     1050 PRINT"THIS IS THE ATTENDANCE FUNCTION.  IF THIS IS
          WHAT YOU"
     1060 PRINT"WERE LOOKING FOR THEN PRESS THE ENTER KEY NOW.
          IF NOT THEN"
     1070 PRINT"TYPE  NO  AND PRESS THE ENTER KEY."
     1080 INPUT VV$
*    1090 IF LEFT$(VV$,1)="N" THEN CLOSE:END
     1100 PRINT"NOW I NEED THE STUDENT'S CLASS ROOM NUMBER.
          PLEASE CALL IT"
     1110 LINE INPUT"240 OR 452 OR 134 OR 022 ETC; ONLY
          NUMBERS !!!" ;A3$
     1120 M$=LEFT$(A3$,1):IF ASC(M$)<48 OR ASC(M$)>57 THEN
          PRINT"SORRY BUT ";A3$;" IS NOT ACCEPTABLE":GOTO 1100
     1130 AA$="C"+A3$+":1"
     1140 GOSUB 1350
     1150 PRINT"YOU HAVE ONLY THREE CHOICES NOW.  THESE ARE"
     1160 PRINT"  (1) MARKING ABSENCES OR LATENESSES"
     1170 PRINT"  (2) PRINTING OUT POST CARDS"
     1180 PRINT"  (3) PRINTING OUT A DAILY ABSENCE LIST"
     1190 INPUT VV$
     1200 IF VV$="" THEN GOTO 1150
     1210 VV=VAL(VV$)
     1220 IF VV<1 OR VV>3 THEN PRINT"SORRY BUT ";VV$;" IS NOT
          ACCEPTABLE":GOTO 1150
     1230 FOR Z=1 TO X
     1240 PRINT"STUDENT ";A1$(Z);" ";A2$(Z)
     1250 IF VV=1 THEN INPUT"ENTER  P IF PRESENT,   A   IF
          ABSENT AND   L IF LATE ";VW$
     1260 IF VV=1 AND VW$="A" THEN B9(Z)=B9(Z)+1 :V(Z)=V(Z)+1
     1270 IF VV=1 AND VW$="P" THEN B9(Z)=0
     1280 IF VV=1 AND VW$="L" THEN A9(Z)=A9(Z)+1
*    1290 IF VV=2 AND B9(Z)>2 THEN LPRINT"TO THE PARENTS OF "
          ;A2$(Z);" ";A1$(Z);TAB(40);"YOUR CHILD HAS BEEN
          ABSENT":LPRINT A4$(Z);TAB(40);"A TOTAL OF ";B9(Z);
          " CONSECUTIVE DAYS.":LPRINTA5$(Z);" "; A6(Z);
          TAB(40); "WHICH TOTALS ";V(Z);" THIS YEAR,"
*    1300 IF VV=2 AND B9(Z)>2 THEN LPRINTTAB(40);"AND LATE
          ";A9(Z);" TIMES."
*    1310 IF VV=3 AND B9(Z)>0 THEN LPRINTA2$(Z);" ";A1$(Z);"
          CLASS ";A3$;"TOTAL TO DATE ";V(Z)
     1320 NEXT Z
```

```
      1330 GOSUB 1610
*     1340 CLOSE:GOTO 1040
      1350 REM *** THIS SECTION READS IN A FILE ***
      1360 OPEN"I",1,AA$
      1370 X=0
*     1380 IF EOF(1) THEN CLOSE:RETURN
      1390 X=X+1
*     1400 LINE INPUT#1,A1$(X)
*     1410 LINE INPUT#1,A2$(X)
*     1420 LINE INPUT#1,A3$
*     1430 LINE INPUT#1,A4$(X)
*     1440 LINE INPUT#1,A5$(X)
*     1450 INPUT#1,A6(X)
*     1460 LINE INPUT#1,A7$(X)
*     1470 LINE INPUT#1,A8$(X)
*     1480 INPUT#1,A9(X)
*     1490 LINE INPUT#1,B1$(X)
*     1500 INPUT#1,B2(X)
*     1510 LINE INPUT#1,B3$(X)
*     1520 LINE INPUT#1,B4$(X)
*     1530 LINE INPUT#1,B5$(X)
*     1540 INPUT#1,B6(X)
*     1550 LINE INPUT#1,B7$(X)
*     1560 LINE INPUT#1,B8$(X)
*     1570 INPUT#1,B9(X)
*     1580 INPUT#1,V(X)
*     1590 INPUT#1,C1(X)
      1600 GOTO 1380
      1610 REM *** THIS SECTION WRITES OUT A FILE ***
*     1620 OPEN"O",1,AA$
      1630 FOR Z=1 TO X
*     1640 PRINT#1,A1$(Z)
*     1650 PRINT#1,A2$(Z)
*     1660 PRINT#1,A3$
*     1670 PRINT#1,A4$(Z)
*     1680 PRINT#1,A5$(Z)
*     1690 PRINT#1,A6(Z)
*     1700 PRINT#1,A7$(Z)
*     1710 PRINT#1,A8$(Z)
*     1720 PRINT#1,A9(Z)
*     1730 PRINT#1,B1$(Z)
*     1740 PRINT#1,B2(Z)
*     1750 PRINT#1,B3$(Z)
*     1760 PRINT#1,B4$(Z)
*     1770 PRINT#1,B5$(Z)
*     1780 PRINT#1,B6(Z)
*     1790 PRINT#1,B7$(Z)
*     1800 PRINT#1,B8$(Z)
*     1810 PRINT#1,B9(Z)
*     1820 PRINT#1,V(Z)
*     1830 PRINT#1,C1(Z)
      1840 NEXT Z
*     1850 CLOSE:RETURN


      1000 REM *** MASS MODIFICATION OF STUDENT RECORDS  ***
*     1010 CLEAR 8000
*     1020 X=150:DEFINT C,V
      1030 DIM A1$(X), A2$(X), A4$(X), A5$(X), A6(X), A7$(X),
```

```
            A8$(X), A9(X), B1$(X), B2(X), B3$(X), B4$(X), B5$(X),
            B6(X), B7$(X), B8$(X), B9(X), C1(X), V(X)
*   1040 CLS:X=0
    1050 REM *** SPECIAL CHANGE FUNCTION ***
*   1060 CLS:PRINT"THE FUNCTION OF THIS SECTION OF THE PROGRAM
            IS THE UPDATING"
    1070 PRINT"OF THE READING OR MATH SCORES OF"
    1080 PRINT"A LARGE NUMBER OF STUDENTS.  FOR ANY OTHER
            UPDATING YOU MUST"
    1090 PRINT"SELECT THE OTHER MODIFY CHOICE (3) FROM THE
            MAIN MENU."
    1100 PRINT
    1110 PRINT"WE ARE GOING TO MASS MODIFY RECORDS NOW.  IF
            THAT"
    1120 PRINT"IS CORRECT THEN PRESS THE ENTER KEY.  IF IT IS"
    1130 PRINT"NOT THEN TYPE NO FOLLOWED BY THE ENTER KEY"
    1140 N$="":LINE INPUT N$
    1150 IF LEFT$(N$,1)="N" THEN END
    1160 PRINT"NOW I NEED THE STUDENT'S CLASS ROOM NUMBER.
            PLEASE CALL IT"
    1170 LINE INPUT"240 OR 452 OR 134 OR 022 ETC; ONLY
            NUMBERS !!!";A3$
    1180 M$=LEFT$(A3$,1):IF ASC(M$)<48 OR ASC(M$)>57 THEN
            PRINT"SORRY BUT ";A3$;" IS NOT ACCEPTABLE":GOTO 1160
    1190 AA$="C"+A3$+":1"
    1200 GOSUB 1410
    1210 CLS
    1220 PRINT"WOULD YOU LIKE TO MODIFY :"
    1230 PRINT"     (1) READING SCORES"
    1240 PRINT"     (2) MATH SCORES"
    1250 INPUT A$
    1260 IF A$="" THEN A$="0"
    1270 A5=VAL(A$)
    1280 CLS:IF A5<1 OR A5>2 THEN PRINTA$;" IS NOT
            ACCEPTABLE " :GOTO 1220
    1290 GOSUB 1420
    1300 IF A5=1 THEN INPUT"THE NEW READING DATE ";Q$
    1310 IF A5=2 THEN INPUT"THE NEW MATH DATE ";Q$
    1320 FOR Z=1TO X
    1330 PRINT"LAST NAME ";A1$(Z)
    1340 PRINT"FIRST NAME ";A2$(Z)
    1350 IF A5=1 THEN B1$(Z)=Q$:INPUT"NEW READING TEST SCORE "
            ;B2(Z)
    1360 IF A5=2 THEN B5$(Z)=Q$:INPUT"NEW MATH TEST SCORE "
            ;B6(Z)
    1370 PRINT
    1380 NEXT Z
    1390 GOSUB 1670
    1400 CLOSE:GOTO 1050
    1410 REM *** THIS SECTION READS IN A FILE ***
*   1420 OPEN"I",1,AA$
    1430 X=0
*   1440 IF EOF(1) THEN CLOSE:RETURN
    1450 X=X+1
*   1460 LINE INPUT#1,A1$(X)
*   1470 LINE INPUT#1,A2$(X)
*   1480 LINE INPUT#1,A3$
*   1490 LINE INPUT#1,A4$(X)
*   1500 LINE INPUT#1,A5$(X)
```

```
*       1510 INPUT#1,A6(X)
*       1520 LINE INPUT#1,A7$(X)
*       1530 LINE INPUT#1,A8$(X)
*       1540 INPUT#1,A9(X)
*       1550 LINE INPUT#1,B1$(X)
*       1560 INPUT#1,B2(X)
*       1570 LINE INPUT#1,B3$(X)
*       1580 LINE INPUT#1,B4$(X)
*       1590 LINE INPUT#1,B5$(X)
*       1600 INPUT#1,B6(X)
*       1610 LINE INPUT#1,B7$(X)
*       1620 LINE INPUT#1,B8$(X)
*       1630 INPUT#1,B9(X)
*       1640 INPUT#1,V(X)
*       1650 INPUT#1,C1(X)
        1660 GOTO 1440
        1670 REM *** THIS SECTION WRITES OUT A FILE ***
*       1680 OPEN"O",1,AA$
        1690 FOR Z=1 TO X
*       1700 PRINT#1,A1$(Z)
*       1710 PRINT#1,A2$(Z)
*       1720 PRINT#1,A3$
*       1730 PRINT#1,A4$(Z)
*       1740 PRINT#1,A5$(Z)
*       1750 PRINT#1,A6(Z)
*       1760 PRINT#1,A7$(Z)
*       1770 PRINT#1,A8$(Z)
*       1780 PRINT#1,A9(Z)
*       1790 PRINT#1,B1$(Z)
*       1800 PRINT#1,B2(Z)
*       1810 PRINT#1,B3$(Z)
*       1820 PRINT#1,B4$(Z)
*       1830 PRINT#1,B5$(Z)
*       1840 PRINT#1,B6(Z)
*       1850 PRINT#1,B7$(Z)
*       1860 PRINT#1,B8$(Z)
*       1870 PRINT#1,B9(Z)
*       1880 PRINT#1,V(Z)
*       1890 PRINT#1,C1(Z)
        1900 NEXT Z
*       1910 CLOSE:RETURN
```

Appendix F: Program Listings: Computer-Aided Instruction

The following seven CAI programs are described in chapter 9. They are examples of software made by teachers for use with their own students. These programs can serve as a model for the creation of other programs or can be modified easily to meet changing needs. For further information about their recommended use please refer to chapter 9 and appendix D.

S T A T E S

```
*     1000 CLEAR 1000
*     1010 CLS
      1020 PRINT"TODAY WE WILL PRACTICE STATE CAPITALS."
      1030 PRINT
      1040 PRINT"PLEASE TYPE IN YOUR NAME AND THEN PRESS THE "
      1050 PRINT"WHITE ENTER KEY."
      1060 INPUT A$
*     1070 CLS
      1080 PRINT"HELLO, ";A$;". I AM A FRIENDLY COMPUTER."
      1090 PRINT "TODAY, WE WILL PRACTICE NAMING CAPITAL CITIES"
      1100 PRINT "OF SOME OF THE STATES."
      1110 PRINT:PRINT"HOW MANY WOULD YOU LIKE TO WORK ON?
           PLEASE TYPE IN"
      1120 PRINT"YOUR ANSWER (A NUMBER BETWEEN 1 AND 10) AND
           THEN"
      1130 PRINT"PRESS THE ENTER KEY."
      1140 INPUT A
*     1150 CLS
      1160 IF A<1 OR A>10 THEN GOTO 1110
      1170 FOR Y=1 TO A
      1180 E=0
      1190 READ B$,C$
      1200 PRINT:PRINT"QUESTION #";Y:PRINT"WHAT IS THE CAPITAL
           OF ";B$;"?"
      1210 INPUT M$
*     1220 CLS
      1230 IF M$=C$ THEN PRINT"WELL DONE, ";A$;"!"
      1240 IF M$<>C$ AND LEFT$(C$,LEN(M$))=M$ THEN PRINT"YOU ARE
           ALMOST CORRECT ."：PRINT"THE CORRECT ANSWER IS "
           ;C$;".":PRINT
*     1250 IF M$<>C$ AND LEFT$(C$,LEN(M$))<>M$ THEN PRINT"YOU
           ARE NOT CORRECT. ":E=E+1:IF E<3 THEN PRINT"PLEASE TRY

           AGAIN. ":GOTO 1200
      1260 IF E=3 THEN PRINT"THE CORRECT ANSWER IS ";C$;"."
      1270 NEXT Y
      1280 PRINT "GOODBYE FOR NOW, ";A$;". I HOPE YOU ENJOYED
           YOURSELF."
*     1290 FOR Y=1TO2000:NEXT:CLS:GOTO1020
      1300 DATA "NEW YORK","ALBANY","NEW JERSEY", "TRENTON",
           "PENNSYLVANIA", "HARRISBURG", "CALIFORNIA",
           "SACRAMENTO", "COLORADO", "DENVER", "ALASKA",
           "JUNEAU", "MASSACHUSETTS", "BOSTON"
      1310 DATA "WASHINGTON", "OLYMPIA", "ILLINOIS",
           "SPRINGFIELD", "MARYLAND", "ANNAPOLIS"
```

A N T O N

```
*    1000 CLEAR 1000
*    1010 CLS
     1020 PRINT"TODAY WE WILL PRACTICE ANTONYMS."
     1030 PRINT
     1040 PRINT "PLEASE TYPE YOUR NAME AND THEN PRESS THE ENTER
          KEY."
     1050 INPUT A$
*    1060 CLS
     1070 PRINT "HELLO, ";A$;", I AM A FRIENDLY COMPUTER."
     1080 PRINT "TODAY I WILL HELP YOU TO PRACTICE ANTONYMS."
     1090 PRINT:PRINT"HOW MANY WOULD YOU LIKE TO WORK ON?
          PLEASE TYPE IN"
     1100 PRINT "YOUR ANSWER (A NUMBER BETWEEN 1 AND 10) AND
          THEN"
     1110 PRINT "PRESS THE ENTER KEY."
     1120 INPUT A
*    1130 CLS
     1140 IF A<1 OR A>10 THEN GOTO 1090
     1150 FOR Y=1 TO A
     1160 E=0
     1170 READ B$,C$
     1180 PRINT:PRINT"QUESTION #";Y:PRINT"WHAT IS THE ANTONYM
          OF ";B$;"?"
     1190 INPUT M$
*    1200 CLS
     1210 IF M$=C$ THEN PRINT "WELL DONE, ";A$;"!"
     1220 IF M$<>C$ AND LEFT$(C$,LEN(M$))=M$ THEN PRINT"YOU ARE
          ALMOST CORRECT .":PRINT"THE CORRECT ANSWER IS ";C$
          ;".":PRINT
     1230 IF M$<>C$ AND LEFT$(C$,LEN(M$))<>M$ THEN PRINT"YOU
          ARE NOT CORRECT. ":E=E+1:IF E<3 THEN PRINT"PLEASE TRY
          AGAIN. ":GOTO 1180
     1240 IF E=3 THEN PRINT"THE CORRECT ANSWER IS ";C$;"."
     1250 NEXT Y
     1260 PRINT "GOODBYE FOR NOW, ";A$;"."
*    1270 FOR Y=1TO2000:NEXT:CLS:GOTO1020
     1280 DATA "HELLO", "GOODBYE", "COLD", "HOT", "TALL",
          "SHORT", "UP", "DOWN"
     1290 DATA "BIG", "LITTLE", "DAY", "NIGHT", "DIRTY",
          "CLEAN", "LARGE", "SMALL", "GOOD", "BAD", "HATE",
          "LOVE"
```

S P E L L

```
*    1000 CLEAR 1000
*    1010 CLS
     1020 PRINT"TODAY WE WILL PRACTICE SPELLING."
     1030 PRINT
     1040 PRINT "PLEASE TYPE YOUR NAME AND THEN PRESS THE ENTER
          KEY."
     1050 INPUT A$
*    1060 CLS
     1070 PRINT "HELLO, ";A$;", I AM A FRIENDLY COMPUTER."
     1080 PRINT
     1090 PRINT "HOW MANY SPELLING WORDS WOULD YOU LIKE TO
          PRACTICE? PLEASE TYPE"
     1100 PRINT"IN YOUR ANSWER (A NUMBER BETWEEN 1 AND 10)
          FOLLOWED BY "
```

```
      1110 PRINT"PRESSING THE ENTER KEY."
      1120 INPUT A
*     1130 CLS
      1140 IF A<1 OR A>10 THEN GOTO 1090
      1150 FOR Y=1 TO A
      1160 E=0
      1170 READ B$,C$,D$
      1180 PRINT:PRINT"QUESTION #";Y:PRINT"WHICH OF THE
           FOLLOWING IS CORRECTLY SPELLED ?":PRINTB$
           ;"    OR    ";D$
      1190 INPUT M$
*     1200 CLS
      1210 IF M$=C$ THEN PRINT"WELL DONE ";A$;"!"
*     1220 IF M$<>C$ AND LEFT$(C$,LEN(M$))=M$ THEN PRINT"YOU ARE
           ALMOST CORRECT .":PRINT"THE CORRECT ANSWER IS "
           ;C$;".":PRINT
*     1230 IF M$<>C$ AND LEFT$(C$,LEN(M$))<>M$ THEN PRINT"YOU
           ARE NOT CORRECT. ":E=E+1:IF E<3 THEN PRINT"PLEASE TRY
           AGAIN. ":GOTO 1180
      1240 IF E=3 THEN PRINT"THE CORRECT ANSWER IS ";C$;"."
      1250 NEXT Y
      1260 PRINT"GOODBYE FOR NOW. ";A$
*     1270 FOR Y=1TO2000:NEXT:CLS:GOTO1020
      1280 DATA "HELLO", "HELLO", "HELO", "BIENG", "BEING",
           "BEING", "FOOD", "FOOD", "FUDE", "TRILE", "TRIAL",
           "TRIAL", "CASE", "CASE", "CAIS", "MOTHE", "MOUTH",
           "MOUTH"
      1290 DATA "BLACK", "BLACK", "BLAK", "WITE", "WHITE",
           "WHITE", "SMAL", "SMALL", "SMALL", "TOOTH", "TOOTH",
           "TUTH"


                          S U M

*     1000 CLEAR 1000
*     1010 CLS
      1020 PRINT"TODAY WE WILL PRACTICE ADDITION."
      1030 PRINT
      1040 PRINT"PLEASE TYPE IN YOUR NAME AND THEN PRESS THE "
      1050 PRINT"WHITE ENTER KEY."
      1060 INPUT A$
*     1070 CLS
      1080 PRINT"HELLO, ";A$;", I AM A FRIENDLY COMPUTER."
      1090 PRINT "TODAY WE WILL PRACTICE ADDITION."
      1100 PRINT:PRINT"HOW MANY EXAMPLES WOULD YOU LIKE TO WORK
           ON?  PLEASE TYPE IN"
      1110 PRINT"YOUR ANSWER (A NUMBER BETWEEN 1 AND 10) AND
           THEN"
      1120 PRINT"PRESS THE ENTER KEY."
      1130 INPUT A
*     1140 CLS
      1150 IF A<1 OR A>10 THEN GOTO 1100
      1160 FOR Y=1 TO A
      1170 E=0
      1180 READ B$,C$
      1190 PRINT:PRINT"QUESTION #";Y:PRINT"WHAT IS THE SUM OF "
           ;B$;"?"
      1200 INPUT M$
      1210 IF M$=C$ THEN PRINT "WELL DONE, ";A$;"!":FOR P=1 TO
           700:NEXT P
```

```
     1220 IF M$<>C$  THEN PRINT"YOU ARE NOT CORRECT. ":E=E+1:IF
          E<3 THEN PRINT"PLEASE TRY AGAIN. ":GOTO 1190
     1230 IF E=3 THEN PRINT"THE CORRECT ANSWER IS ";C$;"."
     1240 FOR P=1 TO 700:NEXT P
*    1250 CLS
     1260 NEXT Y
     1270 PRINT "GOODBYE FOR NOW, ";A$;"."
*    1280 FOR Y=1TO2000:NEXT:CLS:GOTO1020
     1290 DATA "2 AND 3","5","3 AND 1","4","2 AND 2","4","3 AND
          5" , "8", "4 AND 3", "7", "5 AND 7", "12", "7 AND 6",
          "13", "8 AND 7","15","9 AND 8","17"
     1300 DATA "9 AND 9","18"
```

C H A N G E

```
*    1000 CLEAR 1000
*    1010 CLS
     1020 PRINT "TODAY WE WILL PRACTICE MAKING CHANGE."
     1030 PRINT
     1040 PRINT"PLEASE TYPE IN YOUR NAME AND THEN PRESS THE "
     1050 PRINT "ENTER KEY."
     1060 INPUT A$
*    1070 CLS
     1080 PRINT "HELLO, ";A$;", I AM A FRIENDLY COMPUTER."
     1090 PRINT "LET'S PRACTICE MAKING CHANGE."
     1100 PRINT:PRINT"HOW MANY EXAMPLES WOULD YOU LIKE TO WORK
          ON?  PLEASE TYPE IN"
     1110 PRINT"YOUR ANSWER (A NUMBER BETWEEN 1 AND 10) AND
          THEN"
     1120 PRINT"PRESS THE ENTER KEY."
     1130 INPUT A
*    1140 CLS
     1150 IF A<1 OR A>10 THEN GOTO 1100
     1160 PRINT "TYPE EACH ANSWER USING A DECIMAL POINT. OMIT
          THE $."
     1170 FOR Y=1 TO A
     1180 E=0
     1190 READ B$,C$
     1200 PRINT:PRINT"QUESTION #";Y:PRINT"HOW MUCH CHANGE WOULD
          YOU RECEIVE"
     1210 PRINT"IF YOU HAD A $10.00 BILL AND PURCHASED"
     1220 PRINT"GROCERIES FOR $";B$;"?"
     1230 INPUT M$
*    1240 CLS
     1250 IF M$=C$ THEN PRINT "WELL DONE. ";A$;"!"
     1260 IF M$<>C$   THEN PRINT"YOU ARE NOT CORRECT. ":E=E+1:IF
          E<3 THEN PRINT"PLEASE TRY AGAIN. ":GOTO 1200
     1270 IF E=3 THEN PRINT "THE CORRECT ANSWER IS $";C$;"."
     1280 NEXT Y
     1290 PRINT"GOODBYE FOR NOW. ";A$
*    1300 FOR Y=1TO2000:NEXT:CLS:GOTO1020
     1310 DATA "9.50", ".50", "2.80", "7.20", "3.60", "6.40",
          "9.99", ".01", "7.77", "2.23", ".12", "9.88", "5.55",
          "4.45", "1.25", "8.75"
     1320 DATA "9.01", ".99", "6.12", "3.88"
```

T E M P

```
*    1000 CLEAR 1000
*    1010 CLS
     1020 PRINT"TODAY WE WILL PRACTICE READING A THERMOMETER."
```

```
      1030 PRINT
      1040 PRINT"TYPE YOUR NAME AND THEN PRESS THE ENTER KEY."
      1050 INPUT A$
  *   1060 CLS
      1070 PRINT "HELLO, ";A$;", I AM A FRIENDLY COMPUTER."
      1080 E=0
      1090 PRINT
      1100 PRINT"THIS IS A THERMOMETER."
      1110 PRINT "WHAT IS THE NUMBER OF DEGREES AT POINT A?"
      1120 PRINT
      1130 PRINT"              A    B    C         D"
      1140 PRINT"***I****I****I****I****I****I****I****
           I****I***"
      1150 PRINT"   20   30   40   50   60   70   80   90   100"
      1160 PRINT
      1170 PRINT"1) 40"
      1180 PRINT"2) 45"
      1190 PRINT"3) 50"
      1200 PRINT
      1210 PRINT "TYPE EITHER 1, 2, OR 3."
      1220 PRINT"FOLLOWED BY THE ENTER KEY."
      1230 INPUT A
  *   1240 IF A<>1 AND A<>2 AND A<>3 CLS:GOTO 1120
      1250 C=3
  *   1260 CLS
      1270 IF A=C THEN PRINT"WELL DONE, ";A$;"!"
      1280 IF A<>C THEN PRINT"YOU ARE NOT CORRECT. ":E=E+1:IF
           E<3 THEN PRINT"PLEASE TRY AGAIN. ":GOTO 1120
      1290 IF E=3 THEN PRINT"THE CORRECT ANSWER IS ";C;"."
      1300 PRINT"GOODBYE FOR NOW. ";A$
  *   1310 FOR Y=1TO2000:NEXT:CLS:GOTO1020


                      M A I N  I D E A

  *   1000 CLEAR 1000
  *   1010 CLS
      1020 PRINT "TODAY WE WILL PRACTICE FINDING THE SENTENCE"
      1030 PRINT "THAT EXPRESSES THE MAIN IDEA OF A PARAGRAPH."
      1040 PRINT
      1050 PRINT "PLEASE TYPE YOUR NAME AND THEN PRESS"
      1060 PRINT "THE ENTER KEY.":INPUT A$
  *   1070 CLS
      1080 PRINT "HELLO, ";A$;", I AM A FRIENDLY COMPUTER."
      1090 PRINT"READ THE PARAGRAPH THAT WILL APPEAR ON THE
           SCREEN."
      1100 PRINT"AS YOU READ, FIND THE SENTENCE THAT EXPRESSES
           THE"
      1110 PRINT"MAIN IDEA OF THE PARAGRAPH."
  *   1120 FOR P=1 TO 2000:NEXT P:CLS
      1130 E=0
      1140 PRINT "THANKSGIVING DAY DINNER AT GRANDMOTHER'S HOUSE
           WAS FUN."
      1150 PRINT "WE ATE TURKEY, SWEET POTATOES, AND CRANBERRY
           SAUCE."
      1160 PRINT "FOR DESSERT, WE HAD PUMPKIN PIE.  I WATCHED"
      1170 PRINT "THE FOOTBALL GAME ON TELEVISION WITH MY
           COUSIN."
      1180 PRINT "THEN MY UNCLE TOOK US OUT FOR ICE CREAM
           CONES."
      1190 PRINT
```

```
1200 PRINT "WHICH IS THE SENTENCE THAT EXPRESSES THE MAIN
     IDEA"
1210 PRINT "OF THIS PARAGRAPH?"
1220 PRINT
1230 PRINT"1) THANKSGIVING DAY DINNER AT GRANDMOTHER'S
     HOUSE WAS FUN."
1240 PRINT"2) WE ATE TURKEY, SWEET POTATOES, AND CRANBERRY
     SAUCE."
1250 PRINT"3) THEN MY UNCLE TOOK US OUT FOR ICE CREAM."
1260 PRINT
1270 PRINT"TYPE EITHER 1, 2, OR  3.
1280 PRINT"FOLLOWED BY THE ENTER KEY."
1290 INPUT A: FOR P=1 TO 500:NEXT P
1300 IF A<>1 AND A<>2 AND A<>3 THEN GOTO 1270
1310 C=1
1320 CLS
1330 IF A=C THEN PRINT"WELL DONE ";A$;"!"
1340 IF A<>C THEN PRINT"YOU ARE NOT CORRECT. ":E=E+1:IF
     E<3 THEN PRINT"PLEASE TRY AGAIN. ":GOTO 1190
1350 IF E=3 THEN PRINT"THE CORRECT ANSWER IS ";C;"."
1360 PRINT"GOODBYE FOR NOW. ";A$
1370 FOR Y=1TO2000:NEXT:CLS:GOTO1020
```

Appendix G: Glossary

Each career area makes use of a specialized vocabulary. This is the case in the fields of medicine, law, education, entertainment, athletics, and government. It is also the case in the field of computers.

Of necessity, computer specialists have developed a unique vocabulary to facilitate communication. Although it is unnecessary for school administrators and supervisors to be cognizant of every term used by those involved with computers, it is important that they become familiar with those expressions used most frequently. It is uncomfortable, to say the least, when colleagues converse casually in terms that are totally unfamiliar to their supervisors. There is the feeling of being at a disadvantage, particularly when having to make decisions. When one party to a conversation uses terminology that is foreign to the other, communication suffers. A lack of fluency with computer language has the effect of inhibiting the supervisor and eroding the supervisory function. When there is some understanding of the computer language being spoken, there is a much greater sense of security and self-assuredness and a meaningful exchange of ideas may result.

Although we have been careful to provide clear definitions of specialized terms at the time they were introduced in the text, real understanding is not always internalized and when subsequently used out of context, lapses in recall often occur. The following is intended as a concise glossary of computer terms and key words used in programming via the language of BASIC. This glossary may prove helpful in those situations when a quick reference is needed.

Array A collection of variables each of which is identified with the same variable name but having different subscripts. For example, L(1) and L(2) are both variables that are identified as L, but they are different variables and hold different values.

Binary numbers Numbers written in a number system based on the number, 2, rather than on the customary base, 10. Therefore, digits are arranged in a sequence in which those digits to the left are twice the value of those to the right. Binary-numbers place values are sequenced 1, 2, 4, 8, 16, 32, and so on. Digits in the more familiar decimal system are arranged in the sequence 1, 10, 100, 1000, 10,000, and so on. The use of binary numbers permits each number to be written with two symbols, 0 and 1, rather than the more familiar arrangement of ten symbols 0, 1, 2, 3, 4, 5, 6, 7, 8, and 9. The use of binary numbers permits each keyboard character to be adapted to an electronic code based on electronic impulses (ASCII—American Standard Code for Information Interchange). This code serves as the underlying mechanism by which it is possible to program computers. The computer's understanding of the binary system enables it to manipulate data, alphabetic and numeric.

Bit   A single digit in the binary number system. Each number and alphabet character on the keyboard is coded in binary numbers. Each such coded digit is called a bit.

Bug   A defect in a computer program. The word, *bug*, usually connotes an "illegal" or incorrectly arranged statement or sequence of statements in a computer program. Bugs prevent the computer from carrying out the instructions the programmer intended when programming was performed originally. Debugging a program involves the process of locating and correcting the error or errors in the program.

Byte   Each number and alphabet character on the keyboard is configured with a series of wires that permits the transmission of data to the computer via electric signals based on a standardized code of digits. All such collections of digits are stored in a unit called a byte. For example, the byte representing the letter, A, appears as 1000001. The byte representing the letter, B, appears as 1000010. Any comprehensive manual on programming techniques generally offers a chart of the digit code used on all keyboard characters.

CAI   The abbreviation for the term, *computer-aided instruction*. This mode of instruction provides for utilization of the computer in drill-and-practice exercises. Chapter 9 offers comprehensive treatment of this approach to instruction.

CLS   The term, CLS, is a BASIC language statement used in programming that instructs the computer to clear its screen. Its use is analogous to the chalkboard eraser used in classrooms. On some computers, the term, HOME, is used to accomplish the same objective.

Compiler   A program used by a computer to convert languages such as BASIC into a machine language that the computer has been configured to understand. A compiler has the ability to convert an entire program instantaneously into a machine code that the user can either save or run.

Computer   A machine that is constructed of a collection of plastic, glass, silicon, and metal parts. There are primarily four essential parts to a computer, the central processing unit, input devices, output devices, and a memory with provision for either temporary or permanent storage (saving) of information.

CRT   The abbreviation for the term, *cathode-ray tube*, more familiarly known as the standard television-picture tube. Its screen is the most frequently used device for transmitting information from the computer to the user. CRT screens are sometimes known as *monitors*.

Cursor   A character that is visualized only on the computer screen. It permits the user to identify visually the precise location on the screen where information is to be displayed next. As characters of the keyboard are pressed and the characters are instantaneously displayed on the screen, the cursor moves along from character to character and pinpoints the spot where the very next character will be displayed.

Data   Information represented by numbers or words that the computer either retains or manipulates. Computer data may be the names and addresses of individuals or companies. Data may also take the form of specific instructions and programs. Any information that is entered into the computer is referred to as data.

DIM   The term, DIM, is a BASIC-language programming statement that instructs the computer to reserve a desired amount of space in its memory for array variables.

END   The term, END, is a BASIC-language programming statement that instructs the computer that it is to terminate the run of a program and wait for new instructions.

File   A collection of data that has been stored in the computer's memory and saved on external devices such as cassettes or diskettes.

FOR-NEXT   The term, FOR-NEXT, is an extremely powerful BASIC-language programming statement. In programming situations where it is desired that certain commands be repeated a number of times, the FOR-NEXT mechanism is extremely useful. The two words, FOR and NEXT, act as a kind of receptacle, analogous to the bread on a sandwich. When used, the commands that appear between the two words are caused to be repeated a predetermined number of times.

GOSUB   The term, GOSUB, is a BASIC-language programming statement that instructs the computer to break the normal flow of programming instructions and to reroute that flow to a designated place in the program. Once there, the computer performs a specific series of commands. When a RETURN statement is encountered, the computer returns to the designated portion of the program that immediately follows the GOSUB that sidetracked it initially. This is one technique for accomplishing a subroutine.

GOTO   The term, GOTO, is a BASIC-language programming statement that instructs the computer to reroute itself. In regular use, the computer executes commands in line number sequence. The GOTO statement instructs the machine to find a specific line other than the one in the regular sequence of the program and to execute the command on that line.

Graphics   Visual material produced by a computer that may be displayed on a computer screen, a plotting device, or on a printer. Examples of graphics are cartoon characters, pencil drawings, and typewriter characters that have been arranged into a design by the computer.

IF-THEN   The term, IF-THEN, is a BASIC-language programming statement that instructs the computer to evaluate a series of possible options.

The computer is programmed to execute a specific task only if the situation it finds satisfies the condition that has been predetermined by the programmer. The computer evaluates the situation and if the condition is satisfied, it then executes the command it has been given. If, however, the condition it finds is inconsistent with its specific instructions, the computer reroutes itself to the command that follows the IF-THEN statement.

INPUT   The term, INPUT, is a BASIC-language programming statement that instructs the computer to pause and wait for the user to supply information that is needed if the program is to run successfully. This programming mechanism permits the computer to visualize a question on the screen and then wait until the user has supplied an answer. The word also is used to describe a device (input device) that is used in a computer to allow machine users to put information into a computer (that is, keyboard, card reader, and so on).

INT   The term, INT, is a BASIC-language command used to instruct a computer to select only the integral portion (whole number) of a value and to discard the fractional portion.

I/O devices   The abbreviation for the term, *input-output devices*. Such devices are mechanical entities that are connected to the computer's central processing unit. They permit the user to transmit instructions to the computer and allow the computer to reciprocate by returning information to the user. In the same way that the keyboard is the most familiar type of input device, the CRT screen is the most recognized of output devices. Disk drives are able to perform both input and output functions; they permit the user to save data permanently and also serve as the mechanism for loading information that has been saved back into the computer's memory and then visualizing that information on the screen.

Integrated circuit chip   The integrated circuit chip is the heart of the computer. Chips are usually small mechanical devices approximately one inch in length, made of plastic, silicon, and metal, and have a series of electrical wires emanating from them that conduct electrical impulses. Each chip once had the capacity to store only four thousand bits in the early 1970s. Currently, technology permits each chip to hold in excess of a million facts. Microtechnology has permitted the reduction of the size of each chip while at the same time increasing the speed with which the chip is able to transmit information and its capacity.

Interface   A piece of equipment that permits the connection of two devices that are configured to manage data in different ways. The interface acts as a kind of translator that allows such devices to communicate with each other. For example, devices such as the CPU are designed with high transmission rates and can therefore receive and send information rapidly, whereas other devices such as printers, by comparison, can transmit information much more slowly. The interface allows for an exchange of information between the two devices by taking in data at one speed and permitting the data that the computer has manipulated to be sent out at another speed.

Interpreter   An interpreter is similar to a compiler in that it is a program that translates computer languages such as BASIC into an electronic code that the machine has been designed to understand. Interpreters, however, are slower than compilers. Individual instructions to the computer must be translated every time an interpreter is used. Interpreters, however, can usually operate with considerably less memory capacity than can compilers.

Iteration   Iteration refers to the mechanism of counting. When a machine is programmed to count steps in an operation, iteration occurs each time the function is executed.

K   The symbol, K, stands approximately for *thousands*. Therefore, a computer having a designation such as 48K has the capacity to hold approximately 48,000 keyboard characters in memory at any one time. More accurately, 1K actually represents a memory capacity of 1,024 characters but the figure 1,000 is accepted for convenience.

**LEFT$**   The term, LEFT$ (pronounced *left string*), is a BASIC-language instruction that requires a computer to accept only the leftmost portion of a string and to use it for a predetermined programming purpose. It is used as a mechanism for examining either the first letter or first few letters of a word or expression that have been stored in the computer's memory.

LEN   The term, LEN, is a BASIC-language expression that enables the computer to examine the length and identify the number of characters in a string. For example, if A$ is "goodbye," then LEN(A$) is 7.

LIST   The term, LIST, is a BASIC-language programming command to the computer to display the statements in a computer program on the CRT screen.

Machine language   The language computers use to perform operations internally. Machine language is configured to utilize binary numbers that cause electronic switches located inside of a modern computer to open and close. These openings and closings are the computer's activities and through these operations a computer performs all of its functions.

**MID$**   The BASIC-language term, MID$ (pronounced *midstring*), instructs a computer to accept and evaluate only the middle portion of a string. For example, if asked to examine the MID$ of the word *program*, the computer would evaluate only some of the letters (for instance *ogr*) and would ignore the remaining letters in the word.

Modem Represents the concept *MOdulator—DEModulator* and is formed by using the first two letters from the word, *modulator*, and the first three letters from the word, *demodulator*. Its function is to convert information from electrical impulses (which the computer is able to understand) to sound and then to reconvert the sound to its original form. It is used to interface a computer with a telephone line so that a computer can exchange information with another computer located at a significant distance away.

Monitor A computer program that facilitates communication between a user and a machine. It is an integral part of the computer's design. It is the mechanism by which a user's keyboard strokes are transmitted to a computer's input. It then acts as the CPU's funnel for the transmission of data via the computer's output device. The word, *monitor*, also is used to describe a CRT screen.

Numeric The term, *numeric*, means "relating to numbers." The language of computers defines a numeric variable as one that refers to a number that is stored in the memory of a computer.

NEW The BASIC-language term, NEW, is a command to the computer to clear its memory and prepare to receive a new program for storage.

Peripheral Refers to those devices that are an adjunct to a computer. Devices such as tape recorders, disk drives, printers, microphones, and speakers are examples of peripheral equipment.

PRINT The BASIC-language term, PRINT, is a command to the computer to display data (words and/or numbers) on its screen. This is the most commonly used communication term between a user and a computer.

Program A logical, sequential arrangement of instructions to a computer with the singular objective of accomplishing a specific task or related collection of tasks.

Program Documentation Information used to clarify the elements in a computer program. Program documentation appears in two forms: (a) It may appear as printed matter that provides a description of the parameters of a computer program and helps to guide the user with its implementation. (b) It may also appear as a collection of PRINT statements within the program's configuration for the purpose of securing information from the user. Without documentation, a user would be unable to understand the direction a program has been configured to take. Programmers often use REM statements in the computer code to help them understand programs years after they were written.

Programmer An individual who creates a specific sequence of logically and "legally" arranged commands that when communicated to the computer cause it to accomplish a specific objective or collection of related objectives.

RAM The BASIC-language term, RAM, refers to the concept of *Random-Access Memory*, which is the space deliberately set aside by the computer's manufacturer for the temporary storage of specific kinds of program data. This space is accessible to programmers and may also be erased.

RANDOM The BASIC-language term, RANDOM, is used to command a computer to "randomize" a value that has been stored in its memory. For example, if the computer has stored the values one through one hundred in its memory, the use of the RND statement may be used to instruct the computer to select and generate at random a series of numbers within those established parameters.

READ-DATA The BASIC-language term, READ-DATA, is a programming statement that instructs a computer at a desired point in the running of a program to literally read information that is located in another part of that program, which has already been stored in the computer's memory. The computer, after reading the data, may evaluate the responses of a user and then execute a series of other programming commands.

REM The BASIC language term, REM, is an abbreviation of the word *REMark* and is used to instruct the computer to ignore remarks notated by a programmer. REM statements are used by programmers as personal reminders of reasons for having configured portions of a program in a particular fashion. This device enables the programmer to return at a later time to specific portions of a program to effect modifications. The computer, as it processes a program, when identifying a REM statement, will ignore the configured remarks and will continue to execute other commands.

**RIGHT$** The BASIC-language term, RIGHT$ (pronounced *right string*), instructs a computer to accept only the rightmost portion of a string and to use it for a predetermined programming purpose. It is used as a mechanism for examining either the last or last few letters of a word or expression that have been stored in the computer's memory. In effect, the command performs the same function with the last letters of a string that LEFT$ does with the first letters of a string.

RND The BASIC-language term, RND, is used as a command statement in conjunction with the BASIC-language word, RANDOM, to instruct the computer to randomly select and generate a series of numbers the parameters of which have been previously stored in the computer's memory. See *RANDOM*.

ROM The BASIC-language term, ROM, stands for the computer concept, *Read Only Memory*. The computer has deliberately been designed to store such information, which is inaccessible to and cannot be altered by a user. Because ROM is not *true memory* in the sense that it is variable, it cannot be altered unless the programmer possesses unusual technological expertise that will permit the inner workings of the computer to be examined and have some of its parts replaced. For example, compilers and interpreters are often stored in a computer's ROM. Computer language provides synonyms for ROM such as *hardwired software* and *firmware*.

RUN   The BASIC-language term, RUN, is a command statement to the computer to perform its programmed set of instructions.

Simulation   A specific type of computer program that allows a user to interact with the computer in the solving of a problem that resembles one that actually may occur in real life. The program permits the computer to evaluate a variety of responses offered by the user and then presents the user with a new series of options. Users are thereby provided with an academic exercise that simulates a life experience. Simulation is treated in depth in chapter 10.

Software   Organized sets of instructions created by a programmer that are configured to enable the computer to perform specific acts for the accomplishment of desired objectives.

Statements   The logical arrangement of groups of words in series that a computer has been designed to recognize. Such statements are the mechanism that instruct the computer to perform specific tasks. A sequence of such statements comprise a computer program.

String   A collection of keyboard characters in the form of a word or a collection of words. For example, phrases, sentences, or paragraphs may be identified as strings. Addresses, telephone numbers, and Social Security numbers may also be identified as strings.

String Variables   A label that is affixed to a string when the latter is stored in a computer's memory. String variables facilitate the accessing of stored data by enabling a computer programmer to refer to a specific variable.

Subscripted Variable   Synonymous with the term, *array variable* (defined above).

Subroutine   A segment of a computer program that may have to be used frequently. Rather than rewrite the particular portion of the program each time that it is needed, the programmer supplies instructions that cause the machine, on command, to automatically refer to the particular identified segment and then return automatically to the point of origin within the program. This technique facilitates the operation of the program and also reduces its size.

User   The individual who operates a computer that has been preprogrammed by another person in the role of programmer. A computer user generally knows very little or nothing about computers or programming but is able to turn the machine on and then follow the instructions provided in a prepackaged program.

Variable A label that identifies a word or number to be stored in the memory of a computer. The computer has been configured to remember the fact and the label with which it is associated. In this way, the data stored can be accessed, modified, or eliminated.

Word Processor A computer that has been equipped with a specialized program. Such programs allow the user to type data (composed of numbers and alphabet keyboard characters), instantaneously modify that data, and then if desired, rearrange its position automatically within the body of the text. It also permits the data to be saved and printed.

Word Processing The techniques for preparing written documents with the aid of a computer that has been equipped with a specialized program.

Index

About the Authors

Stephen Radin is a computer-education coordinator for Community School District 22 in New York City. He is author of two books and numerous magazine articles in the school computing field and is an adjunct assistant professor in both The City University of New York and St. John's University. He has served as a consultant to educational and business organizations in the field of computer education. For the past twenty-two years, he has developed courses and trained teachers and administrators in many states, covering grades from prekindergarten through graduate school.

Harold M. Greenberg has been a teacher in the New York City school system for the past twenty-five years. As chairman of the Social Studies Department at South Shore High School for the past thirteen years, he has developed both traditional and elective courses and supervised and administered the largest high-school social-studies department in the nation. He has taught on the college level and in both public and parochial institutions.